T0320171

Corruption, Grabbing and Development

Corruption, Grabbing and Development

Real World Challenges

Edited by

Tina Søreide

Faculty of Law, University of Bergen, Norway

Aled Williams

U4 Anti-Corruption Resource Centre, Chr. Michelsen Institute (CMI), Bergen, Norway

Edward Elgar

Cheltenham, UK • Northampton, MA, USA

Published by
Edward Elgar Publishing Limited
The Lypiatts
15 Lansdown Road
Cheltenham
Glos GL50 2JA
UK

Edward Elgar Publishing, Inc.
William Pratt House
9 Dewey Court
Northampton
Massachusetts 01060
USA

A catalogue record for this book
is available from the British Library

Library of Congress Control Number: 2013947147

This book is available electronically in the ElgarOnline.com Social and Political Science Subject Collection, E-ISBN 978 1 78254 441 8

ISBN 978 1 78254 440 1 (cased)

Typeset by Columns Design XML Ltd, Reading
Printed and bound in Great Britain by T.J. International Ltd, Padstow

Contents

Figures

Tables

Contributors

EDITORS

Tina Søreide is a postdoctoral researcher in law and economics at the Faculty of Law, University of Bergen, on leave from the Chr. Michelsen Institute. From 2008 to 2010, she worked for the World Bank, Washington DC, on their Governance and Anti-Corruption agenda. She teaches political economy for the Department of Economics, University of Bergen, and the economics of corruption for the International Anti-Corruption Academy. She holds a PhD in economics from the Norwegian School of Economics and Business Administration and a master's from the Department of Economics, University of Bergen. Her current research addresses challenges in criminal law. The main themes of her publications are political economy, corruption, industrial organization and governance. Recent titles include the *International Handbook on the Economics of Corruption Volume 2* (Edward Elgar, 2013), co-edited with Susan Rose-Ackerman.

Aled Williams is a political scientist with interests in aid and development, corruption, governance and natural resource management. He is Senior Advisor for the U4 Anti-Corruption Resource Centre at the Chr. Michelsen Institute, where he coordinates research and training portfolios on corruption in natural resource management and in forest- and climate-related aid. He has previously served as a policy researcher for the anti-graft NGO Transparency International based in Berlin, where he developed the organization's first working and policy paper series. He has consulted for the British, Norwegian and German governmental aid agencies on anti-corruption and development issues.

AUTHORS

Inge Amundsen is a political scientist and Senior Researcher at the Chr. Michelsen Institute focusing on democratic institutionalization, parliaments, political parties, political corruption and natural resources (petroleum resource management and revenue management). His main study area is francophone West Africa, Ghana, Angola, Tanzania, Nigeria and

Bangladesh. Amundsen was Research Director at CMI from 2000–03 and Director of the U4 Anti-Corruption Resource Centre from 2002–06. He has also coordinated three CMI institutional cooperation programmes. Amundsen teaches extensively on corruption prevention and good governance in the petroleum sector.

Jens Chr. Andvig is an economist and Research Professor at the Norwegian Institute of International Affairs. His main research interests are in the interactions between formal institutions and family life. He has published on corruption and child labour including child soldiering. Outside of this he has contributed to the history of macroeconomics.

Tiberius Barasa is a lecturer at Maseno University, Nairobi, Kenya. He has previously been affiliated with the Institute of Policy Analysis and Research and with Moi University, Kenya.

Germà Bel is Professor of Economics at the Universitat de Barcelona. His main interest is the interaction between governments and markets, and his research focuses on the economics and politics of public sector reform. He has paid special attention to infrastructure economics and policy, and to local public services. His last two books are *Infrastructure and the Political Economy of National Building in Spain (1720/2010)* (Sussex Academic Press, 2012), and *The Economics and Politics of High-Speed Rail: Lessons from Experiences Abroad* (Lexington Books, 2012, with Daniel Albalate).

Blessings Chinsinga is based at Chancellor College, University of Malawi, as an associate professor at the Department of Political and Administrative Studies and Deputy Director at the Centre for Social Research (CSR). His main research interests include the political economy of development, public policy analysis and institutions and development.

Lucy Corkin completed her PhD at SOAS, University of London, on Chinese public infrastructure financing in Angola, which was published as *Uncovering African Agency: Angola's management of China's credit lines* by Ashgate in February 2013. Since 2006, Lucy has participated in research on China's relations with African countries, particularly in the construction and finance sector. She writes extensively and provides commentary to local and international media on this subject. Lucy speaks English, Portuguese, French, Afrikaans and Mandarin Chinese. She currently works at Rand Merchant Bank, a South African investment bank.

Antonio Estache has a PhD in economics from the Université Libre de Bruxelles. Until the end of 2007 he was Chief Economist of the Sustainable Development Network of the World Bank where he worked for 25 years. He joined the European Centre for Advanced Research in Economics and Statistics full-time as the beneficiary of the Bernard Van Ommeslaghe Chair on 1 January 2008. He is also associated with the Centre for Economic Policy Research in London. He currently teaches public economics, regulatory economics, development economics and environmental economics.

Renaud Foucart is a postdoctoral research fellow at Nuffield College and the Department of Economics at the University of Oxford. He received his PhD from the European Centre for Advanced Research in Economics and Statistics (Université Libre de Bruxelles). His research interests are in applied microeconomic theory, with strong connections to public economics.

Siri Gloppen is Professor of Comparative Politics at the University of Bergen, Senior Researcher at CMI and Research Coordinator of Pluri-Courts, Faculty of Law, University of Oslo. With a research focus in the intersection between law and politics her work spans legal mobilization and the role of courts in social transformation, democratization and institutionalization of accountability structures, constitution-making, election processes, human rights, transitional justice and reconciliation. Her main empirical focus is Southern and Eastern Africa.

Svein-Erik Helle is currently a PhD student at the Department of Comparative Politics at the University of Bergen, Norway, where he also completed his master thesis on political funding in Uganda and Angola. He has previously worked as a research assistant at the Chr. Michelsen Institute on projects related to elections and democratization in sub-Saharan Africa. In his PhD project he focuses on access to money, media and the state in electoral authoritarian regimes in sub-Saharan Africa in the post-Cold War era.

Karen Hussmann is a public policy expert with 17 years' experience in anti-corruption, accountability and governance fields. She is an external advisor to the U4 Anti-Corruption Resource Centre hosted by the Chr. Michelsen Institute, and works as an independent consultant on anti-corruption policy-making at national and sector level. She is currently based in Colombia and holds an MA in public policies and management from the University of Chile. Her publications focus on how to address corruption in different contexts and are written for the OECD, Norad, DFID, UNDP and Transparency International, among others.

Eirik G. Jansen has had a long and varied career in aid and development. He holds a PhD in social anthropology and, since the 1970s, has written extensively on the Lake Victoria fisheries and Bangladesh. He has worked at the Norwegian embassies in Dhaka (1987–90) and Dar es Salaam (2003–07) and published several articles on aid and corruption in Bangladesh during the 1980s and 1990s. He has worked on evaluating development programmes in the Ministry of Foreign Affairs and Norad in Oslo for more than 8 years.

Philippe Le Billon is Professor at the University of British Columbia with the Department of Geography and the Liu Institute for Global Issues. Working on linkages between environment, development and security, he has published widely on natural resources and armed conflicts, the political economy of war, resource governance and corruption. His two latest books are *Wars of Plunder: Conflicts, Profits and the Politics of Resources* (Columbia University Press, 2012) and *Oil* (Polity Press, 2012, with Gavin Bridge).

Ida Lindkvist is an advisor at Norad's evaluation department and is working within areas of health and education using impact evaluation as an evaluation methodology. She holds a PhD in economics from the University of Bergen, and has previously worked as a researcher at the Chr. Michelsen Institute, where she conducted research on health-care quality and informal payments in Tanzania.

Jean-François Marteau is a Transport Specialist at the World Bank. He has co-authored a book on the costs of being landlocked, and has managed projects including port and customs reforms components in Africa, Europe and Central Asia. He is now coordinating infrastructure projects and technical assistance for the World Bank in Eastern Europe and the Baltic Countries.

Muriel Poisson is Programme Specialist at the International Institute for Educational Planning (IIEP-UNESCO). Since 2002, she has been the task manager of the Institute's project 'Ethics and corruption in education'. She is responsible for research and training activities in this area, including on subjects such as academic fraud, teacher codes of conduct and public expenditure tracking surveys. Prior to working with IIEP-UNESCO, she conducted research on non-formal education in Asia. She has worked on recommendations for curriculum reform for the International Bureau of Education in Geneva, and participated in UNESCO's follow-up to the Dakar World Conference on Education for All. She has co-authored a number of articles and books, including: *Corrupt Schools, Corrupt Universities: What Can be Done* (UNESCO, 2007).

Gaël Raballand is a Senior Public Sector Specialist at the World Bank. He holds a PhD in economics and has co-authored three World Bank books on transport in Africa, including one on cargo dwell time. He has also been involved in customs reforms and co-authored a book on the costs of being landlocked. He is now working on public spending efficiency, public investment management, governance and aid-effectiveness issues.

Lise Rakner is a political scientist focusing on the issues of democratization and human rights, economic reform, taxation, institutional change and international aid, with a particular emphasis on Southern and Eastern Africa. Her current research interests concern electoral administration and party developments in sub-Saharan Africa and more generally the relationship between the political and economic processes of reform, accountability and the development of political institutions. Rakner is Professor of Comparative Politics at the University of Bergen.

Juan Carlos Rivillas is National Coordinator of Health Observatories at the Ministry of Health and Social Protection in Colombia. His main interests are health economics, health policy analysis and health system research. He holds an MSc in health economics and policy from the University of Turin, and has worked as Junior Researcher to the Italian Epidemiology Service exploring the role of socio-economic conditions in health outcomes. He has recently received several grants from the Erasmus Medical Center and the Colombian Agency for Junior Research.

Ingvild Aagedal Skage is a PhD student at the Department of Comparative Politics at the University of Bergen, Norway, where she also received her MA. At the Chr. Michelsen Institute, Skage was part of a Norad-commissioned study on the uses and abuses of per diems in Ethiopia, Malawi and Tanzania in connection with workshops and seminars. Other research interests include democracy movements, political mobilization, party politics and urbanization in sub-Saharan Africa.

Arne Strand is a political scientist focusing on peace, conflict and aid, with a particular emphasis on Afghanistan. He holds a PhD in post-war recovery studies. His present research focuses on aid coordination, forced migration and reintegration, peace-building and security sector reform, and humanitarian and development assistance. He has extensive management experience from NGOs and research institutes, and has also been involved in developing management and professional capacities of Afghan NGOs and peacebuilding organizations. He is currently Deputy Director of the Chr. Michelsen Institute.

Arne Tostensen is a Senior Researcher at the Chr. Michelsen Institute and a sociologist currently focusing on governance and human rights research. Tostensen's professional profile and research interests include labour migration (Kenya), regional integration in Eastern and Southern Africa, poverty and institutional analysis, research policy, the research–policy nexus, governance and democratization, human rights, development assistance and urbanization (Africa). Tostensen has more than 30 years of experience in research and consultancy work, principally in Eastern and Southern Africa, and has acted as team leader internationally, including for European aid agencies and the UN. Between 1988 and 1994 he served as the Chr. Michelsen Institute's director.

Jill Wells is a social scientist with a significant record of research and publications on economic and social issues related to construction. She has had a long career that has straddled work in academia, government, international agencies, the private sector and civil society, but has seldom deviated far from study of the interface between construction and development. She is currently employed by Engineers Against Poverty and has played a key role in the Construction Sector Transparency (CoST) pilot project.

Liam Wren-Lewis is a Research Fellow at the Paris School of Economics, with research interests that include land rights and corruption. He previously worked as an Economist in the Ministry of Economic Planning and Development in Malawi. He completed his PhD at the University of Oxford, and has worked as a consultant to the World Bank and the Institute for Fiscal Studies.

Acknowledgements

This project was created at the Chr. Michelsen Institute (CMI) in Bergen, Norway, a multidisciplinary research institution focused on development challenges around the globe. CMI researchers study a large number of sectors and state functions in many different countries. It has become apparent that some form of grabbing far too often stands in the way of development. With this project we have managed to present the insights of researchers and practitioners, at CMI and internationally, so that governments and the anti-corruption community can draw on their experiences and perspectives for more efficient reform. As editors, we are deeply grateful that our idea for this book project could be brought to life. Tara Gorvine at Edward Elgar Publishing has offered support and guidance from the day she heard about the proposal and we are very grateful to the publisher for working with us. Thanks also to their anonymous reviewers who contributed useful advice. We are grateful to our colleagues at CMI, who have contributed with many useful comments; special thanks to Ottar Mæstad, Siri Gloppen, Arne Strand, Ivar Kolstad, Odd-Helge Fjeldstad and colleagues at the CMI-hosted U4 Anti-Corruption Resource Centre, particularly Liz Hart and André Standing who provided both space and moral support for Aled's involvement as co-editor. Susan Rose-Ackerman has played an important role as a mentor, particularly in terms of Tina's experience of co-editing another volume with her (*International Handbook on the Economics of Corruption Volume 2*, Edward Elgar, 2013). At the Faculty of Law, University of Bergen, where Tina now works, Linda Gröning and Jørn Jacobsen have been steady sources of support and feedback. Most important, however, is how the project has depended on the many authors of this volume who wanted to contribute with their distinct experiences. In addition to writing their own chapter, they all acted as reviewers on other chapters in the volume, thereby improving overall quality. We have appreciated a very good collaboration with each one of them and thank them for their openness to our comments and willingness to meet what was, at times, a demanding production schedule.

Introduction

Tina Søreide and Aled Williams

There are many reasons why there are differences across the globe in terms of how well opportunities for development and a good life are secured. One of the things we know, however, is that *grabbing,* and perceived risks of grabbing, distort many interactions and exchanges in a society, largely because it reduces trust and perverts allocation mechanisms. The consequences are particularly detrimental in developing countries, where institutions and structures in place to prevent and counter it are often weak. We also know that the extent of grabbing in a society correlates with its government's ability and willingness to secure framework conditions that are conducive to development. What we need to know more about is what we can do to more efficiently curb propensities to grab and hinder its harmful impacts on development, including in societies where government representatives themselves benefit from some form of grabbing. With this volume we want to reinforce awareness of grabbing as an obstacle to development.

GRABBING

Grabbing is when someone seizes something that he or she is not entitled to, or takes *more* than what is his or hers formally, informally or tacitly allocated share. Stealing, embezzlement, corruption and fraud are obvious forms of grabbing, while also being acts that are usually regulated by penal law. Cheating, swindling and deceiving can be illegal in some situations and legal in others, but are all acts that we associate with grabbing. The term refers to clearly legal acts as well. It would be seen as grabbing if someone takes too large a share of a cake, although the allocated share is not defined by the host. Securing for oneself too big a share is a selfish act conducted at the expense of others and thus seen as a violation of social norms, regardless of legal definition. The inclination to grab is one of the bad traits of human nature and therefore difficult to eradicate. It can be observed among children in a kindergarten, among neighbours, at sporting events, among civil society activists, elected politicians, civil servants at all levels of state administration, in all sectors of the economy and in all countries.

From the perspective of evolutionary psychology, natural selection would be expected to favour selfishness, in other words, grabbing. Given free rein, a selfish mutant would quickly outproduce altruistic competitors, as explained by Pinker (1997: 337). Evolution of selfless behaviour is what requires special explanation, an explanation which, according to Trivers (1971), has to be reciprocation, in other words, the mutual benefits obtained by trading favours with other members of a society, including recognition of ownership and other rights. However, these benefits outweigh the 'benefits of grabbing' primarily in societies with a high level of group identity. In societies with weak cohesion and a general distrust, the lack of group identity may stimulate selfish behaviour and grabbing.[1]

Our tendency to define some acts as grabbing reflects our sense of fairness. Members of any society have some common views on what is fair, which indeed can vary across cultures, for example because of different views on how power and rights should be allocated between gender, ethnicity, caste and age. What is grabbing in one culture can be accepted in another. The meaning of grabbing is nevertheless the same, since it can be understood as a violation of the specific fairness norms that have developed in a given society.

However, our views on what forms of self-seizing acts are acceptable or not is shaped also by the idea of a 'social contract', which allows someone to rule on behalf of society at large simply because this usually secures better framework conditions than anarchy. The idea refers to the fundamental agreement about how society is organized, including how political, legal and physical power should be allocated to certain institutions steered by individuals who are selected through more or less agreed upon procedures. These individuals are entrusted to oversee state operations and institutions, and given bureaucratic hierarchy; their responsibilities are delegated and shared by a large number of trusted individuals. For society as a whole there are usually clear benefits in the existence of such a state organization, particularly if it offers protection, essential services and an allocation mechanism for rights and scarce resources. The downside of accepting these benefits is the risk that some (or many) of those entrusted individuals cannot be trusted after all, because they are in a position to grab. Hence, when the power to administer state functions and rule on behalf of society is misused for personal benefit, facilitating grabbing instead of hindering such behaviour, it violates the underlying agreement in society, as well as laws that are even more fundamental than a country's constitution.[2] This perspective on society implies that serious violations of these norms by those entrusted with political power are illegitimate, regardless of how the acts are legally defined. Grabbing at this level can make a government illegitimate, even if its grabbing occurs within its self-designed legal framework. These are logical and well-known arguments and yet, governments around the world are recognized and treated as legitimate despite their grabbing, particularly if they control important resources or if friendship is strategic in other ways. The question of high-level grabbing is thus a complex one and not necessarily a question of country-specific responsibilities only.

When grabbing refers to the bribes demanded by decision-makers entitled to allocate resources on behalf of others, we call it *corruption*. It is often defined as the misuse of office for personal benefit, a definition that largely overlaps with what we have characterized as *grabbing*. An important characteristic of corruption, more specifically, is the element of a 'deal'.[3] A decision-maker demands or accepts bribes for offering services or decisions that he or she controls, usually involving some divergence from official procedures. The bribe compensates the decision-maker for the risk and moral cost of deviating from what he or she would otherwise decide. If this 'otherwise' would have been consistent with development, corruption is harmful to development. Grabbing focuses on the selfish act of seizing benefits, while corruption is typically an illegal trade in decisions, usually with the same motivation as grabbing, and thus, the words are close synonyms.[4] The term corruption is in many contexts less applicable than grabbing, however. Corruption is a legal definition that reflects the opportunity to pursue a violation of rules in the judicial system. The word is also used more loosely, describing a situation where institutions cannot be trusted and where benefits are unfairly allocated, although alleged acts of corruption cannot necessarily be identified or proven. Its dual meaning combined with recognition of the legal principle that no individual, company or institution is guilty unless otherwise proven, should imply caution in how we use the word. We should not bandy about unverified allegations of grabbing either, but since grabbing is not a legal definition, this term is perhaps less sensitive when referring to the misuse of authority for personal benefits and the unfair allocation of rights and values.[5] The term is imprecise, and still, it refers quite specifically to the act of selfishly securing benefits at the expense of others.[6] It is also clear that when grabbing occurs at scale and affects the function of important institutions and norms, it harms the development of a whole society.

A COLLECTION OF CASE STUDIES

This book is a collection of 16 case studies of various forms of grabbing. The cases are studied and presented by highly qualified experts, most of them from academic institutions and development organizations. The authors have studied how the phenomenon distorts development in specific sectors and the functions of state institutions. Many of them have been responsible for or advisors to research and/or development aid programmes, and have chosen to present some of their experiences and policy recommendations in this volume. All cases are studied in an analytic perspective with an aim to understand the underlying mechanisms at play and use this understanding to propose policy recommendations. We hope this collection of case studies will be useful for government representatives seeking solutions to their own challenges, students with an academic interest in governance, researchers of several social science disciplines, as well as representatives of the development aid community.

We have categorized the chapters in four sections according to what form of approach and level of governance is addressed. The first category describes how certain characteristics of some sectors and state functions create opportunities for grabbing. As the chapters explain, we see similar mechanisms at play in many countries, and the challenges discussed are not primarily context specific. Change may demand a new way of thinking about organization or regulation of the functions or services exposed to risk, and the solutions found in one country may thus be applicable to others.

The second category of chapters presents cases of grabbing in a country-specific context. These cases point primarily to how a solution to grabbing needs improvements at the level of sector governance or the administration of state functions. Political will is always a condition for change, particularly if representatives of the top level of governance themselves benefit from grabbing. In this category of cases, the challenges and solutions are nevertheless described without relating them to political level characteristics.

The third category of chapters addresses cases where grabbing at the political level is indeed the main challenge and must be addressed to curb grabbing at the sector level or within state functions. In these cases, the challenges are likely to continue regardless of how the administration or sector is organized or reformed and, therefore, bottom-up approaches to secure development may easily be wasted.

The fourth category of chapters includes cases when interaction with international players, who are present in a country with the intention of promoting development, creates opportunities for grabbing. Even if we have known for some time that aid is exposed to rent-seeking behaviour, we still struggle with balancing the modes of financial support, external control and independence needed to create sustainable solutions and promote accountability. The chapters in this category present examples of how these challenges can occur and what solutions may need to look like.

All the chapters explain a specific phenomenon of grabbing and present unique proposals for development. We will now briefly point out some of their arguments and results, following the categories just described.

Grabbing Explained by Characteristics of a Sector or State Function

In the first chapter, Jill Wells explains why grabbing is a challenge in the construction sector. To some extent explanations are found in the fact that contracts in this sector are particularly large, and often involve political decisions and complex financial solutions that are difficult for outsiders to evaluate. Adding to these factors, Wells explains how construction sector regulation and decision-making procedures rely on certain conditions which in practice are not necessarily met. When it comes to procurement procedures, for example, it is assumed that construction designs can be completed before the bidding procedure begins. It is also often assumed that bidders can calculate costs ahead of start-up, and that governments have budgeted sufficient resources. In practice these criteria may not have been fulfilled, and thus, contract management procedures can easily be manipulated since they will in any case need to deviate from original intentions and formal procedures in order to adjust to project realities. Moreover, the pressure on contractors to make unreasonable promises about prices when the true expenses are unknown, may nurture tolerance for collusion and corruption. In her policy debate, Wells points to a need for rethinking how large construction contracts are awarded, in particular by making better use of information that is available to decision-makers. More weight can safely be placed on contractors' past performance when ranking candidates, she argues, and payments can be tied up to *ex-post* reviews of work done.

Chapter 2, by Gaël Raballand and Jean-François Marteau, describes challenges in the port sector. It is well known that ports in many countries are inefficient and a typical arena for facilitation payments, for example in the form of bribes demanded from ships when they arrive to unload freight. Based on empirical studies of ports in sub-Saharan Africa, Raballand and Marteau provide a far more nuanced picture. Analysing decision-making procedures, asymmetric information and incentives along the sector value chain, they describe the opportunities for various forms of collusion between players in the private and public sector, which in turn explain very long average cargo dwell times and rampant corruption. In fact, weak performance in ports can be very much subject to collusion among private players in the clearing and forwarding profession; and is not explained by corruption on the side of civil servants alone. What they also find is that delays in ports are used strategically to keep competitors away in various domestic markets, and is thus applied as an informal form of trade protectionism. The illegal benefits accruing to civil servants in the port sector, who are paid to condone weak performance or actively demand bribes, have made such positions attractive, and therefore, handy for politicians involved in patrimonial barter games. However, by offering such positions because of the informal benefits associated with them, these politicians also have to make sure the grabbing can take place, regardless of complaints or controls. For this reason, the control system for ports is impeded so that there are few, if any, consequences for those involved if the corruption is revealed.

In Chapter 3, Philippe Le Billon adds important nuance to the characterization of how governance failure distorts the returns to society from natural resource production. Instead of relying on macroeconomic figures and broad generalizations, he depicts an unholy trinity consisting of corruption (often at political or regulatory level), illegal exploitation of resources and tax evasion. Combined, as he argues they often appear to be, these challenges amount to the creation of a 'resource grab' – a phenomenon that has meant lower income countries with significant natural resource deposits have still failed to benefit from a recent boom in commodity prices. Le Billon explains that the main beneficiaries are not only corrupt governments. Tax evasion may benefit parent or holding companies while illegal resource exploitation is often the business of domestic firms. Moreover, the different risks of corruption, illegal exploitation and tax evasion play out very differently at different stages of the sector value chain. Anti-grabbing initiatives should depend on what forms of risks are more pronounced at different stages, and match an understanding of who the players and beneficiaries are. These insights are not enough for reform, however. Change depends on the willingness of players who may benefit from the status quo. Pressure from international players, for example in the form of the Extractive Industry Transparency Initiative (EITI), improved taxation capabilities, sector regulation, financial reform and corporate responsibility is critically important in many countries. Yet concrete gains in terms of preventing *resource grabbing* and holding those who engage in such activity accountable still appear too distant in some countries

Muriel Poisson, in Chapter 4, focuses on multiple forms of grabbing in the education sector in developing countries, drawing on cases and research she has engaged with while working to support developing countries' education systems. The discussion of grabbing mechanisms is illustrated by three cases: the misallocation of funds in a school improvement programme in Indonesia, the uncovering of the use of 'ghost teachers' through an educational reform programme in Sierra Leone and corruption in the purchasing of textbooks in the Philippines. The severe implications of these types of grabbing are clear: educational goals are undermined, which in turn undermine national development prospects. Yet, in the search for effective policy solutions, the author stresses we should be mindful of a number of trade-offs. Finding the right balance between equity and transparency in the process of allocating educational resources, for instance, is not straightforward. Decentralizing procedures to empower local and schools authorities and thus improve their accountability, can introduce local bias. While fostering community participation – often regarded as a key tool for promoting social control – can also inadvertently mean fostering the interplay of local influence. Flexibility is therefore needed that allows for simple and easy control, while making initiatives match the needs of end users of education. The importance of strong education management information systems to limit grabbing opportunities is emphasized throughout.

In Chapter 5, the last chapter in this category, Siri Gloppen describes the risk of grabbing in the justice system. In order to serve their function in society, courts are given authority to judge independently. However, those who are trusted with this authority are also individuals who can sometimes be persuaded to let a certain legal decision be steered in exchange for personal benefits. The scale varies, Gloppen explains, from facilitation payments, charged as informal fees, to substantial bribes offered by powerful members of political or private sector elites in search of immunity. Moreover, judges are subject to extortion, and sometimes used in dirty power games instructed by politicians as well as mafia leaders. They also engage in self-censorship knowing that adverse rulings may jeopardize their future career. While all forms of corruption in courts will leave societies in doubt about how rules will be enforced and rights protected, we must separate between forms of judicial corruption when designing policy initiatives. It is important to see the difference between (1) corruption in interactions between judicial personnel and society,

(2) pressure on judges by political power-holders seeking personal or party benefits, and (3) undue pressure by the judicial leadership on lower rank judges. Gloppen explains how the role of courts as a pillar of integrity can be strengthened through reforming the process of appointing judges, the rules regarding terms and conditions of tenure, and the regulation of finances, including judges' salaries and benefits – while it also requires changes in professional norms and attitudes. She explains how more professional collaboration across borders can strengthen norms of judicial independence and integrity by facilitating learning and creating professional communities where reputation matters.

Gloppen's analysis of weaknesses and proposals are general in character, and thus relevant to any country that wants to strengthen the integrity of its courts. The next category of chapters addresses cases where challenges in state functions or sectors are studied and understood in a specific country context, although the analysis of challenges and solutions may apply to other countries as well.

Grabbing at the Level of Sector and State Functions in a Country Context

Law enforcement is also the theme in Chapter 6, by Jens Andvig and Tiberius Barasa, who describe the problem of police corruption in Kenya. While crime in general is a significant challenge in the country, grabbing-related forms of crime like theft and robbery, in particular, reduce general trust in the police. It is not uncommon that police officers misuse their authority to demand bribes, for example in exchange for administrative assignments (like registering a crime), in exchange for the release of an offender or by blaming innocent citizens for crimes and letting them go only if they pay a bribe. Andvig and Barasa explain the police corruption in light of the country's colonial past. The police force, as an institution, was introduced by the British. With the intention of discouraging violent rebellion, they ensured police officers were placed in areas where they were strangers to local citizens, and thus assumed to be less sympathetic towards them. For the same reason, police officers were also rotated frequently around the country. According to Andvig and Barasa, it is exactly this intended detachedness that has nurtured a culture of police grabbing. Emotional distance from victims keeps the moral costs associated with such corruption low. The benefits accruing to the police officers have become an expected bonus, the illegal practices a norm. Largely, the police force in Kenya has failed to develop a sound sense of accountability to the citizens they patrol. The illegal benefits have become lodged in the whole law-enforcement system, and reforms will need to address the whole sector's accountability pyramid.

Blessings Chinsinga and Liam Wren-Lewis explore, in Chapter 7, the role that grabbing in Malawi plays in creating a highly unequal and frequently inefficient distribution of land. They focus on various forms of malpractice, corruption and opportunistic behaviour associated with land transfers, and show how the present land framework still closely resembles that which existed under colonial rule. Pernicious forms of grabbing, they argue, are perceived to include the allocation of public lands based on considerations other than need and date of application. Common allegations surrounding customary land involve petty bribes given to community leaders to settle local conflicts, echoing Muriel Poisson's concerns about the potential for unpredictability in decentralization reforms. Characteristic of this form of grabbing, however, is that it is very visible in society who has obtained land-related benefits through grabbing, and this problem will easily trigger the negative consequences associated with reduced trust in politics and state administration. The authors discuss how policy changes are difficult; since a more transparent and understandable land allocation system would probably worsen the terms on which elites presently obtain this resource. Civil society and international donors have important roles to play in this regard, by transmitting information on land use and telling the stories of the dispossessed.

Ida Lindkvist, in Chapter 8, presents a sophisticated analysis of data collected on informal payments in the Tanzanian health sector. Informal payments have been known for some time to lower demand for health care, reduce trust in health workers and switch their attention from patients' health to their ability to pay informal fees. A common policy prescription to address these problems has been to increase health worker salaries: a wage differential supposedly increases the opportunity costs of engaging in corruption. But evidence to support the effectiveness of such policies has been mixed. One explanation for this is that previous studies have not controlled for the skill level of health workers, an important omission given that highly skilled workers may both have better opportunities to engage in corruption and have higher salaries. Lindkvist finds that the correlation between salary and informal payments crucially depends on the inclusion of skills. More broadly, her analysis illustrates the difficulties of using higher salaries for anti-corruption purposes, showing how the intended impact may depend on how such policies are combined with performance-based promotion mechanisms.

In Chapter 9, Karen Hussmann and Juan Carlos Rivillas describe how growing levels of grabbing in the Colombian health system contributed to a profound crisis of legitimacy and financial sustainability in the early 2000s. Analysing the case of the public health insurance fund, the authors find that the unjustified use of health-care reimbursements through the fund grew rapidly between 2002 and 2010, depleting the health-care system of scarce resources. Early warning signals went unheeded by relevant public and private actors, leading to questions concerning why. The story portrays a conflict in which the country's checks and balances are challenged. Specifically, the Colombian Constitutional Court addressed the country's government with clear requests for better audits and control of the health sector and demanded investigations and arrests. From the side of the government, there have been some responses, including further investigations, an updating of the health insurance package, and the design of a strategy to control future reimbursements. But, according to the authors, there are also mixed signals of political will. Several early waning signals were not reacted to, investigations of high-ranking civil servants were stopped and there is still a clear need for further policy actions. In their view, these actions should include guidance on how information relating to resource flows for health reimbursements is to be made available to the public.

When Political Grabbing Prevents the Performance of a Sector or State Function

We now turn to cases where grabbing can be understood only as a result of incentive problems in politics. In Chapter 10, Germà Bel, Antonio Estache and Renaud Foucart describe over-spending on infrastructure in Spain as the result of a 'somewhat incestuous relationship' between politics and the construction industry. Spurred by World Bank loans in the 1960s and 1970s, when infrastructure upgrading was vitally needed, a period of huge government investment began. The political will to invest in infrastructure persisted, eventually, and Spain is now one of the countries with the most comprehensive infrastructure networks in the world. According to Bel, Estache and Foucart, this infrastructure has not only been excessively expensive and overly subsidized, it has also been constructed without enough thought for users' needs. This failure has left many transport routes inefficient, too expensive and/or hardly used. The characteristics of the construction sector, as discussed by Jill Wells, make it easy to hide corruption in complex financial schemes, procurement rules, and a general lack of competence with regard to technical or financial solutions. However, even if several grand-scale corruption cases involving politicians have been revealed in Spain, particularly over the last two decades, Bel, Estache and Foucart find it likely that collusion between large construction companies and politics still occurs within legal terms. Whether this will change depends on voters' ability to recognize how the grabbing distorts sector governance.

In Chapter 11, Inge Amundsen discusses the phenomenon of buying parliamentary nominations and seats in Bangladesh. He argues that this *political grabbing* has led to an influx of businessmen into Bangladeshi politics. This is a challenge for the proper functioning of parliament, including its ability to secure development benefits for the country at large. The problem is not the fact that the individuals in question are businessmen per se; it is the general impression that they are seeking their positions primarily to facilitate their own personal enrichment. One important reason why these rent-seekers get these positions is the country's lack of direct public funding for political parties. While there are hardly any public sources of funding for election campaigns, these aspiring candidates pay for their candidature, and thus, they offer a welcome short-term benefit for the party in question. These financial challenges contribute also to explaining a tendency to manipulate political campaign expenses, a challenge addressed by Svein-Erik Helle and Lise Rakner in Chapter 13 too. Though rules and laws exist to regulate such expenses, they are not necessarily put into proper operation. The main policy challenge here, according to Amundsen, is that the general rules of the political game in Bangladesh have yet to be defined: the exercise of politics exists in a confrontational climate and is viewed by those involved as a zero-sum game. Properly defined and enforced rules and sanctions for misbehaviour are needed.

Lucy Corkin, in Chapter 12, draws on her research into the mechanisms and implementation process of the China Exim Bank credit line in Angola to argue that the Angolan political elite has used the credit to enhance its grip on power. Although the credit line has indeed helped underpin the rebuilding of physical infrastructure in the country after years of conflict, it has not, the author contends, allowed for the general participation of Angolans in reconstructing their nation. Corkin explains severe constitutional distortions in the Angolan government, directed by the president himself. High-ranking officials have been allowed to misuse public authority as long as they have had the president's support.[7] The author describes how corruption has become institutionalized, and how, for example, government officials use their position to direct contracts to their own companies. What becomes clear, is that Angola's *resource curse*[8] is not a result of the revenues from the oil sector alone; the misuse of revenues must also be understood in light of the huge loans from abroad and the space for political manipulation of infrastructure contracts in the country's highly needed reconstruction process. As a consequence of this grabbing, only a small and select group appears to be benefitting from the economic gains brought about by the reconstruction process, with the rebuilding of 'soft infrastructure' (in the form of institution and capacity building) taking a back seat. Existing political and economic elites have retained a monopoly on credit-backed rebuilding projects to reduce the potential threat posed by other economically empowered actors. Under these circumstances, fiscal reforms (which are in any case under way) cannot be expected to bring about much change. It is difficult, too, to see how pressure from ordinary citizens could lead to reform. At the same time, preventing the country's unemployed youth from accessing the economic benefits associated with reconstruction may, in the long run, prove even more detrimental to political stability.

In Chapter 13, Svein-Erik Helle and Lise Rakner show how the integrity and quality of electoral processes can be threatened by the role of money in politics. Drawing from their research into the 2011 parliamentary, presidential, and local elections in Uganda, they argue that vote buying and the use of state resources for partisan purposes had both damaging economic and political consequences. These forms of *election grabbing* affected, in the case of Uganda, not only electoral accountability, but also the country's financial and political stability through higher rates of inflation and related social unrest. The chapter points at how an incumbent political party, which exploits its discretionary authority to use state revenues for its election campaign, may not only enhance its opportunities to win the next election, but also contribute to bolster its power, and for each election, make it increasingly more difficult for the opposition to take over. In light of their findings, the authors propose that national and international stakeholders must pay attention to the quality and not only to the quantity of elections in Uganda. This reminds us that the steps towards greater democratization are many and should include an enhanced appreciation of the principles and not just the mechanisms of democratic accountability.

Risk of Grabbing Due to Interaction with International Players

International players, particularly in the development aid community, have a clear goal of preventing crime, corruption and other forms of grabbing. Despite their ambition to support governments in their development goals, however, their actual presence and the funds they provide often create circumstances that may in fact aggravate grabbing-related challenges. Cases of such unforeseen consequences are presented in this last category of chapters.

Arne Strand explains in Chapter 14 how the intervention of NATO (North Atlantic Treaty Organization) forces in Afghanistan, coupled with huge amounts of donor money and a tendency to accept governance weaknesses if necessary to maintain dialogue with the government, laid the foundations for a case of large-scale fraud and political corruption. Drawing on his long experience as a researcher and development practitioner focused on Afghanistan, Strand tells the story of how the first Afghan private bank, Kabul Bank, which administered the salaries of about 80 per cent of Afghan public officials and which was financed by donors through the Afghan Reconstruction Trust Fund, became a vehicle for the illicit enrichment of the country's small and interconnected elite. He points to how, once the scandal broke, the same elites managed to protect themselves by placing the blame on those actors and institutions who did not uncover the wrongdoing earlier. The NATO forces, with their extensive intelligence analysis, may have known about this collusion between the banking sector and the political elite, but were apparently unable to react.[9] This bank fraud and related political grabbing had wide-ranging implications for the country's political stability and economic future. The main policy implication is that international military and development aid actors must be aware that buying short-term peace may not be conducive with long-term state-building goals.

In Chapter 16, Eirik G. Jansen addresses the difficult balance of controlling the use of funds transferred for specific development purposes while at the same time, encouraging accountable governance by allowing recipient responsibility. The chapter presents a specific case where Norway offered around USD 60 million for a natural resource management programme in Tanzania over a period of 12 years. A careful audit of the programme revealed weak documentation of the spending, significant fraud in terms of misreported travel expenses, and large sums transferred to the Ministry of Natural Resources without good explanation. Jansen describes inadequacies in the Norwegian government's response to the alleged fraud, and lists reasons why a development partner may have weak incentives to conduct efficient oversight of programme performance, and thus, be in position to reveal and address such crime. Norway, as a development partner, places significant weight on recipient responsibility and the start-up of new projects, rather than implementation and control of initiated projects, and the question is if it goes too far in protecting its good dialogue with partner governments. Like Arne Strand, Jansen argues that integrity has to be expected from the first dollar offered, and practised with independent audits and hands-on involvement in the implementation processes of large development programmes.

In Chapter 16, the last chapter of the volume, Ingvild Aagedal Skage, Tina Søreide and Arne Tostensen detail how aid money offered for competence-raising programmes, like the Tanzania programme described in Chapter 15, are exposed to grabbing. The chapter presents a qualitative study of the uses and abuses of travel compensation systems in the state administrations of three developing countries: Ethiopia, Malawi and Tanzania. For efficiency purposes, the travel compensation systems use standard per diem rates supposed to cover most daily expenses, and civil servants can pocket the difference between actual expenses and per diem payments. However, there are also numerous opportunities for mis-reporting, and civil servants can easily obtain higher reimbursements than they are supposed to receive. According to Skage, Søreide and Tostensen, such practices are often condoned by the manager, sometimes to offer an extra bonus, or to buy loyalty, for example if he or she has more serious offences to hide. While cases of per diem abuse seem trivial when considered in isolation, the problem is widespread and likely to cause significant distortions both in terms of how aid money is spent and how civil servants spend their time. Skage, Søreide and Tostensen explain why development partners tend to reinforce such malpractices. The reason is not only negligent controls and a lack of will to react, but also due to some donors offering high per diem payments and sitting allowances, simply to attract civil servants to attend their training.

LESSONS LEARNED FOR GOVERNANCE AND SECTOR REGULATION

In principle, the problem of grabbing should not be too difficult to combat. The risk of grabbing can usually be explained as the result of information asymmetries, weak allocation of responsibilities, failed accountability mechanisms, lack of functioning markets, or some kind of coordination failure. For each of these diagnoses we have solutions in the literature, and a good approach would be to prioritise anti-grabbing strategies according to the seriousness of the consequences of grabbing. What the cases presented in this book suggest, however, is that the development of strategies to combat many types of grabbing is tricky in practice. Standard solutions will not necessarily work. The challenge observed might be only one among multiple obstacles to development and it may be difficult to isolate and categorize the issue in order to determine counter-measures from an analytic perspective. Efficient reform depends on a comprehensive understanding of contextual realities.

However, there are also cases where we have a good understanding of the challenges and we are still unable to provide clever guidance.

For the most clearly delimited cases of grabbing, the authors list policy recommendations very much in line with recommendations in the existing literature. For example, in Chapter 1, Jill Wells argues increasing information about firms' past performance in fulfilling construction contracts is likely to lead to improved contracting decisions. In Chapter 9, Karen Hussmann and Juan Carlos Rivillas suggest enhancing information flows to remedy grabbing, this time in terms of guidance on how resources for health reimbursements are to be made publically available. Muriel Poisson, spells out in Chapter 4, however, that even when introducing the most obvious anti-corruption remedies, there are trade-offs in implementation, or even counter-intuitive effects. Ingvild Aagedal Skage, Tina Søreide and Arne Tostensen explain in Chapter 16 how the introduction of a standard travel compensation system, supposed to enhance administrative efficiency, has in fact created opportunities for grabbing and mismanagement. Likewise, Ida Lindkvist in Chapter 8 points at nuances in the use of compensations schemes, since in practice civil servants' motivation is steered by a relationship between several factors, and not monetary benefits alone. Eirik G. Jansen explains in Chapter 15 how development partners' intentions of promoting sector governance accountability may weaken their own control of the funds transferred. Hence, even in cases when an anti-corruption initiative appears to be wise when considered in isolation, there can be framework conditions or indirect effects which hamper the intended impact of the initiative or even lead to counter-productive impacts.

We all recognize the fundamental importance of ensuring law enforcement systems function in an accountable way. But, as described by Siri Gloppen in Chapter 5 and Jens Andvig and Tiberius Barasa in Chapter 6, this challenge has few straightforward solutions. Also for these state functions there might be a complex set of reasons why grabbing occurs. In particular, many of the chapters present examples of situations where members of the political elite and other influential players in society have likely been informed about the problem, but they have chosen not to intervene, possibly because there are direct or indirect benefits for them to tacitly condone or actively support grabbing. Consider for example the cases of apparent constitutional weaknesses and grand collusion, as described by Inge Amundsen in Chapter 11 on Bangladesh and Arne Strand in Chapter 14 on the grand fraud and corruption connected to Kabul Bank in Afghanistan. Very relevant examples of high-level incentive problems are the case of Angola presented by Lucy Corkin in Chapter 12 and the governance of resource production discussed by

Philippe Le Billon in Chapter 3: here grabbing seems to distort a range of mechanisms and involves a set of powerful players. In such cases, the true power structures might be blurred, grabbing has been allowed to continue and several societal integrity pillars malfunction.[10] If the law has also been altered to facilitate grabbing, it can be difficult to differentiate between what is legal and what is illegal, and thus, who can be held legally responsible for what.

Even if many of the *sector problems* presented appear defined, and apparently solvable, reform very often depends on the political willingness to act. Problems that are well understood and explained, such as in the chapters by Blessings Chinsinga and Liam Wren-Lewis in Chapter 7 on land grabbing and Gaël Raballand and Jean-François Marteau in Chapter 2 on governance failure in the ports sector, can be solved if governments decide to do so. The obvious challenge is the governments' monopoly on political power, which may be a challenge even in well-developed democratic countries. This explains why the narrow interests behind infrastructure priorities in Spain, as described by Germà Bel, Antonio Estache and Renaud Foucart in Chapter 10, seem to make the authors somewhat disillusioned, as they conclude with a need for better-informed voters and democratic reaction to signs of governance failure. Likewise, Jens Christian Andvig and Tiberius Barasa explain in Chapter 6 that while the problem of grabbing in Kenya's police forces can be somewhat reduced with certain practical initiatives, the sector as a whole has a long way to go to secure accountability, actions for which have to start at the top. A main lesson from the volume is therefore that standard anti-corruption strategies targeted at specific and usually isolated forms of grabbing, may not be enough. Grabbing as an obstacle to sector development is rarely *one* challenge; it is a complexity that must be understood from the perspective of many different players. The obstacles to reform must also be analysed and addressed, and this is where anti-corruption starts to get really difficult. Several of the chapters in this volume more or less explicitly accentuate the inadequacy of familiar policy approaches – like better control, transparency, auditing, checks and balances, civil society and democracy – while the main reason why they fail to deliver might be that they are not implemented well enough or comprehensively enough.

Most of the guidance we have in the literature on underlying incentive problems at high levels of governance is referred to as *political economy*. A practical side of this literature tells us how to map incentive problems, how to understand them analytically, what terms we can use to describe what we find, and how we might find directions towards reforms.[11] How to actually implement reforms in cases of fundamental dysfunctions is usually not so clear. Economic regulation theory adjusted for institutional weaknesses offers solutions (see Laffont, 2005, and Laffont and Tirole, 1991), but its application to politics is not sufficiently spelled-out in the literature, and besides, it tends to assume a benevolent principal. New institutional economics (see North, 1986, and Williamson, 2000) is rarely specific enough on how to actually address governance complexities. Mancur Olson (1996) and Ellinor Ostrom (2000), in their different ways, explain collective action problems, and how improved collaboration is needed for a society to escape a bad equilibrium, but again, we are missing a more practical view of how to go about escaping such an equilibrium.[12]

In order to bring us further on the more complex governance challenges, Susan Rose-Ackerman has developed a useful typology for analytic understanding of options for anti-corruption reform and explains how the choice of initiatives should be determined by the traits of government dysfunctions. She (1) provides logical categories of consequences of corruption and explains their implications for anti-corruption priorities (see Rose-Ackerman, 1999); (2) reviews anti-corruption solutions presented in the literature and describes how their relevance depends on macro-institutional characteristics (see Rose-Ackerman and Truex, 2013); and (3) provides an analytic discussion of how and when international players can make a difference, depending on given circumstances and goals (see Rose-Ackerman, 2013). With these contributions she provides a good starting point for a constructive approach, including for the most serious forms of anti-corruption challenges, and depicts a direction for further thinking and research. Since the real challenges are often related to implementation and reform processes, and not so much the design of optimal institutions, we need more research that outlines the steps towards improved state functions or sector governance. More specifically, we need sophisticated advice that addresses combinations of governance failures and weak framework conditions, and describes the dynamics of reform under imperfect circumstances. We hope this volume will motivate more research in such a direction.

NOTES

1. The term *rent-seeking* is much applied to describe investment of time and money to secure benefits for oneself in ways that are not beneficial to society at large. Among important contributions to the literature on rent-seeking are Krueger (1974), Rose-Ackerman (1978), Buchanan, Tollison and Tullock (1980) and Bhagwati (1982). While rent-seeking behaviour overlaps with our grabbing terminology, rent-seeking includes many legitimate acts like lobbying and marketing. The word *grabbing*,

however, refers more strongly to selfish acts in securing benefits for oneself and are, informally or formally, illegitimate acts. See Lambsdorff (2002b) and Harstad and Svensson (2011) for analyses of these nuances.

2. The Genevan philosopher Jean-Jacques Rousseau, who presented the idea of a social contract more than 250 years ago, said in his classic text that these laws '*are such that, though perhaps never formally stated, they are everywhere the same, everywhere tacitly admitted and recognized; and if ever the social pact is violated, every man regains his rights and, recovering his natural freedom, loses that civil freedom for which he exchanged it*' (Rousseau 1762 [2004]: 15).

3. Lambsdorff (2002a) explains how this deal requires reciprocity and therefore significant trust between those involved in the corruption.

4. The correlation between corruption and development has been studied and largely verified by econometric analyses, see among others Svensson (2005) and Aidt (2009).

5. Perhaps this is why Andrei Shleifer and Robert W. Vishny used the term in their much cited book, *The Grabbing Hand* (2002).

6. Grey zone areas could be to skip volunteer work for a neighbourhood ('grabbing the benefits while others make the effort') or playing music too loudly in a public area (which could be thought of as 'grabbing the atmosphere and the choice of music').

7. According to the author, the president replaces high-ranking officials frequently and in that way prevents any other individual from gaining too much influence. The 2010 Constitution secures for the president wide authority to replace and recruit civil servants, including all high-level positions in government and the judiciary.

8. See Chapter 3 by Philippe Le Billon for an explanation.

9. Many allegations in the media support this assumption. See, for example, the *Financial Times*, 30 April 2013, for the story 'Karzai admits CIA sent cash to Afghan intelligence agency'.

10. Transparency International has conducted National Integrity System (NIS) studies in many countries, in which *integrity pillars* in society, meaning the many checks, balances and controls in governance, are examined in terms of how they should operate in theory and in terms of actual practice. The results for European countries were disappointing, particularly since the studies revealed that corruption at the top level of states can take place far more easily than many of us had expected. See Transparency International's website for the studies.

11. Drazen (2000), Mueller (2003) and Besley (2006) among others present relevant theories. Sturzenegger and Tommasi (1998) offer experience-based explanation of challenges. There are also sector-specific literatures, such as for natural resource production, see Estache and Wren-Lewis (2009), see Frankel (2010) for a review. The World Bank offers practical guidance on how to identify and assess governance challenges, see their website for reports.

12. See Andvig and Moene (1990) for an explanation of the dynamic mechanisms at play behind good and bad corruption equilibria.

REFERENCES

Aidt, T. (2009), Corruption, institutions, and economic development. *Oxford Review of Economic Economic Policy*, **25** (2), 271–291.

Andvig, J. C. and K. O. Moene (1990), How corruption may corrupt. *Journal of Economic Behavior and Organization*, **13**, 63–76.

Besley, T. (2006), *Principled Agents? The Political Economy of Good Government*. Lindahl Lectures. Oxford: Oxford University Press.

Bhagwati, J. N. (1982), Directly unproductive, profit-seeking (DUP) activities. *Journal of Political Economy*, **90** (5), 988–1002.

Buchanan, J. M., R. D. Tollison and G. Tullock (eds) (1980), *Toward a Theory of the Rent-Seeking Society*. College Station, TX: A&M University Press.

Drazen, A. (2000), *Political Economy in Macroeconomics*. Princeton, NJ: Princeton University Press.

Estache, A. and L. Wren-Lewis. (2009), Toward a theory of regulation in developing countries: following Jean-Jacques Laffont's Lead. *Journal of Economic Literature*, **47** (3), 729–770.

Frankel, J. A. (2010), The natural resource curse: a survey. NBER Working Paper 15836. National Bureau of Economic Research, Cambridge, MA.

Harstad, B. and J. Svensson. (2011), Bribes, lobbying and development. *American Political Science Review*, **105** (1), 46–63.

Krueger, A. O. (1974), The political economy of the rent-seeking society. *American Economic Review*, **64** (3), 291–303.

Laffont, J. J. (2005), *Regulation and Development*. Cambridge and New York: Cambridge University Press.

Laffont, J. J. and J. Tirole (1991), The politics of government decision making. A theory of regulatory capture. *Quarterly Journal of Economics*, **106** (4), 1089–1127.

Lambsdorff, J. G. (2002a), Making corrupt deals: contracting in the shadow of the law. *Journal of Economic Behavior and Organization*, **48** (3), 221–224.

Lambsdorff, J. G. (2002b), Corruption and rent-seeking. *Public Choice*, **113**, 97–125.

Mueller, D. C. (2003), *Public Choice III*. Cambridge: Cambridge University Press.

North, D. C. (1986), The New Institutional Economics. *Journal of Institutional and Theoretical Economics*, **142** (1), 230–237.

Olson, M. (1996), Bigbillsleft on the sidewalk: why some nations are rich, and others poor. *Journal of Economic Perspectives*, **10**, 3–24.

Ostrom, E. (2000), Collective action and the evolution of social norms. *The Journal of Economic Perspectives*, **14** (3), 137–158.

Pinker, S. (1997), *How the Mind Works*. New York: W. W. Norton and Company.

Rose-Ackerman, S. (1978), *Corruption: A Study in Political Economy*. New York: Academic Press.

Rose-Ackerman, S. (1999), *Corruption and Government. Causes, Consequences and Reform*. Cambridge: Cambridge University Press.

Rose-Ackerman, S. (2013), Introduction: the role of international actors in fighting corruption. In S. Rose-Ackerman and P. Carrington. (eds), *Anti-Corruption Policy: Can International Actors Play a Constructive Role?* Durham, NC: Carolina Academic Press, pp. 3–38.

Rose-Ackerman, S. and R. Truex. (2013), Corruption and Policy Reform. In B. Lomborg (ed.) *Global Problems, Smart Solutions: Costs and Benefits*. Cambridge: Cambridge University Press, forthcoming.

Rousseau, J. J. (1762 [(2004)], *The Social Contract*. London: Penguin Books.

Shleifer, A., and R. W. Vishny. (2002), *The Grabbing Hand: Government Pathologies and Their Cures.* Cambridge, MA: Harvard University Press.

Sturzenegger, F. and M. Tommasi (1998), *The Political Economy of the Reform.* Cambridge, MA: The MIT Press.

Svensson, J. (2005), Eight questions about corruption. *Journal of Economic Perspectives*, **19** (3), 19–42.

Trivers, R. (1971), The evolution of reciprocal altruism. *Quarterly Review of Biology*, **46**, 35–57.

Williamson, O. E. (2000), The New Institutional Economics: taking stock, looking ahead. *Journal of Economic Literature*, **38** (3), 595–613.

PART I

Grabbing explained by characteristics of a sector or state function

1. Corruption and collusion in construction: a view from the industry

Jill Wells

Investment in capital projects is essential for economic growth and development. Yet there is widespread dissatisfaction with the outcomes of construction investment. Major challenges in developing countries include inappropriate projects, high prices, poor quality, excessive time and cost overruns, inadequate maintenance and low returns. These problems impact negatively on development and poverty alleviation and have led to a search for ways to get better 'value for money' from the construction industry.

At least a part of the explanation for poor construction outcomes in low-income countries relates to mismanagement, but corruption is also an issue that has to be addressed. The construction sector is widely reported as one of the most corrupt globally. Public works and construction repeatedly top the charts of Transparency International's Bribe Payer's Index, perceived as the sector most likely to engage in bribery (Hardoon and Heinrich, 2011). Estimates of 20–30 per cent of project value lost through corruption are widespread. In the most comprehensive review of corruption in the construction industry to date, Stansbury (2005) outlines 13 features of construction projects that make them particularly prone to corruption. Most relevant are: size, uniqueness, complexity and the fact that projects are structured through various phases and contractual links that disperse accountability among numerous separate agents.

This chapter will explain the various processes involved in the delivery of a construction project, highlighting the project delivery stages from planning through to completion. A simplified version of the stages is presented in Table 1.1, showing the risks of corrupt behaviour at each stage and the participants involved. The focus of the discussion is on developing countries, particularly the countries in sub-Saharan Africa (SSA) and on the delivery of publicly owned construction projects.

Table 1.1 Stages in the delivery of a construction project

	Project identification	Project preparation	Tender and selection	Construction and quality control	Handover, operation and maintenance
Risks	Political influence or lobbying by private firms that biases selection to suit political or private (individual or company) interests Political influence to favour large projects and new construction over maintenance Low estimate of costs to get projects approved without economic justification	Poor planning and inadequate compensation for loss of land and livelihoods Costly designs which increase consultants', fees and contractors' profits Design to favour a specific contractor Incomplete designs leaving room for changes which can be manipulated High estimate of costs to provide a cushion for later diversion of funds	Bribery to obtain contracts, (which means costs have to be recovered at the next stage) Deliberate underestimation of costs to win tender Collusion among bidders to allocate contracts and/or raise price (may be with assistance from procurement officers) Interference by procurement officers to favour specific firms or individuals	Agreement between contractor and the supervising engineer (with or without knowledge of the client) to accept lower quality materials, overlook substandard work Agreement between contractors and supervising engineer to increase the contract sum or reduce the scope of work through variations, in order to make extra profit, cover potential losses or recover money spent on bribes	Agreement by the supervising engineer to accept poor quality work or work below the specification, leading to rapid deterioration of assets Problem exacerbated by lack of funds for maintenance as new construction takes precedence in project identification stage
Main participants	Government ministers, politicians and senior civil servants + private sector consultants	Client + consultants, (planners, designers, engineers, surveyors)	Client + procurement officers + consultants + contractors + supervising engineers	Client + Contractor + subcontractors + supervising engineers	Client + supervising engineer + contractor

1.1 DELIVERING A CONSTRUCTION PROJECT

Once a project has been identified and included in government budgets, responsibility for delivery is under the direction of the client or a separate procuring agency working on the client's behalf. While in the past much public construction work in developing countries was planned, designed, priced and constructed 'in house' by professional staff employed in a government ministry or local authority, it is increasingly the practice to engage private companies to provide these services. The majority of developing countries have copied from the higher-income nations a system based on the separation of key functions. Separate contracts are signed with participants based on historically defined roles for the architect, engineer, quantity surveyor and builder, with separate responsibilities for planning and designing the structure, constructing the asset and supervising the construction. Hence responsibility for delivery is divided among a large number of people who, while performing essentially complementary activities, belong to quite separate commercial units.

The participants have to comply with various control mechanisms the purpose of which is to ensure accountability. Where the control mechanisms are weak, or have broken down, an environment is created where any two parties can enter into an agreement to bend the rules. The question that arises is why the controls so frequently break down?

A fundamental problem is that the separation of functions means that the control mechanisms at each stage (planning, design, construction, and so on) are independent. It is assumed that the functions are sequential and that one stage is completed before the next begins, but in practice the functions overlap and there is interdependence among the participants from different stages. Ground-breaking research into the British building industry in 1966 found that the non-continuous and sequential application of the control functions conflicts with the management requirements on the ground (Tavistock Institute, 1966: 45–46).[1] In practice the formal system cannot be closely followed and is replaced by informal procedures that produce more realistic phasing of decisions, more continuous application of controls and more flexibility in the face of the inevitable uncertainties. These procedures are never written down and yet they are universally understood and widely followed (*ibid.*).

Research by the author into the construction industry in Kenya at around the same time echoed these findings, revealing problems of inadequate capacity but also a formal system for delivering projects that was simply not working and in many instances not workable (Wells and

Rado, 1968). Informal practices developed as participants tried to get around the many obstacles inhibiting project delivery (inadequate planning, inflated expectations, incomplete design, delayed payment). Recent findings from the Construction Sector Transparency (CoST) initiative[2] have revealed that little has changed in many countries.

1.2 THE SYSTEM OF COMPETITIVE TENDER

Nowhere are problems with the formal control systems more apparent than in the practice of putting the contract for construction (the works contract) out to competitive tender after the design has (in principle) been developed. According to the multilateral development banks (MDBs) and most developing countries with reformed procurement procedures, the default option for the procurement of works contracts is open tendering (usually conducted through a sealed bid auction) with the contract awarded to the bidder offering to complete the project for the lowest price (open tender/lowest price).[3] Opening bidding to all and evaluating bids solely on the basis of price is preferred by international agencies as it is presumed to reduce the exercise of discretion, thereby avoiding favouritism and corruption in contract award.[4]

However, the award of construction contracts to the lowest bidder through sealed bid auctions is based on a number of key assumptions, which are summarized in Table 1.2. Most important is that all aspects of the project have been finalised before tender and specified in detail in the tender documents. In practice, designs are rarely complete before tender and it has been argued that the need for feedback from contractors means it is unlikely that designs can ever be complete before construction starts (Tavistock Institute, 1966). One-quarter (26 per cent) of problems found in the delivery of construction projects in the eight countries involved in the CoST pilot were at the pre-tender stage. These included poor quality and incomplete design with items missing, failure to survey sites, and so on (CoST, 2011). In this situation changes to the client's brief continue to be fed into the construction process as it evolves, requiring renegotiation of the contract between the supervising engineer and the contractor. The latter is in a powerful position post-contract to engage in opportunistic behaviour and this may be facilitated by a corrupt engineer. Late payment of contractors' invoices further weakens the bargaining power of the client and is a major reason why contracts are not enforced. The CoST project identified poor payment practices as a major problem in many countries and a factor limiting the effectiveness of the control mechanisms in the contract for managing time and cost (CoST, 2011).

Table 1.2   Assumptions in the open tender/lowest price method of contract award and their implications

Assumption	Implication
Design is complete before tender	Incomplete design means that changes are needed post contract, which opens the door to post-contract negotiation and opportunistic behaviour over variations and claims
	It also means that costs cannot be estimated with any degree of accuracy
Bidders can accurately estimate costs at tender stage	Estimating errors may lead to the acceptance of unrealistically low tender prices, which means insufficient funds in the contract to deliver to the specification
	A contract price below the estimated cost means that something has to give – either prices are inflated to cover real costs or work has to be accepted below specification
	Inability to estimate costs accurately, and the danger of predatory pricing by others, drives contractors to bribe or collude in order to win contracts
	Bribery and low contract prices both encourage cheating during construction
Government has budgeted well	Late payment weakens the bargaining power of clients and is a major reason why contracts are not enforced.

A second assumption behind the award of construction contracts to the lowest bidder is that contractors can make accurate estimates at the time of tender of costs to complete the work. But this is also unrealistic, particularly when design is incomplete. Estimating errors are unavoidable. There is substantial evidence that competitive tendering through sealed bid auctions forces contractors to price work at unrealistically low levels (Brockman, 2011). In addition to normal estimating errors,[5] bid prices will reflect local market conditions at the time the tender is launched and when the market is slack contractors may bid low to keep their foremen employed and labour gangs together. In SSA, where there are often no significant barriers to entry to the industry, it is common for inexperienced contractors to win contracts through the submission of unrealistically low bids.

A bid that is too low to cover costs can land the winning contractor in serious trouble, which is why it is often referred to as the 'winner's curse'. It might lead to the contractor making a loss or even to default and collapse, but generally contractors will seek ways to cover potential losses, by squeezing their subcontractors, putting in claims and becoming more aggressive in negotiations with the client. The more unscrupulous may cheat on the materials, compromise on quality and deliver below the specification, leading to poor quality assets and high maintenance costs. Both inflated claims and poor performance require collaboration between the contractor and the supervising engineer and hence further breakdown of the checks and balances embodied in the control system. Forty per cent of the concerns raised during the CoST pilot occurred during implementation (CoST, 2011).

1.3 WHY DO CONTRACTORS BRIBE OR COLLUDE TO WIN CONTRACTS?

Submitting a low bid to win a contact may also be adopted as a deliberate tactic. Brockman (2011) argues that competing in a sealed bid auction is the worst situation a seller can be in. Contractors must submit a bid without any knowledge of the other bidders' behaviour – and with open tender, no knowledge of their competitors. The chance of making a profit increases with a higher price, yet the chance of winning the competition decreases (Drew, 2011). The situation is further complicated by the fact that s/he does not know with any certainty what the costs are going to be. Submitting an unrealistically low bid and recovering potential losses through claims is one way in which contractors fight back against what they regard as an unfair pricing system. Alternative ways are paying a bribe or colluding with other bidders to agree who will win the contract and at what price.

1.3.1 Bribery to Win Contracts

Bribery to win a contract is the most visible form of corrupt activity. The best evidence comes from talking to those involved in paying and receiving bribes. Discussions with local contractors in Ghana and Nigeria (Ladbury, 2003) revealed that they pay bribes first to get onto tender lists (when tender is by invitation only) and then to win a contract. There are similar findings from discussions with contractors in Tanzania (TACECA, 2007) and in the water sector in South Asia (Davis, 2004). A large majority (83 per cent) of respondents to the survey in Tanzania said that the major contributing factor is the high level of competition for small-value contracts due to ease of entry into the industry, the prevalence of open tender procedures and large firms moving down market to bid for smaller contracts. A contractor who wins one contract may not be able to win another for many years yet a regular flow of contracts is essential if a firm is to survive.

Bribery to win a contract leads to further compromises during contract implementation similar to those resulting from unrealistically low prices. Evidence from Tanzania suggests a direct link between bribery at tender stage and lax supervision during construction. Contractors interviewed in the TACECA (2007) study said that they paid bribes of 10–15 per cent to win contracts in return for a 'conducive environment' for recovering the shortfall through delivery of substandard works. Similarly, contractors in Ghana and Nigeria report they pay between 10 and 20 per cent in bribes to win a tender after which supervising engineers and contractors agree to use fewer materials and split the savings (Ladbury, 2003). While, in South Asia, Davis (2004) found contractors paying additional bribes (kickbacks) during construction of between 5–11 per cent of contract value, in part to cover low-quality work.

Often overlooked is corruption in the award of contracts with professional consultants (architects, engineers, surveyors, and so on) appointed to design, manage or supervise the construction. This may be because the contract sums involved are smaller, but the value of the consultant's contract is not significant as consultants may conspire with the contractor to facilitate the extraction of rents from the construction contract and share in the proceeds (Mawenya, 2007).

1.3.2   Collusion to Allocate Contracts

An alternative to bribery to gain access to contracts is colluding with other bidders to 'fix' the competition.[6] Evidence of collusion among contractors during the tender process – whereby it is agreed to let one contractor win in return for a percentage payment or similar support on another contract – is overwhelming. Hard evidence from investigations into cartels comes mostly from developed countries. But the integrity department (INT) of the World Bank reports that collusion is rife in the roads sector in a large number of developing countries, including Kenya, Tanzania, Uganda, Cambodia, Philippines, Indonesia, Nepal, Pakistan, some states in India, as well as in Columbia and Peru (World Bank, 2011). In some of these countries, cartels are well established and have operated for many years. The effect on tender prices is believed to be significant (up to 30 per cent) and higher than when cartels operate in developed countries.

But collusion does not necessarily result in higher prices. Suppliers collude to decide two issues: who should win the contract and at what price. There is a rationale to allocating contracts among a group of bidders. Contractors involved in collusion in the Dutch construction industry maintained that it made their businesses less vulnerable to predatory pricing and helped to reduce uncertainty about future workload fluctuations (Dorée, 2004). It reduced rivalry and created a more stable and predictable market environment. Collusion in bidding also means considerable savings on estimating costs that are inevitably passed on to clients in the longer term. When a fair price is bid the client may also benefit by avoiding the negative consequences that flow from a price below the real costs of construction.

1.4 CHECKS AND BALANCES, COMPROMISES AND INFORMAL SYSTEMS

I have argued that the formal systems of control that have been established in the construction industry involve a number of contra-dictions, chief of which is the pretence that design and construction are separate and sequential tasks and that a cost and time for completion of the works can be set with certainty at tender stage. The contract agreement is a legally binding agreement between client and contractor, yet all know that it is impossible to predict the time it will take to complete a project and the cost involved. Because the formal system cannot work as intended informal procedures have developed which are not necessarily corrupt, but pretending to still adhere to the formal system when everybody knows that it cannot work involves *collusion in acceptance of unreality by all parties* (Tavistock Institute, 1996: 49).

On the basis of discussions with contractors and project managers in Ghana, Nigeria and the UK, Ladbury (2003) found informal systems that involve practices that are common to all three countries' construction industries. These include: bribery to get onto tender lists or to win contracts, submitting false information in documents, forming a cartel, submitting several bids from the same contractor under different names, front-loading the tender, putting in a low bid and then making claims or skimping on materials, not making good defects and foregoing retention. Many of the informants in Ghana and Nigeria did not see these practices as corrupt, while in the UK a recent survey by the UK Chartered Institute of Building (CIOB, 2006) found that: *collusion between bidders for market sharing purposes* and *leaking of information to a preferential bidder* was considered only moderately corrupt or not at all corrupt by 60 per cent of respondents and *production of fraudulent timesheets and invoices* was considered only moderately or not at all corrupt by around

50 per cent of respondents[7]. Ladbury (2003) concluded that the opportunities for manipulation and the standards used to classify activities as 'corrupt' appear to be more specific to the construction industry than to what most citizens associate with the term. Actions regarded elsewhere as corrupt are seen by the industry as simply the way of doing business.

1.5 POLICY IMPLICATIONS

The current approach to address the issue of corruption in the construction sector suggests that the practices described above could be prevented by tighter regulation, perhaps also with more transparency and civil society oversight such as envisaged in the CoST programme.[8] But a question that is raised by Ladbury (2003) is whether current anti-corruption strategies take account of the nature of the relationships in the informal system. She argues that many of the above practices:

> do not involve procedures that can be 'tightened up' because they are based on institutionalized systems of social – as well as financial – relations which are not always visible to the outside eye … Any organisation intending to move a system from the informal end of the continuum towards the formal end will need to take account of the enmeshed nature of these relationships and their lack of visibility. (Ladbury, 2003: 30)

Regulation could be tightened, given the political will, despite the difficulties in this sector. But tackling the problem of corruption in the construction industry will also require a move to a formal system that can actually work. If corruption is to be reduced there is need for a more rational system for awarding contracts and a more transparent way of paying contractors for the work done. It must recognize interdependence between the various participants and the uncertainty that underlies all construction processes.

There is a better way of doing business and it involves a lot more trust and cooperation among the parties within the construction team. Writing in the aftermath of a major corruption scandal in the Netherlands in 2002, Nijhof et al. (2009) argue that trust can be built within the tender requirements with more transparency about the performance that is to be delivered and about past performance. If the award of a contract was based on the company's record on past contracts (and not just on the price, which is currently the case) there would be an incentive to perform well in order to obtain more work in the future. There should be particular scrutiny of the past performance of engineering consultants appointed to supervise the construction work as it is they who control most of the avenues through which corruption can occur.

Recognition of interdependence will require more integrated forms of contract. This could be through a 'design-build' approach where there is a single point of responsibility, or where the relationship is based on a common financial interest as the parties share in any cost savings or losses. In many developed countries it is now common practice to engage a contractor during the design stage and to make payments on the basis of the actual costs of construction, through a 'cost-plus' contract. The danger of escalating costs can be addressed by 'open book' accounting and the client and contractor agreeing a target cost once the design is substantially complete. Any difference between the final cost and the target cost is then split according to a 'pain/gain' formula set out in the contract. Such arrangements are now routinely adopted on major UK public construction projects using the New Engineering Contract (NEC) developed by the UK Institution of Civil Engineers. NEC contracts are increasingly used in the Gulf States, South Africa, Botswana, Australia, New Zealand and Hong Kong. There is growing interest in other countries in SSA.

The current insistence on awarding construction (works) contracts solely on the basis of price is clearly ineffectual in dealing with corruption in the construction industry. The argument made here is that it may even be encouraging it. The components of a more rational system are already available and tested and developing countries need to be allowed a little more room to experiment. While there will always be greedy people and corruption will still exist, at least some of the major causes will have been eliminated with a change to a more rational procurement system.

NOTES

1. These findings have been confirmed by a number of subsequent studies commissioned by or on behalf of the UK government, see for example Latham (1994) and Egan (1998).
2. The Construction Sector Transparency (CoST) initiative aims to improve value for money in infrastructure programmes by increasing transparency in the delivery of construction projects. It was piloted between 2008 and 2011 in eight countries (Ethiopia, Guatemala, Malawi, the Philippines, Tanzania, the UK, Vietnam and Zambia) with support from the UK Department for International Development (DFID) and the World Bank. A new expanded programme was launched in late October 2012. The author has been involved in the initiative from the start.

3. In principle the 'lowest evaluated bid' but in practice the lowest responsive bid as consideration of issues other than price is not allowed by the MDBs in the evaluation of tenders for works contracts.

4. Contracts are awarded either on the basis of a lump sum (estimated on close scrutiny of the drawings and specification) or in the form of an agreed 'schedule of rates' or priced 'bill of quantities', whereby provision is made for re-measurement of each item of work as construction proceeds. There may be conditions in the contract to increase the sums paid to the contractor due to price escalation. But essentially these are fixed price contracts, as opposed to cost-plus arrangements.

5. Brockman (2011) has shown that, while the distribution of errors among the bidders may be unbiased overall, this is not so for the lowest bid which will inevitably lie below the mean. Hence the contractor who wins the contract is the one with the largest estimating error.

6. Collusion among bidders is not always regarded as corruption, although it is often linked to corrupt officials in the procurement agency (Lambert-Mogiliansky, 2011).

7. A second survey by the CIOB into corruption in the construction industry will be published shortly (see www.ciob.org). The key finding is that 49 per cent of respondents believe that corruption is common in the UK construction industry, a 2 per cent decrease form the first survey published in 2006.

8. The CoST programme has interpreted transparency as the disclosure of detailed construction project information into the public domain. While this may provide useful information on failures in the delivery of construction projects it seems unlikely (in the author's opinion) to reveal much about the reasons for the failure or about how the informal system actually works.

REFERENCES

Brockmann, C. (2011), Collusion and corruption in the construction sector. In G. D. Valence (ed.), *Modern Construction Economics: Theory and Application.* Oxford: Spon Press, pp. 29–62.

CIOB (2006), Corruption in the UK Construction Industry, Chartered Institute of Building, Ascot, UK. Available at: http: //www.ciob.org.uk/sites/ciob.org.uk/files/WEB-INF/files/documents/CIOBCorruption.pdf (accessed 8 March 2013).

CoST (2011), Report on information disclosure and assurance team findings: international comparison. Available at: http: //www.constructiontransparency.org/_db/_documents/27._International_AT_report.pdf (accessed 8 March 2013).

Davis, J. (2004), Corruption in public service delivery: experience from South Asia's water and sanitation sector, *World Development*, **32** (1), 53–71.

Dorée, A. G. (2004), Collusion in the Dutch construction industry: an industrial organisation perspective, *Building Research and Information,* **32** (2), 146–156.

Drew, D. (2011), Competing in construction auctions: a theoretical perspective. In G. D. Valence (ed.), *Modern Construction Economics: Theory and Application.* Oxford: Spon Press, pp. 63–79.

Egan, J. (1998), Rethinking construction. Report of a construction taskforce chaired by Sir John Egan, HMSO, London.

Hardoon, D. and F. Heinrich (2011), *Bribe Payers Index 2011*. Berlin: Transparency International Secretariat. Available at: https://www.kpk-rs.si/download/t_datoteke/2017 (accessed 8 March 2013).

Ladbury, S. (2003), Annex 1. Informal practices in the construction industry: findings of an empirical study. Beyond bureaucratic solutions: the political economy and informal systems approach to corruption. Unpublished report.

Lambert-Mogiliansky, A. (2011), Corruption and collusion: strategic complements in procurement. In Susan Rose-Ackerman and Tina Soreide (eds), *International Handbook on the Economics of Corruption, Volume II*. Cheltenham, UK and Northampton, MA: Edward Elgar, pp. 108–140.

Latham, M. (1994), Constructing the team: final report of the government/industry review of procurement and contractual arrangements in the UK construction industry. London: HMSO.

Mawenya, A. S. (2007), Challenges of delivering value for money [from] consulting engineering services in corruption prone sub-Saharan African countries. Paper presented at the 14th GAMA conference, Gaberone, Botswana, 14–17 May.

Nijhof, A., J. Graafland and O. de Kuiper (2009), Exploration of an agenda for transparency in the construction industry, *Construction Innovation*, **9** (3), 250–267.

Stansbury, N. (2005), Exposing the Foundations of Corruption in Construction. In *Corruption in Practice, Transparency International Global Corruption Report 2005*. Transparency International: Berlin, Chapter 2. Available at: http://archive.transparency.org/publications/gcr/gcr_2005 (accessed 8 March 2013).

TACECA (2007), Study on the state of corruption in the procurement of construction contracts and proposals for mitigation, Final Report, Tanzania Civil Engineering Contractors Association, Dar es Salaam.

Tavistock Institute (1996), *Interdependence and Uncertainty*. London: Tavistock Publications.

Wells, E. J. and E. R. Rado (1968), Constraints and costs in the Kenya building industry, Staff Paper no. 22, Institute of Development Studies, University of Nairobi, Kenya.

World Bank (2011), *Curbing Fraud, Corruption and Collusion in the Roads Sector*. Washington DC: World Bank.

2. Rents extraction in the sub-Saharan Africa port sector

Gaël Raballand and Jean-François Marteau

Ports are critical for trade facilitation. One of the specificities of ports in sub-Saharan Africa (SSA) on top of their small size is their long dwell time: on average cargo spend 3 weeks there compared to less than a week in high income regions (see Table 2.1). Long cargo dwell times in ports are a critical issue in SSA countries since they result in slow import processes and are bound to constrain trade.

Table 2.1   Average cargo dwell time in sub-Saharan Africa (in days)

Durban	Douala	Lomé	Tema	Mombasa	Dar es Salaam	Average (Durban excluded)
4	19	18	20	11	14	16

Source: Raballand et al. (2012a).

Findings of recent research (Raballand et al., 2012a[1]) point to the crucial importance of private sector behaviours, such as the common practice of some shippers of using ports as a storage area, to explain long cargo dwell time. Rather than being advocates of reforms, numerous private operators are actually among those responsible for the failures of many initiatives to facilitate trade and reduce corruption.

Corruption is often rampant in ports[2] in SSA (customs brokers and/or importers usually pay bribes to customs, controlling agencies and port authorities to reduce tariff duties and handling fees) and results in a low equilibrium of collusion between public agents and cartelized private operators (at the expense of final consumers since brokers charge importers for the bribes paid to public agents and operators, and importers increase their selling prices due to high prices of brokering). Long dwell times are also used de facto as one of the natural barriers to prevent competition and maintain rent extraction (by preventing competition from foreign or local structured investors) for some companies.

2.1 THE PERVASIVENESS OF CORRUPTION IN THE PORT SECTOR IN SSA

A well-known example of tariff evasion taking place in ports is Panalpina World Transport (Holding) Ltd. and Panalpina US, who admitted having violated the Foreign Corrupt Practices Act's anti-bribery provisions. Both companies paid bribes to various foreign officials on behalf of numerous customers in the oil and gas industry (in order to evade tariff duties and speed up processes). The purpose of bribes was to avoid local rules and regulations connected to the import of goods. For example, Panalpina Nigeria provided an express courier service through which it made corrupt payments on behalf of its customers to Nigerian customs officials in order to evade the normal customs process and, thereby, expedite delivery. Specifically, between 2002 and 2007, both corporations paid bribes totaling at least USD 27 million to foreign officials (Igbanugo, 2012).

Due to the high number of stakeholders, it is important to describe each institution/organization's role in a port.[3]

- The Port Authority usually owns port infrastructure and sometimes still operates conventional terminals. It is usually responsible for managing and developing ports in a country, often provides marine services and rules on navigation restrictions. It usually decides on vessels call sequence.
- Container terminal operators are usually private concessionaires, in joint venture or not with local partners. They are in charge of investing in handling equipment and charge handling and storage fees (if applicable). They usually have a monopoly on containers traffic in SSA since most of the time, there is only one container terminal per port. Monitoring of port charges by authorities is usually weak. Container terminals are usually very profitable due to high tariffs.
- Customs and other controlling agencies: they are responsible for collecting tariff duties and excise taxes and VAT (when applicable) and make sure imports comply with various local regulations (health, standards, veterinary, phytosanitary, security …).
- Other private stakeholders include: import and export companies, freight forwarders and customs brokers (who are usually the

intermediate in charge of organizing transport and clearance of goods), shipping lines (companies in charge of transporting goods) and their local representatives (shipping agents), owners of containers depots, truckers and transporters.

It is worth differentiating petty corruption, which is usually between public and private operators (and sometimes among private stakeholders) in order for instance to speed up processes, from grand corruption, which involves high-level politicians and/or bureaucrats (to evade tariff duties for instance). Grand corruption may be less visible but can have more severe impacts.[4]

In many instances, corruption and rent-seeking behaviours stem from the existence of information asymmetry[5] between several key stakeholders, the most common being between some agents or customs brokers and some customs officials at the expense of the importer and the treasury. An importer will often use an agent to organize transport and clearance of imports, and in some countries it is even compulsory to use an intermediate. In many cases, customs brokers do not give their customer (in other words, the importer) a breakdown of the various fees. The shipper is therefore aware of the total cost but not of what corresponds to overheads and bribes since tariffs are usually not public.

In several countries, access to the Clearing and Forwarding (C&F) profession is restricted to large foreign companies and a limited number of individuals, who have strong connections with some customs officials. Most of the time, access to intermediation is not based on professional criteria. One consequence of this easy or non-rationalized access is 'suitcase' companies with low capacity, low training and low professionalism (but strong political connections). In such situations, customs clearance, dwell time and uncertainty increase significantly. The responsibility for this low performance is then due to private firms in C&F, and not to public parastatals such as port authorities or customs. Statistical evidence from Cameroon suggest that more than 50 per cent of dwell time in the Port of Douala is caused by C&F low capacity to fulfill documentary requirements properly or the inability to provide the necessary payments or securities. When the Cameroon Facilitation Committee tried to set quality criteria for clearing agents in 2005, less than 10 per cent managed to fulfill them even after one year, and the process had to be stopped. There are few incentives for agencies and operators to be transparent in their cost breakdown since the most important profits for brokers derive from information asymmetry: as long as the importer does not know the real cost of procedures and tariff duties, the broker can continue to overcharge the importer (Arvis et al., 2010).

On the administration side, procedures (and especially additional control procedures) are often non-selective as they affect all shipments and are essentially independent of the nature of the consignment. Even compliant shippers or consignees can fail to obtain fast track processes. Conversely, consignees using the service of non-professional freight forwarders might be better off and can sometimes get faster clearance through informal practices.

Another recurrent feature is that, in many countries, small-scale traders often start to clear imported goods only when they have been pre-sold, thereby using the port as a free or cheap storage space even when they are located several hundreds (or thousands) of kilometres away. In many cases, price and availability of cash is the only criteria for the importer, who is ready to leave cargo (or even abandon it) if duties are not substantially reduced. Therefore, a bargaining process between the importer/broker and customs officials can last for several days. In these cases, port storage tariffs are a critical incentive. If there is no tariff escalation and tariffs are low, it can be an incentive for an importer to bargain longer and leave the cargo in the port. Using a typical private storage cost, we estimate that storage in the port of Douala is cheaper than outside the port storage for 22 days, meaning 11 days more than the container terminal's free time (Raballand et al., 2012a)![6] It is also worth noting that storage fees, despite low unit prices, can be a major source of revenues for container terminal operators. Therefore, long dwell time increases revenues for terminal operators (as long as there is no severe congestion) and is cost-neutral for importers.[7]

Moreover, customs auction practices[8] can indirectly incentivize importers to extend their port dwell time. Cargo owners or importers, who are often unable or unwilling to pay very high duty on their high-value goods, deliberately delay formal procedures to take advantage of customs auction practices. This becomes possible when the auction processes are rigged and limit selling prices. Under the alternative (illegal) auction practice, the importer buys back his/her own goods at an artificially low price in return for paying a commission to the customs agency (Raballand et al., 2012a).

The import process in ports can become a chain of rents and bribes: first, the importer reduces tariff duties through negotiations, but is often able to charge high prices to consumers (due to cartelized markets) and second, the broker/freight forwarder extracts rents by benefitting from information asymmetry and reducing what he pays to customs or other agencies involved in imports. These two factors have the largest impact on port governance and on the state, and can possibly be verified by using mirror customs statistics to see the discrepancy in declared value

(Raballand et al., 2012b). Moreover, the broker can overcharge the importer, while on other elements of the logistics chain the terminal operator limits investments to its minimum, tries to secure its monopoly and charges high port tariffs (and redistributes part of it in exchange for loose control from local authorities). These weaknesses are even more profitable for an 'integrated' company (port operator, freight forwarder, transporter) since business units can subsidize each other and the opacity of tariffs can be higher. Finally, customs officers take bribes to reduce the tariff duties paid. The benefits of corruption are then shared by everybody in the logistics chain.

The consequences of these phenomena are multiple: (1) long dwell time because of the bargaining process time as well as the use of pre-sell goods to limit cash exits; (2) high maritime transport costs because, for example, ships have to wait for a berth and increase their prices because of immobilization costs; (3) practices lead to low actual taxation and low public revenues since tariff duties bargaining are done at the expense of the treasury.

2.2 WHAT CAN EXPLAIN THE PERVASIVENESS OF CORRUPTION?

Ports in Africa remain one of the biggest sources of fiscal revenues (import dues and VAT, and sometimes export dues), which justifies an abundance of control processes that multiply opportunities of direct contacts between importers (or their agents) and various officials. Simplification of processes is often resisted by some customs officers and even some customs brokers and cannot be completely offset by full automation if access to some professions (especially customs brokers) is itself fraudulent. This is an example of how local business is distorted with an adverse selection effect: the ones remaining in business are the best connected and usually not the most professional.

This overall situation is in a stable equilibrium because the overwhelming majority of port users have an interest in keeping the status quo, especially customs brokers and freight forwarders. Large international companies can overcharge clients and can resort to specific arrangements with high-level officials, and in many cases obtain decent dwell time to get their goods out if need be. Small and inefficient operators also bribe their way out of import processes and can also get fast clearance if they need to, or withstand very long dwell times on purpose for storage or to later re-buy goods. This translates into the long average dwell time observed, and in daunting figures of uncertainty in dwell time (sometimes 2 or 3 times more than the already long dwell time). As a result of both behaviours, the main losers are mid-size structured local firms or potential newcomers, who would have to go through the long and non-selective 'normal' processes, pay high duties and potentially also a few extra illegal fees to get their goods.

The system is also based on the fact that duties are underestimated in quantity and in value in many countries. To get importers to pay the real tariff for real quantities in many countries would mean (1) customs staff having to explain huge variations in revenues, including why it was lower (unless everybody is changed in the customs administration), (2) potentially run the risk of inflation in key imported goods price with the associated social impact when actual duties are applied (there are still many countries with tariff categories over 20 per cent). Besides, importers are often players in these arrangements, and thus, local business communities in general are not necessarily going to be supportive of changes in fear of short-term impact (unless enforcement is accompanied by a decrease in customs tariffs). Complying with rules would therefore mean a loss for many. Moreover, the level of undervaluation of duties is still often such that customs authorities can still achieve improvements (vis-à-vis the International Monetary Fund or their own ministry of finance) without tackling substantially the issue of transactions at import.

In practice, discretion remains important in the import control process and few administrations have the means to completely control their frontline staff because traditionally appointment of officers is often decided at a very high political level given the associated benefits. This also means that normal sanction processes in the administrations will not function as intended and the decisions are not assessed by controlling authorities. Customs brokers professions are not really controlled, and securities or guarantee mechanisms are often not called or they are ineffective. Finally, in many instances judicial systems do not provide enough guarantees for addressing economic related crimes or fraud, because of influence peddling or simple overcrowding of courts.

2.3 WHAT ARE THE CONSEQUENCES OF CORRUPTION IN PORTS?

The extreme impact of corruption in ports is economic paralysis, even if it does not happen frequently. The most well-known examples are Cameroon in the mid-1990s and Nigeria in the early 2000s. In both cases, agents' behaviours described above resulted in further increases in dwell time beyond the low equilibrium usually experienced, and significant congestion, which had a rollover effect on maritime transport (therefore triggering actions from international shipping lines) and exponential development of additional side-bribes and rent extraction processes that affected the whole economy.

In both cases, it led to widespread actions coming from the macroeconomic level (adjustment programme in Cameroon, privatization of port operations in Nigeria). However, while in both cases the situation is now better than it was at the peak of their respective crises, they are back at the equilibrium described above (3 weeks dwell time, less than optimal governance situation). The reforms did not tackle the most important leg, for example, the clearance process itself and its integrity. We see a similar situation in many countries, with actions being taken only when congestion becomes an additional barrier, while in fact normal dwell times would imply that these ports would not be congested. With a few exceptions, measures taken are targeting infrastructure or port operations, and not the process that causes the situation or the lack of professionalism among C&F agents.

Another consequence is the vicious circle between dwell time and trade diversification through low trade volumes. Indeed, dwell time is equivalent to a barrier at entry and leads to a selection bias in favour of the incumbent importers and manufacturers, which are not necessarily the most competitive. Low trade volumes and low diversification make it easier for 'monopolists' to capture a rent or a sector. Thanks to collusion with the public sector, some barriers at entry are put in place in order to prevent external and internal competition. A lack of competition enables the monopolist to inflate selling prices thanks to a dominant position and perpetuate rents. This dominant position of a monopolist in a sector favours a status quo and then weakens the coalition of interest in favour of major reforms (and the ones in favour of reforms are too weak to achieve any major impact). This then translates into inflated prices in most sectors, undermines competitiveness and hence diversification remains a challenge and low volumes enable the monopolists to prosper (Cardozo et al., 2013).[9]

Data seem to confirm this vicious circle. Based on firms' surveys, it was demonstrated that firms engaged in manufacturing and assembling have a much shorter dwell time than small and medium retailers (8 days against 18 days)[10] probably due to the fact that being in competition with the rest of the world, for survival reasons, they cannot afford too long dwell times (despite the fact that 8 days is already long by world standards). This is different for retailers since they will charge the inefficiency to the consumers, who know neither the real reason for the surplus nor the amount of the price surplus (Raballand et al., 2012a). Therefore, poor governance related to port and trade sectors could possibly explain why export concentration remains the norm in SSA. As long as most companies remain protected from worldwide competition thanks to barriers at entry (illustrated by long cargo dwell time), trade diversification is unlikely to happen.

2.4 WHAT SHOULD BE DONE TO IMPROVE PORTS GOVERNANCE?

Market incentives are usually too weak for supply-side measures to drive radical changes in trade logistics efficiency and governance in this area. Rather, actors in the trading, industrial, and logistics sectors exhibit risk-averse behaviours because they are operating in a context of oligopoly in brokering where significant adjustments do not translate into obvious gains for them (Raballand et al., 2012a).

Findings from firm surveys and political economy analyses indicate that most measures, starting with building more storage capacity, often do not have the expected positive impact on dwell time (Raballand et al., 2012a). A public information campaign to consumers, which would explain why prices sold to consumers are so high, is needed to disseminate findings on the main causes of long dwell times. In most cases, the perceived causes, such as lack of terminal capacity, do not hold, and structural issues need to be addressed. Even if investments were made, without structural changes, dwell time would probably remain the same.

In this context, the main tools to get out of the vicious cycle of long dwell time and systematic transactions in import processes will come from the public sector. The exception may be when a country's development is such that the industry is of a substantial enough size to be heard in terms of requirements for efficient clearance time and where a strong coalition can be created. This is, for example, the case of the foreign-owned automotive industry in South Africa, which has pushed for drastic reforms of Durban port. Another enabling measure is to try to limit peaks or high customs tariffs to reduce incentives to undervalue. But in most cases, public authorities have a major role to break the collusion as no or little private incentives are usually in place for the largest winners in the system. In conditions where a dynamic and demanding private sector exists, professionalization of freight forwarders can be imposed. However, in non-conducive environments the first actions need to come from within the state administrations themselves, with the view to influence the rest of the players.

With this end in view, innovative schemes for frontline officers' management, such as we have seen developed in several customs services can be useful since it strengthens internal controls and the hierarchical chain. Consider, for example, how human resource policies were at the core of the reform processes in Cameroon. In 2007, Cameroon customs launched a reform and modernization initiative. The reform began with the installation of ASYCUDA (Automated System for Customs Data), a customs clearance system that allows the administration not only to track the processing of each consignment but also to measure a substantial number of criteria relevant to the reform, such as compliance with the deadline for recording the manifest by consignees. For almost 2 years, upper management and frontline officers in Cameroon customs shared the same reality thanks to indicators that measured how the reforms initiated by the former were applied by the latter. But, while the initial quantification phase bore fruit, its impact later stalled since there were no compulsory performance changes.

Beginning in 2010, Cameroon customs introduced a system of individual performance contracts to measure the actions and behaviours of customs officers operating at two of the seven Douala port bureaus, using indicators extracted from ASYCUDA. The performance contracts were introduced as an experiment, with a treatment group of individuals offered the performance contracts and a status quo control group. After almost two years of implementation, the Cameroon customs bureaus in the treatment group showed better results than the control group on indicators related to reduction of corruption, collection of revenue, and facilitation of trade. The additional revenues generated during the experiment were an estimated USD 25 million on a yearly basis.[11]

To reduce long-term cargo dwell time and corruption, customs auction practices need to be amended in many countries, and doing so should be at the core of any plan to tackle cargo dwell time. Auctions should be transparent, published in the press and online, and organized after a delay of four to six weeks. Moreover, in order to reduce ports corruption, senior officials should (1) strive to generate benchmark reliable data; (2) refrain from supporting investment infrastructure without first trying to support structural reforms to change the behaviour of stakeholders and (3) not hesitate to combine macroeconomic level actions (on tariffs for example) and on the ground actions on agents' behaviour.

NOTES

1. For more information on data collection methodology, see Raballand (2012a: 1).
2. In the largest possible definition of ports, including several institutions, public and private, as described below.
3. It can obviously vary port by port but we describe how most ports in SSA are structured and organized.
4. For a description of this phenomenon, see Sequeira (2011).
5. A situation in which one party in a transaction has more or superior information compared to another. This often happens in transactions where the seller knows more than the buyer, although the reverse can happen as well. Potentially, this could be a harmful situation because one party can take advantage of the other party's lack of knowledge (http://www.investopedia.com/terms/a/asymmetricinformation.asp).
6. Due to free time for 11 days and low port storage tariffs, an importer saves on storage tariffs (compared to private warehouses) if s/he leaves the cargo in the port for less than 22 days, which is a huge incentive to use the port as a storage area.
7. This is not per se a corrupt practice and does sometimes help traders that are far from the port, but it does make transactions possible in some cases.
8. If duties are not paid, after several weeks or months, customs take possession of cargo and auction them in order to pay for duties and storage costs.
9. This is confirmed by Musila and Sigue (2010), who demonstrated that corruption adversely affects international trade.
10. Beuran et al. (2012).
11. For more details, see Cantens et al. (2011).

REFERENCES

Arvis, J.-F., G. Raballand and J.-F. Marteau (2010), *The Cost of Being Land-locked*. Washington DC: The World Bank.

Beuran, M., M. H. Mahihenni, G. Raballand and S. Refas (2012), The impact of demand on cargo dwell time in ports in SSA. Policy Research Working Paper Series 6014, The World Bank, Washington DC.

Cantens, T., G. Raballand, S. Bilangna and M. Djeuwo (2011), Reforming customs by measuring performance: a Cameroon case study. In O. Cadot, A. Fernandes, J. Gourdon and A. Matto (eds), *Where To Spend the Next Million? Applying Impact Evaluation to Trade Assistance*. Washington DC: The World Bank, pp. 183–205.

Cardozo, A., G. Masumbu, C. Musonda and G. Raballand (2013), Growth, employment, diversification and the institutional context of private sector development in Zambia. In P. Collier (ed.), *Zambia*. Oxford: Oxford University Press.

Igbanugo, H. A. (2012), Assessing and minimizing customs-related corruption risk in sub-Saharan Africa's ports. Mimeo. Available at: http://gcs.dowjones.com/wp-content/uploads/2012/03/Assessing-Minimizing-Customs-Related-Corruption-in-SSA-Ports-2012.pdf.

Musila, J. and S. Simon (2010), Corruption and international trade: an empirical investigation of African countries. *The World Economy*, **33** (1), 129–146.

Raballand, G., S. Refas, M. Beuran and G. Isik (2012a), *Why Does Cargo Spend Weeks in Sub-Saharan African Ports?* Directions in Development Series, Washington DC: The World Bank.

Raballand, G., T. Cantens and G. Arenas (2012b), Mirror trade statistics, a tool to help identify customs fraud. In T. Cantens, R. Ireland and G. Raballand (eds), *Reform by Numbers.* Directions in Development Series, Washington DC: The World Bank.

Sequeira, S. (2011), Transport costs and firm behaviour: evidence from Mozambique and South Africa. In O. Cadot, A. Fernandes, J. Gourdon and A. Matto, (eds), *Where To Spend the Next Million? Applying Impact Evaluation to Trade Assistance.* Washington DC: The World Bank, pp. 123–162.

3.   Resource grabs

Philippe Le Billon

Most developing countries do not reap the full benefits of their natural resource wealth, a major issue given the opportunities that arose from high primary commodity prices over the past decade. One major reason for this situation is a *resource grab* that benefits domestic elites and foreign corporations rather than local populations, thereby contributing to the *resource curse* (see Humphreys et al., 2007; Collier, 2010). This resource grab not only takes the shape of corruption but also illegal resource exploitation and tax evasion, which together constitute the main sources of illicit financial flows – money illegally earned, transferred, or used – draining wealth away from producing countries. Besides financial impacts, resource grabs also have many indirect effects, including negative environmental, social and political impacts. Many initiatives have sought to prevent such grabs, from tougher implementation of anti-corruption laws and resource nationalisation to revenue transparency norms. Recent high-profile cases included a USD 1.2 billion settlement imposed by US authorities on oil and gas service companies accused of corruption in Nigeria (Department of Justice, 2010). Presenting anecdotal evidence and conceptual interpretations, this chapter first highlights the three main ways of *grabbing development* from resource revenues and then discusses some counter-measures.

3.1   EXTRACTIVE SECTORS AND ILLICIT FINANCIAL FLOWS

Extractive sectors currently generate about USD 3.5 trillion in annual gross revenue, corresponding to around 5 per cent of global gross domestic product (GDP), the proportion of 'extractive products' – fuels, metals and minerals – rising from 23 per cent to 34 per cent of global international trade between 2001 and 2011 (UNTACD, 2013). Potential annual net revenues are estimated at about USD 1 trillion for low-income and lower-middle-income countries, or about USD 200 per capita for a total population of 5 billion.[1] Producing countries, however, lose much of this money through illicit financial flows. Fuel exporters accounted for nearly half of the illicit financial flows from Africa between 1970 and 2008, with Baker and Kodi (2010: 12) stressing that 'acceleration in illicit outflows was undoubtedly driven by oil price increases.' Most recently, Boyce and Ndikumana (2011) found a statistically significant positive relationship between oil exports and illicit financial flows; for each extra US dollar in oil exports, they estimate that an additional 11 to 26 cents leaves the country as illicit capital flight. More broadly, high natural resource dependence reduces the level of transparency and increases corruption (Williams, 2010).

Several factors make extractive sectors prone to illicit financial flows, including high-level discretionary political control, frequent blurring of public, shareholder, and personal interests, limited competition among firms resulting in complicit behaviour, complex financial structures requiring stringent auditing, high volume but limited import channels opening lucrative opportunities for illicit financial flows (Gillies, 2010). Illicit financial flows are derived from three main sources: proceeds of corruption, involving the abuse of public authority for personal interest at the expense of the broader community; revenues from illegal resource exploitation in which the state is blocked from receiving its legal share; and tax evasion. These three sources are often combined, with for example, a company paying a bribe to illegally exploit a resource to avoid taxation. Yet these practices mostly reward different beneficiaries (see Table 3.1).

Table 3.1   Main types of illicit financial flows and beneficiaries

	Corruption	Illegal exploitation	Tax evasion
Main financial flows	Facilitation payments (bribes) paid by companies, money embezzled from tax collection and budgetary allocation	Undeclared corporate revenues from illegal resource exploitation	Inflated costs deducted from taxable revenues, smuggling of resources
Main beneficiaries	Corrupt government officials and companies gaining undue advantage	Domestic companies, local subsidiaries of foreign companies	Parent or holding companies, exporting companies

3.1.1 Corruption

Of the three sources, corruption is often presented as '*the* development problem in resource-rich countries, rather than just one of a number of problems' (Kolstad and Søreide, 2009: 214, emphasis added). Large resource revenues facilitate rent-seeking and patronage, resulting in higher levels of corruption, diversion of time and talent from productive activities, inefficient public spending, and low political accountability. There is evidence that illicit financial flows are intimately linked to large-scale corruption in developing countries (Reed and Fontana, 2011). Illicit financial flows from many developing countries derive from the poor governance of extractive industries. Of the 'top 10' corrupt political leaders in developing countries identified by Transparency International (2004), three ruled in extractive sector-dependent countries: Nigeria, Indonesia and Zaire (now Democratic Republic of the Congo). In Egypt, former energy minister Sameh Fahmy was arrested in relation to a 15-year gas supply deal with an Israeli company that would have brought a USD 714 million loss for the Egyptian state, equivalent to 10 per cent of the annual education budget. The deal would reportedly have resulted in massive kickbacks for Egyptian officials and handsome profits for Mubarak's business ally Hussein Salem (Carlisle, 2011).

Corrupt practices, in turn, are frequently linked to the two other sources of illicit financial flows. The bribing of midlevel resource management officials, for example, enables illegal resource exploitation outside of concession areas. Corruption also facilitates tax evasion, with bribes undermining the maximization and collection of various forms of tax revenues. In some sectors, such as logging and diamond mining, production companies and exporters routinely bribe officials to under-report the volume or value of resources. Corruption can take place at all levels of the value chain, beginning with the initial bidding and contractual process (see Table 3.2). Resource income (measured as resource rent per capita) is associated with higher levels of perception of corruption, and in turn with poor economic performance (Leite and Weidmann, 2002). This relationship is stronger for extractive sectors, more so for fuel than non-fuel mineral exports. The correlation is most robust for countries with low-quality democratic institutions (Bhattacharyya and Hodler, 2010).

3.1.2 Illegal Resource Exploitation

Illegal exploitation in extractive sectors includes a broad range of practices, many of which contribute directly to illicit financial flows. These include operating outside the confines of licensed areas, such as by extracting resources from outside a concession, or beyond contractual limitations, such as by extracting extensive quantities of mineral under an 'exploration' license that only authorizes sampling – a common practice in medium-scale mining of shallow deposits of high-value minerals (for example, relatively small and poorly monitored open-cast diamond mines). Theft is a common issue in extractive industries. About 30 tons of gold were suspected of being stolen from South African mines every year in the mid-1990s, with the government losing approximately 13 per cent of its potential revenues from the sector (Gastrow, 2001).

Underreporting the volume or quality of resource produced (for example, through biased oil volume measurements or misreporting of ore grade) is also common, especially when measurement involves technical expertise and equipment. Accurate volume reporting for tax purposes is a major concern in many countries, including such high-profile cases as Iraq and Nigeria (McPherson and MacSearraigh, 2007). More broadly, illegal resource exploitation also includes failure to respect environmental and social regulations, such as policies on wastewater disposal or on workers' exposure to chemicals. Compliance with environmental and social regulations is costly for companies and thus open to corruption through compliance avoidance, lowering of standards, or demand for 'facilitation payments' by officials. Arguably, non-compliance also generates illicit financial flows benefitting the company by illegally increasing profits (especially if these are not taxed or companies declare false compliance expenses).

The Democratic Republic of the Congo and Nigeria are among the countries most affected by the illegal exploitation of resources. Several Congolese commissions and UN panels of experts have documented illegal mineral exploitation and exports, some of which finance armed groups in the Democratic Republic of the Congo, especially in the eastern part of the country. Even in the diamond sector, which comes under international monitoring through the Kimberley Process (see below), about 30–50 per cent of the production by value is reported to be exported without proper declaration or valuation (World Bank, 2008; Solvit, 2009). Estimates of fraudulent exports, oil theft or bunkering in Nigeria reached at times as high as 300 000 barrels per day between 2001 and 2008, about 12 per cent of production. In both cases, the notion of illegality needs to be complemented by perspectives on the licit character of such exploitation, with oil 'bunkering' offering local populations a means of accessing oil revenues and a cheaper source of fuel for the domestic market. In some estimates, 85 per cent of illicit oil flows result from elite corruption rather than militant operations, although the two are difficult to disentangle (Asuni, 2009; Vanguard, 2011).

3.1.3 Tax Evasion

Taxation is a core area for revenue maximization. Extractive companies often seek to minimize taxation, starting with the negotiation of contracts set within the broader framework of extractive sector taxation policy. Companies seek a 'favourable investment climate' with low taxes via broad fiscal reforms or specific contractual arrangements. While this can increase foreign direct investment and production volumes, it can be fiscally sub-optimal and arouse the frustration of local populations, decreasing the legitimacy of domestic authorities and resource companies (Campbell, 2012).[2] Additionally, contracts are frequently negotiated not with resource companies in their home country but with subsidiaries incorporated in low- or no-tax jurisdictions. This insures companies against tax payments agreed under bilateral tax treaties. Profits routed through the subsidiaries' low-tax jurisdictions are then passed on to the company's group, often through the proceeds of high-interest loans, in order to also avoid taxes in the home country (Taylor et al., 2011). Both host and home countries lose, while untaxed profits accrue to the subsidiary in the tax haven (Palan et al., 2010).

Such advantageous fiscal terms are most often the result of general policies of liberalisation pursued since the early 1990s (Bridge, 2004). But they are also sometimes the result of corruption, with payments by companies to public officials to secure better terms. Investors seeking higher returns who find corrupt elites willing to accept direct bribes or similar benefits such as lucrative service contracts can initiate such corruption. Very attractive investment conditions can also be offered by political elites in the hope of generating large initial payments, such as signature bonuses, which can be embezzled (or used to address short-term priorities unrelated to the long-term national interest). Similar mechanisms can be behind the privatization of public companies, re-negotiation of contracts, or reallocation of concession areas. This could have been the case recently in the Democratic Republic of the Congo, where USD 23.7 million may have been embezzled from a USD 100 million signature bonus for a copper mining contract (Global Witness, 2011).

Once a contract is in place, a second stage of 'tax optimization' involves aggressively seeking all possible tax advantages (Benari, 2009). Tax avoidance turns into tax evasion when tax regulations are broken, and into tax fraud when falsified declarations are involved. Common practices include costs inflation that reduces taxable earnings through over- or under-invoicing – a practice that can partly be avoided through benchmarking costs. Transfer mispricing advantageously setting prices for internal transactions between two subsidiaries of the same corporation are also frequent (Hollingshead, 2010). Typically, a subsidiary in the producing country purchases goods and services (such as mining equipment and geological expertise) needed for resource production, or sells resources (such as mineral ore) to another subsidiary located in a low-tax jurisdiction. The main objective of transfer pricing is to determine the fair (or arm's length) price of a good or service sold across jurisdictions within a business group in order to avoid a double taxation of its revenues. However, parent companies can abuse the system to reduce the taxation of profits. Such tax abuses are common, long recognized, and costly to producing countries (Sikka and Willmott, 2010). Several reports focusing on Southern Africa's mining sector highlight tax regimes unfavourable to host-governments, lack of auditing, and cases of tax evasion and fraud (Christian Aid, 2009a; Kangamungazi, 2009). Underreporting was estimated at up to 74 per cent in a silver mine in the Philippines, while revenues lost through the non-payment of royalties were assessed at about USD 140 million per year in Peru between 2004 and 2006 (Christian Aid, 2009b). Glencore and First Quantum Minerals have faced allegations of financial accounts manipulation of their Mopani Copper Mines in Zambia to evade taxation while operating within a 'highly attractive fiscal environment' that featured exemptions on customs duties, a 0.6 per cent royalty tax rate, a corporate tax rate limited to 25 per cent, and a 20-year stability clause; claims denied by Mopani Copper Mines (Doward, 2011; OECD Watch, 2011).

To sum up, illicit financial flows derive from different sources and reward different actors; while IFF occurrence risks vary along the value chain, during the project cycle, the institutional context of operations, and according to different types of resources and modes of extraction (see Le Billon, 2011).

Table 3.2   Revenue grabbing risks along the resource value chain

Activity	Risk level		
	Corruption	Illegal exploitation	Tax evasion
Licensing	High, through award criteria, information access, and selection process	Low, except for overriding normally prohibited resource exploitation (e.g. in national park)	High, through setting fiscal framework
Exploration	Low, except for ensuring investment schedule and presentation of survey results	Low, except for medium- scale placer mining of high-value minerals	High, through expenditure inflation
Development	High, through contract amendments, cost-recovery and production-profile plans, and construction phase	High, through agreement on future production monitoring	High, through procurement over-invoicing
Production	High, through application of production regulations and contract amendments	High, including through fraudulent measurements and underreporting	High, through transfer mispricing and over-invoicing
Trading and transportation	High, through resource purchase contracts, shipment authorisation, and pipeline access	High, through diversion of resource flows and racketeering by transporters	High, through transfer mispricing and under-invoicing
Refining and marketing	Medium, through circumventing price controls and award of importing and retailing contracts	High, through diversion of refined resources and racketeering by transporters	Medium, through smuggling of untaxed or subsidised products
End phase	Low, except for decommissioning expenditures including environmental mitigation	Low, except for post-decommission 'illegal' exploitation	High, through early exit or false bankruptcy

	Risk level		
Activity	Corruption	Illegal exploitation	Tax evasion
Revenue allocation	High, through embezzlement, 'pork-barrelling', 'white elephant' projects, and inefficient 'populist' policies	Low, except through effect of low revenue allocation to regulation of extractive sectors	High, through under-invoicing of imports

Sources: McPherson and MacSearraigh (2007), Al-Kasim et al. (2008), Kolstad and Søreide (2009) and author.

3.2 ENDING THE GRAB

Sound management of resource revenue is now widely recognized as crucial to development outcomes, and many donors are focusing on greater financial self-reliance by developing countries. In this context, issues relating to corruption and tax evasion, both related to illicit financial flows, are gaining attention. Several international initiatives are attempting to address these problems by improving transparency and accountability in resource revenue flows. The Extractive Industry Transparency Initiative, for example, fosters public reporting on financial flows between resource companies and governments. Combining management principles with capacity-building and peer-pressure activities, these initiatives have targeted countries where tax payments by companies are confidential, budgeted expenditure and actual outcomes not compared, and audit reports not prepared – a situation that, for example, long characterized oil-rich Angola (Isaksen et al., 2007: vii). These initiatives include revenue and contract transparency instruments, resource certification instruments, broad governance standards, and tax reform initiatives (Taylor et al., 2011).

Several factors have contributed to the relative success of these initiatives in gaining support and acceptance within the international policy community (see also Le Billon, 2011). First, is greater awareness of the resource curse in the context of the recent commodity boom. Many stakeholders are anxious to ensure that the long-term developmental failure associated with the 1970s commodities boom will not be repeated. Second is the high-level backing by prominent politicians (especially former UK Prime Minister Tony Blair) and business leaders (especially George Soros and, in the case of the KPCS, the diamond company De Beers); by several developed countries (especially the UK and Norway);

and by well-funded and effective civil society organizations (especially Revenue Watch Institute, Global Witness, Partnership Africa Canada and Publish What You Pay (PWYP)). Third, these have adopted a slow but sustained, constructive, and voluntary multi-stakeholder approach backed by national legislation. Fourth, there is relative complementarity between these initiatives, generally embedded in a unifying 'good governance' framework. Fifth, public pressure due to the legitimacy enjoyed by this cause is making companies reluctant to reject these initiatives publicly, and once adopted, companies can choose either to undermine their application or to help promote their wider adoption to ensure uniform impacts across the industry. Overall, these initiatives have led to greater transparency and more effective involvement by civil society. However, tangible impacts both in terms of prevention and accountability have yet to be demonstrated (Mejía Acosta, 2011; Søreide and Truex, 2013).

In conclusion, curbing illicit financial flows from extractive sectors is a high-stakes endeavour. These flows are massive and are closely connected with governance and developmental issues in producing countries and internationally. Not only do illicit financial flows directly divert revenues from development, but their indirect effects undermine poverty reduction while reducing ruling elite and corporate accountability. Extractive sector revenue issues have gained increasing attention over the past decade, and some significant progress has been made. Some of the initiatives reviewed in this chapter are already transforming the development *potential* of resource-dependent economies and reshaping relations between resource-exporting and -importing countries. Yet there is little robust evidence of the effectiveness of existing institutions, while much more can and should be done, particularly with respect to overlooked components of the extractive sector related to illicit financial flows, such as tax evasion and revenue expenditure. Specific initiatives could seek more effective anti-corruption measures for resource companies within and beyond OECD countries, fostering better practices in national resource companies, require the awarding of contracts to companies incorporated in fair tax and high disclosure jurisdictions, and instituting principles of tax payment maximization for companies operating in low-income producing countries.

NOTES

1.   Average annual rent estimated between 2000 and 2008 for countries with per capita GDP below USD 4000. See World Bank Wealth of Nations database (http://data. worldbank.org/data-catalog/wealth-of-nations).

2. Examples include long tax holidays (10 years is frequent), full write-off of capital costs, exemption from import and often export duties as well as many other domestic taxes, special transfer pricing arrangements (including resource pricing based on costs and fixed mark-ups rather than international market price), capitalization through 'debt' with financial institutions affiliated to the same company and located in a low-tax jurisdiction, minimal royalties (3.5 per cent), and low corporate profit tax (15–20 per cent).

REFERENCES

Al-Kasim, F., T. Søreide and A. Williams (2008), *Grand Corruption in the Regulation of Oil*. U4 Issue 2008: 2. U4 Anti-Corruption Resource Centre. Bergen: Chr. Michelsen Institute.

Asuni, J. B. (2009), *Blood Oil in the Niger Delta*. Washington DC: United States Institute of Peace.

Baker, R. and M. Kodi (2010), Illicit financial flows from Africa. Meeting Summary, Chatham House, London, 10 May.

Benari, G. (2009), *Tricky Tax: Transfer Pricing*. Brussels: Tax Justice Network.

Bhattacharyya, S. and R. Hodler (2010), Natural resources, democracy and corruption. *European Economic Review*, **54** (4), 608–621.

Bridge, G. (2004), Mapping the bonanza: geographies of mining investment in an era of neoliberal reform. *Professional Geographer*, **56** (3), 406–421.

Boyce, J. K. and L. Ndikumana (2011), *Africa's Odious Debts: How Foreign Loans and Capital Flight Bled a Continent*. London: Zed.

Campbell, B. (2012), Corporate social responsibility and development in Africa: redefining the roles and responsibilities of public and private actors in the mining sector. *Resources Policy*, **37** (2), 138–143.

Carlisle, T. (2011), Corruption inquiry focus on Egyptian gas contract. *The National*, 26 April.

Christian Aid (2009a), *False Profits: Robbing the Poor to Keep the Rich Tax-Free*. London: Christian Aid.

Christian Aid (2009b), *Undermining the Poor: Mineral Taxation Reforms in Latin America*. London: Christian Aid.

Collier, P. (2010), *The Plundered Planet: How to Reconcile Prosperity with Nature*. London: Penguin.

Department of Justice (2010), Snamprogetti Netherlands B. V. resolves Foreign Corrupt Practices Act investigation and agrees to pay $240 million criminal penalty. Press Release, 7 July. Department of Justice, Washington DC. Available at: http: //www.justice.gov/opa/pr/2010/July/10-crm-780. html.

Doward, J. (2011), Glencore denies allegations over copper mine tax. *Observer* (London), 16 April.

Gastrow, P. (2001), *Theft from South African Mines and Refineries: The Illicit Market for Gold and Platinum*. Monograph 54. Pretoria: Institute for Strategic Studies.

Gillies, A. (2010), Fuelling transparency and accountability in the natural resources and energy markets. Paper presented at 14th International Anti-Corruption Conference, Bangkok, 10–13 November.

Global Witness (2011), *China and Congo: Friends in Need*. London: Global Witness.

Hollingshead, A. (2010), *The Implied Tax Revenue Loss from Trade Mispricing*. Washington DC: Global Financial Integrity.

Humphreys, M., J. Sachs, and J. E. Stiglitz, eds (2007), *Escaping the Resource Curse*. New York: Columbia University Press.

Isaksen, J., I. Amundsen, A. Wiig and C. Abreu (2007), *Budget, State and People: Budget Process, Civil Society and Transparency in Angola*. R 2007: 7. Bergen, Norway: Chr. Michelsen Institute.

Kangamungazi, E. (2009), *Tax Avoidance and Inequitable Mine Contracts: Case Study Zambia*. Geneva: United Nations.

Kolstad, I. and T. Søreide (2009), Corruption in natural resource management: implications for policy makers. *Resources Policy*, **34** (4), 214–226.

Le Billon, P. (2011), *Extractive Sectors and Illicit Financial Flows: What Role for Revenue Governance Initiatives?* U4 Issue 13. Bergen: CMI.

Leite, C., and J. Weidmann (2002), 'Does Mother Nature corrupt?' In G. T. Abed and S. Gupta (eds), *Natural Resources, Corruption, and Economic Growth: Governance, Corruption, and Economic Performance*. Washington DC: International Monetary Fund, pp. 159–196.

McPherson, C. and S. MacSearraigh (2007), Corruption in the petroleum sector. In J. E. Campos and S. Pradhan (eds), *The Many Faces of Corruption: Tracking Vulnerabilities at the Sector Level*. Washington, DC: World Bank, pp. 191–221.

Mejía Acosta, A. (2011), *The Impact and Effectiveness of Accountability and Transparency Initiatives: The Governance of Natural Resources*. London: Department for International Development.

OECD Watch (2011), Sherpa et al vs. Glencore International AG. OECD Case. Available at: http://oecdwatch. org/cases/Case_208.

Palan, R., R. Murphy, and C. Chavagneux (2010), *Tax Havens: How Globalization Really Works*. Ithaca, NY: Cornell University Press.

Reed, Q. and A. Fontana (2011), *Corruption and Illicit Financial Flows: The Limits and Possibilities of Current Approaches*. U4 Issue 2011: 2. Bergen, Norway: U4 Anti-Corruption Centre.

Sikka, P., and H. Willmott (2010), *The Dark Side of Transfer Pricing: Its Role in Tax Avoidance and Wealth Retentiveness*. Colchester, UK: University of Essex Business School.

Solvit, S. (2009), RDC: *Rêve ou illusion: Conflits et ressources naturelles en République Démocratique du Congo*. Paris: L'Harmattan.

Søreide, T and R. Truex (2013), Multi-stakeholder groups for better sector performance: a key to fighting corruption in natural-resource governance? *Development Policy Review*, **31** (2), 203–217.

Taylor, G., G. Tower and J.-L. W. Van der Zahnet (2011), The influence of international taxation structures on corporate financial disclosure patterns. *Accounting Forum*, (1), 32–46.

Transparency International (2004), *Global Corruption Report 2004: Special Focus: Political Corruption*. London: Pluto Press.

UNTACD (2013), Statistics database. Available at: http://unctadstat.unctad.org/.

Vanguard (2011), Nigeria oil bunkering: politicians, military behind it – Wikileaks. *Vanguard* (Nigeria), 13 April.

Williams, A. (2010), Shining a light on the resource curse: an empirical analysis of the relationship between natural resources, transparency, and economic growth. *World Development*, **39** (4), 490–505.

World Bank (2008), Democratic Republic of Congo: growth with governance in the mining sector. Report 43402-ZR, World Bank, Washington DC.

4. Grabbing in the education sector

Muriel Poisson

Grabbing in the education sector can take multiple forms, from the use of school premises for private purposes, to the capture of funds or resources aimed at constructing or equipping schools, or the collection of illegal fees from parents. Multiples cases demonstrate the effects of such practices on access, quality and equity issues. In the case of Pakistan, for instance, the existence of thousands of ghost schools (13 000 according to the 2005 National Education Census, and 30 000 according to media) automatically reduces educational opportunities for thousands of children (Save the Children UK, 2010). Similarly, the fact that a quarter of school equipment never reaches schools in Burkina Faso (26 per cent of school supplies, 24 per cent of didactic materials and 35 per cent of specific materials such as chalk, paper, rulers or glue in 2010–11) has a detrimental impact on the learning process (Oubda, 2013). Finally, the results of several tracking surveys prove that capture of funds between central and frontline service delivery levels is more likely to affect the poorest schools: in the case of Uganda, a 10 per cent increase in household income increased the amount of public funding reaching the school by 3 percentage points (Reinikka and Smith, 2004).

The short-term effects of grabbing on policy priorities, on the quantity and quality of services provided, as well as on their costs and efficiency are very significant. However, their longer-term impact on global development remains to be fully assessed from different perspectives. First, by impeding the access of underprivileged groups to schools and universities or to the benefits of quality education, grabbing of resources in education tends to widen social inequalities and to feed the poverty cycle (UNDP, 2011). Second, by reducing opportunities for talented children and adolescents to gain access to good quality education – while at the same time making it easier for those who are less talented to take advantage of corruption to get through the system – it results in a significant loss in the human capacity of society and reduces the supply of quality skilled labour (Rumyantseva, 2005). Third, by showing the younger generation that favouritism, manipulation and bribery are common practices and part of the daily operation of the education system, it can undermine their acquisition of ethical values and, as a result, hamper the development of societies built on a belief in transparency, integrity, and social justice (Hallak and Poisson, 2007).

For the past 50 years, the International Institute for Educational Planning (IIEP-UNESCO) has been directly involved in educational planning and management in a large number of countries worldwide. As a staff member of IIEP, I have been in position to analyze all kinds of grabbing occurring in the education sector at all levels of the system. Some of these instances have been thoroughly analysed and discussed as part of the Institute's Project on Ethics and Corruption in Education, conducted for nearly a decade. This chapter draws on experiences documented within this framework. Three domains deserve particular attention and will be covered: (1) the leakage occurring in the flows of resources, especially from the Ministry of Education down to the schools; (2) distorted practices in the management of teaching staff – which represents the single-most expensive item of the education budget – in particular, ghost teachers; and (3) corruption in public procurement: the case of textbooks will serve as an example. An effort has been made to bring in stories from one country per domain, and to describe both the challenges and approaches to address them.

4.1   GRABBING IN EDUCATION: CASES FROM INDONESIA, SIERRA LEONE AND THE PHILIPPINES

The following three examples of grabbing in the education sector have been selected according to three criteria: (1) they refer to past experiences that have been duly studied; (2) they involve huge amounts of resources, including international aid funds; and (3) attempts have been made to address the issues in different ways; even though the problems have not been solved, much may be learned from the strategies used in trying to tackle them. The first example deals with the case of extra allocation for school reconstruction in Indonesia; the second, with ghost teachers in Sierra Leone; and the third, with corruption in the textbook industry in the Philippines.

4.1.1   School Reconstruction in Indonesia

The School Improvement Grants Programme (SIGP), a multi-donor-funded project of approximately USD 60 million, was introduced in

Indonesia after the economic crisis that hit the country at the end of the 1990s. Under the SIGP, grants were provided directly to the schools, in order to assist them in upgrading their facilities, obtaining learning materials and supplementing teaching capacity. Three-quarters of the grants were given to the poorest schools, located in the country's poorest districts most affected by the crisis. More specifically, about one-quarter of the grants by value were provided to help schools cope with the influx of internally displaced pupils or the physical consequences of natural or social catastrophes, while the rest were allocated according to a poverty index based on the number of pupils from poor families, the level of school fees, and the status of communities in the government's existing poverty alleviation scheme. Altogether more than 8000 schools benefitted from these grants. But even though the SIGP registered significant results in improving teaching and learning conditions, allegations of grabbing were reported in the course of its implementation.

Baines (2005) reports a number of cases where schools which were not supposed to receive extra funds still received them, while schools supposed to receive them did not. Grabbing was put forward as one of the major factors explaining this misallocation of funds. The selection process of the beneficiaries of the grants had been decentralized to local committees, and instead of securing a better allocation mechanism it made the process vulnerable to local influences, lobbying, and trade in favours. The Central Independent Monitoring Unit (CIMU) in charge of programme supervision, managed to establish a list of the schools which had benefitted from rehabilitation funds despite already being in good condition. In most cases, it turned out that the manipulation had been made possible because the head teacher or owner of the school was influential at the local level – for example, he was the chairman of a local party, or the chairperson of the commission for education at the local parliament. There were also cases where local officials had accepted bribes to influence the selection of school grant recipients. Moreover, it was discovered that a significant amount of resources had been lost through capture of funds, purchase of inappropriate goods, illegal payments, collusion with providers of goods and services, and so on.

4.1.2 Ghost Teachers in Sierra Leone

All aspects of the Sierra Leone education system have been severely affected by the conflict that hit the country in the 1990s: school infrastructure, teaching force, management capacities, data record keeping, and so on. In order to get an accurate picture of the state of the sector, the Ministry of Education endeavoured to build a new Education

Management Information System (EMIS) and to collect an updated and complete set of data. Between 2001 and 2005, it tried to carry out a school census. In 2006, it set up a new information system with the assistance of the UNESCO Institute for Statistics (UIS). In 2007, the first annual school census was carried out, followed in 2008 by a physical headcount of teachers with the support of the UK Department for Foreign Investment (DFID). EMIS Staff were deployed in 50 centres to this end. Hamminger (2008) explains that, in order to minimize the danger of fraud (for example, individuals who were not teachers presenting themselves as such), a counting and registration process was carried out near the schools, under the control of local authorities and communities. The recording of digital thumb prints was expected to help detect cases of teachers registered in more than one school.

This whole process revealed that resources aimed at teacher salaries in the country were grabbed in different ways: the official payroll included both 'ghost teachers' (teachers who did not physically exist, or who never showed up in any school), and teachers receiving salaries from several schools. The funds attracted in this way were then kept by the school for its daily functioning, or captured for private purposes. Hamminger (2008) reports cases where the total number of teachers quoted by a school was understated in *one* of its reports (for the purpose of requesting more teachers) and overstated in *another* (for the purpose of getting a higher amount for salaries). It took some time for the Ministry of Education to acknowledge the gravity of the situation. However, in 2011, it disclosed in the media that more than 5000 ghost teachers had been unduly collecting salaries from the Consolidated Fund.

4.1.3   Textbook Industry in the Philippines

In the 1990s, the Department of Education, Culture and Sports (DECS) of the Philippines used to be considered among the most corrupt public institutions, together with the Department of Public Works and Highways. Corruption had begun to escalate in the 1970s when loans and grants from development partners and banks flew into the departments for procurement of educational materials. As the DECS central office could not use up all its funds, regional offices were created and it spread money to the field offices. Textbook purchases were negotiated directly with the private sector at regional level. In the process, corruption was also decentralized. In 1999, the Philippine Center for Investigative Journalism published a book denouncing high-level corruption within the textbook industry. In 2001, Government Watch, a civil society organization, started to review public sector performance in textbook delivery

(Aceron, 2009). In the following years, several media disclosed multiple forms of grabbing in this sector.

Testimonies converged to describe various forms of grabbing during local procurement procedures, which led to capture of public resources, payment of bribes, delayed delivery of textbooks, failed distribution of textbooks, ghost deliveries, and so on. It is estimated that payoffs ate up 20–65 per cent of textbook funds. Bribes given to the regional office and school divisions could represent 20 per cent of a contract, with the administrative accounting officer and auditor each receiving 0.5–1 per cent. Moreover, collusion between regional officers and private publishers implied a large number of unapproved books and unauthorized reprints purchased by corrupt local authorities for distribution in the classrooms (Chua, 1999). In addition, the prices of the textbooks procured by DECS were unreasonably high, and the physical quality of the books was poor, with the apparent use of substandard materials in their production. As a result, a critical shortage of textbooks was noticed in nearly all of the country's 40 000 public schools; on average, each textbook was shared by six pupils in elementary schools and by eight in high schools.

4.2 FOCUS ON THREE EXPLANATORY FACTORS: WEAK INFORMATION SYSTEMS, LOCALIZATION OF PROCEDURES AND COMMUNITY BIAS

Analysis shows that there are both internal and external factors conducive to the development of corrupt practices within the education sector. Internal factors are linked to the decision-making and management structure of the education system itself, whereas external factors are linked to the overall environment in which the education sector operates. Several of these factors are summarized in Figure 4.1. With reference to the experiences described above, three factors will be addressed in more detail in what follows, namely: (1) weak EMISs; (2) localization of procedures, in a context of poor governance and control; and (3) community involvement in the management process, despite weak capacities.

4.2.1 Weak EMISs

Difficulties in collecting reliable and up-to-date data on the state of the education sector clearly enable grabbing opportunities in the three countries under analysis. In Indonesia, lack of reliable data on the

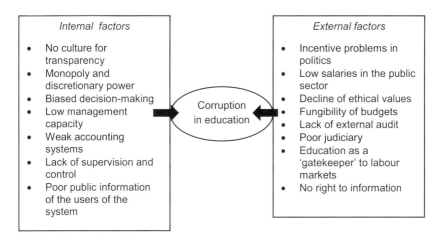

Source: Adapted from Hallak and Poisson (2007).

Figure 4.1 Internal and external factors conducive to corrupt practices in education

physical conditions of the schools as well as on the socio-economic profile of their catchment areas made bias in resource allocation much easier. Similarly in Sierra Leone, the absence of a baseline on the existing number of teachers and their postings, combined with the impossibility of checking the accuracy of lists of vacancies communicated by head teachers, led to all kinds of manipulations. Moreover, in both cases, poor information management did not allow cross-checking of data and the detection of anomalies. In Sierra Leone, the roster of teachers held by the Ministry could thus not be reconciled with that of the teachers' payroll. This explains why in both cases follow-up measures were taken to review the exact criteria used to select programme beneficiaries (Indonesia); to reconcile data from various sources (Sierra Leone); and to use new information technologies such as biometric data to limit inconsistencies in the future (Sierra Leone).

4.2.2 Localization of Decision-making Procedures

Decentralization of management procedures to local authorities or to schools is another factor that can partly explain the rapid spread of grabbing practices in the countries under review. In the case of the Philippines, the decision to decentralize the procurement of textbooks to regional offices was often put forward as a key element to explain the 'decentralization of corrupt procedures' to a much wider number of entities. Similarly in Indonesia, the direct transfer of funds to the schools opened up new opportunities for the latter to siphon away resources and to collude with local building contractors. This does not mean that a centralized management of these programmes would have helped solve all problems. Indeed, if the direct transfer of resources to schools did not solve problems of corruption in Indonesia, it still helped avoid most of the risks of diversion or capture of funds that existed in the previous system (in other words, funds could no longer be pilfered as they passed through several administrative layers). Analysis shows that the nature of corruption and its diffusion simply changed. Remedial measures included the design of more comprehensive guidelines on the procedures to be followed by schools (Indonesia); the development of management capacities at local level (Indonesia); and the establishment of independent monitoring and control mechanisms (Indonesia and Philippines).

4.2.3 Community Involvement in the Management Process

Communities were involved in the management of the SIGP programme in Indonesia in different ways: they were represented in multi-sectoral committees in charge of the selection of grant beneficiaries at district level, and in school committees responsible for the implementation of the programme at school level. Members of the CIMU noted in their conclusions a correlation between high community participation and low incidence of corruption. But they also emphasized that community involvement did not always operate as expected (Baines, 2005), as illustrated by the incidents of lobbying, bribing, capture of resources, and so on, described above. Several explanatory factors were highlighted, for example, low representativeness of committees (over-representation of local influential people, political appointees, head teachers, and so on.), turnover of committee staff, lack of training of some of their members, low ownership, social ponderousness, and so on. Lessons learnt included the need to clarify the composition of committees; to better specify their roles; to further develop their skills; to provide greater guidance on how they should operate in practice; and to consider their payment.

4.3 POLICY OPTIONS TO REDUCE GRABBING OPPORTUNITIES IN EDUCATION

As emphasized by Hallak and Poisson (2007), three strategic axes can be considered in order to reduce grabbing opportunities in education, namely: setting transparent regulatory systems; strengthening management capacities; and promoting enhanced ownership of management processes by users. Within this framework, the following key policy issues can be emphasized: (1) how to find the right balance between equity and transparency in resource allocation; (2) how to minimize local bias favoured by the introduction of decentralized procedures; and (3) how to promote community participation without fostering local influence interplay.

4.3.1 Equity Versus Transparency

Greater equity in the education sector requires the channelling of funds towards those most in need. At the same time, it is difficult to target resources when accurate data are lacking, or when local allocation processes cannot be fully trusted, in which case equity measures prove hard to operationalize. Due to grabbing, pro-poor targeted mechanisms, if not properly monitored, can thus sometimes appear even less equitable than universal schemes. At the same time, scholarships, conditional cash transfers, or free school meals may be considered as the most adequate response to local needs, especially in contexts of vast and diverse territory and budget constraints (Poisson, 2013). There is no obvious policy response here, but rather a dilemma to be solved by decision-makers: how to find the right balance between a simple and transparent formula which is difficult to bypass and a more sophisticated formula that can help focus resources according to needs but can also be more opaque and likely to entail fraudulent practice. If solutions have to be adapted to each specific context, certainly in low governance settings, the simpler they are the better.

4.3.2 Local Empowerment Versus Accountability

Decentralization of educational management is often presented as a prerequisite for introducing flexibility in the system, better responding to needs, and improving accountability. At the same time, experience shows that the localization of decisions and procedures can also contribute to opening up new opportunities for corrupt practices at intermediate and school level, particularly in contexts of weak capacities (Levačić and Downes, 2003). The challenge faced by decision-makers here is the following: how to promote local empowerment regarding management processes, without creating new corruption risks that will be particularly difficult to address given their spreading across the national territory. This does not mean that the centralization of financing and management of resources is a panacea, especially in contexts where high-level corruption prevails at central level. In such a context, a proper balance should be found between centralization and decentralization of procedures, duly taking into account existing norms and procedures, central and local capacities, monitoring and complaint systems, and the state of the judiciary.

4.3.3 Social Control Versus Local Influences

Social control can be seen as a powerful tool to address grabbing issues – as noted by Karim (2004), 'an empowered citizenry is the mainstay of a country's national integrity system'. Yet local influences can also follow from community and civil society participation. The dilemma for policymakers is how to promote better social control over the allocation and use of public funds, while not submitting public decisions to the interests of a few individuals acting as representatives of social interest of communities they control. Innovative partnerships experienced in the Philippines may show the way forward. Since 2003, the 'textbook count' project mobilizes citizens to ensure that the right quantity and quality of textbooks are delivered to the right people at the right time. It relies on a partnership between the Department of Education, the Ateneo School of Government and the Textbook Count Consortium of civil society organizations. So far, it has helped improve transparency in textbook delivery. Yet, community mobilization remains a challenge, which requires 'long-term capacity-building efforts, including addressing citizen's immediate concerns and priorities that are economic in nature' (Aceron et al., 2012).

REFERENCES

Aceron, J., G. ven der Linden and J. Tonn (2012), *Improving Education and Curbing Corruption by Monitoring Textbook Deliveries in the Philippines.* Washington DC: Partnership for Transparency Fund.

Aceron, J. (2009), G-Watch's textbook count story. a public–private partnership fairy tale? Presented during a Regional Seminar on Good Practices in Corruption Prevention, organized by the Commission Against Corruption Macao (CCAC) and the ADB/OECD Anti-Corruption Initiative for Asia and the Pacific, Macao, 25–26 March 2009.

Baines, S. (2005), *Towards More Transparent Financial Management: Scholarships and Grants in Indonesia.* Ethics and Corruption in Education Series. Paris: IIEP-UNESCO.

Chua, Y. T. (1999), *Robbed. An Investigation of Corruption in Philippine Education.* Quezon City, the Philippines: Philippine Center for Investigative Journalism (PCIJ).

Hallak, J. and M. Poisson (2007), *Corrupt Schools, Corrupt Universities: What Can Be Done?* Ethics and Corruption in Education Series. Paris: UNESCO Publishing.

Hamminger, L. (2008), The power of data: enhancing transparency in the education sector in Sierra Leone. *U4 Brief*, No. 22. U4 Anti-Corruption Resource Centre, Chr. Michelsen Institute, Bergen.

Karim, S. (2004), Report card surveys in Bangladesh. In *Transparency in Education. Report Card in Bangladesh. Quality School Programme in Mexico.* Ethics and Corruption in Education Series. Paris: IIEP-UNESCO, p. 69.

Levačić, R. and P. Downes. (2003), *Formula Funding of Schools, Decentralization and Corruption. A Comparative Analysis.* Ethics and Corruption in Education Series. Paris: IIEP-UNESCO.

Oubda, F. (2013), Public expenditure tracking survey in Burkina Faso. Reducing leakages and improving information systems in the education sector. *IIEP Newsletter*, Vol. XXX, No. 2, July–December 2012.

Poisson, M. (ed.) (2013), *Achieving Transparency in Pro-poor Education Incentives. Lessons from Experiences Conducted in Africa, Asia and America.* Ethics and Corruption in Education Series. Paris: IIEP-UNESCO.

Reinikka, R. and N. Smith (2004), *Public Expenditure Tracking Surveys in Education.* Ethics and Corruption in Education series. Paris: IIEP-UNESCO.

Rumyantseva, N. L. (2005), Taxonomy of corruption in higher education. *Peabody Journal of Education*, **80** (1), 81–92.

Save the Children UK (2010), Case studies on the role of politicisation of education in conflict-affected countries. Background paper prepared for the Education for All Global Monitoring Report 2011. The hidden crisis: armed conflict and education. UNESCO, Paris.

UNDP (2011), *Fighting Corruption in the Education Sector. Methods, Tools and Good Practices.* New York: UNDP.

5. Courts, corruption and judicial independence

Siri Gloppen

A well-functioning justice system is crucial to address corruption effectively, which in turn is important for development. But judicial institutions are themselves corruptible. Surveys show that experiences with and perceptions of corruption in the courts are widespread (Afrobarometer, 2010; Latinobarometer, 2010; Eurobarometer, 2011; TI, 2011; GCR, 2012: 303; World Justice Project, 2012). In its 2011 Annual Report, Transparency International (TI) noted that, globally, almost half of those surveyed (46 per cent) perceived their judiciary as corrupt. According to the Eurobarometer (2012), around a third of Europeans think corruption is widespread in their judicial services (32 per cent). In Bangladesh, 88 per cent reported having experienced corruption when dealing with the courts (TI, 2012: 23), 85 per cent of Peruvians had little or no confidence in their judiciary (Latinobarometer, 2010), and in countries as diverse as Afghanistan, Bolivia, Bulgaria, Cambodia, Croatia, Ethiopia, Georgia, the Former Yugoslav Republic of Moldova, Morocco, Peru and Ukraine, the judiciary was seen as the most corrupt of all public institutions (TI, 2012: 19). Corruption and perceptions of corruption in the judiciary not only undermines the courts' credibility as corruption fighters. More generally, it erodes trust in the courts' impartiality, harming all the core judicial functions, such as dispute resolution, law enforcement, protection of property rights and contract enforcement. In addition, it harms the broader accountability function that the judiciary is entrusted with in democratic systems – upholding citizens' rights, securing the integrity of the political rules of the game, and sanctioning representatives of other branches when they act in contravention of the law.

While there is broad consensus that corruption in the court system is destructive and should be addressed, there are particular challenges involved in fighting judicial corruption. Anti-corruption efforts may jeopardize the independence of the judiciary and thus undermine judges' ability to fulfill their accountability functions. In fact, limiting judicial independence may be the real motive behind such measures. So while we should care about corruption in the court system, we should also keep in mind that corruption charges and measures against judicial corruption may serve as a way to rein in bothersome judges.

The first section of this chapter explores different facets of corruption in the judicial sector and how this undermines real and perceived independence of the judiciary and threatens the very core of the judicial function, where trust plays a crucial role. The second section discusses governments' use of corruption charges and investigations as tools that now and then are misused in political power games. The third section presents common approaches to address corruption problems in the judicial sector and examines how they balance the need for increased accountability with respect for judicial independence.

5.1 IMPLICATIONS OF CORRUPTION FOR JUDICIAL INDEPENDENCE

Corruption is commonly defined as the misuse of public office or entrusted power for private gain. When we talk about judicial system corruption (judicial corruption for short) the paradigmatic image is that of judges taking bribes. Judicial corruption is a lot more, however. It includes *all forms of inappropriate influence* that may damage the impartiality of justice, and may involve any *actor* within the justice system, including lawyers and administrative support staff. The question of corruption is not only a matter of relations between judicial personnel and 'court users' (public and private parties in civil cases, prosecutors and accused in criminal cases); it is also about internal relations in the judiciary. The 'gain' need not be material. It can also be sexual favours, or the offered 'furtherance of political or professional ambitions' (TI, 2007: xxi), and may also take the form of avoiding something undesired, in the form of threats. Biased decision-making is thus not only a matter of the personal integrity of judicial personnel, but concerns the structural protection of judicial independence and the insulation of judicial decision-makers from illegitimate political and hierarchical influence.

5.1.1 Petty Corruption

Systemic petty corruption or bribery in the judicial system is a problem in many developing countries as well as in more developed economies. A 2006 survey asked people who had been in contact with the judiciary over the past year, whether they had paid a bribe. One in ten reported this to be the case: including 21 per cent of Africans, 18 per cent of Latin Americans, 15 per cent in the Asia-Pacific region and the former Soviet Union, 9 per cent in South East Europe – but only 1 per cent in Western Europe (TI, 2007: 11). Bribes offered by users of the legal system may take many forms, including illegal 'fees' that court personnel levy to do what they should do anyway. Court users pay just to get their case through the system, to influence the outcome of a given case, or to delay it. Bribes may be paid to the judge, or to assistant staff or lawyers to remove files or get the case assigned to a particular judge.

Where petty corruption is prevalent it creates an additional barrier for ordinary citizens to access the justice system. For poor people the sums involved may be prohibitive. Even where it does not directly affect case outcomes (and even more so when it does), bribery adds to the class bias of the justice system and strengthens exclusionary patterns based on gender, race, ethnicity, caste and so on. Widespread bribery also erodes trust in the courts and distorts their ability to perform their functions as impartial arbiters of disputes, guarantors of contracts and enforcers of the law. Bribery is not only a problem in formal judicial institutions, but commonly also in alternative administrative and judicial institutions (variably termed informal, traditional, customary, community, or non-state) that most people in the developing world turn to for lack of access to or trust in the formal justice system (Golub, 2007; Nyamu-Musembi, 2007).

The share of respondents who report having experienced bribery when being in contact with the judiciary is alarming. Still, a much higher percentage perceives their judiciary to be corrupt (TI, 2007: 42). Media reports of high-profile corruption scandals and allegations of political bias among judges contribute to shaping citizens' perceptions of corruption.

5.1.2 Undue Political Influence

Judges' political bias and people's perceptions of such undermines the role of the judiciary as protector of citizens' rights vis-à-vis the state in its various manifestations. It leaves ordinary people without effective recourse to justice when the state is the offending party, and with scant protection when the state presses charges. The political bias is not necessarily consistent across all types of cases. It tends to tick in when the stakes are high, such as when the executive or other power-holders feel their position threatened. It is thus particularly damaging for the courts' political accountability function, their ability to impartially enforce the rules of the political system, for example in relation to election fraud (Gloppen et al., 2004; Gloppen, 2010).

Illegitimate political influence on judges take different forms, some are clearly illegal (bribes, blackmail, threats, violence/murder), while other forms of undue influence stem from the ways in which relations between the judiciary and other arms of government are organized, or reflect a legal culture where judges are expected to defer to political authorities.

Structural sources of political bias in the judiciary are related to procedures for *appointment* of judges and judicial leadership; terms and conditions of *tenure* for judges; and budgetary and *financial* regulations, including salaries and benefits:

Judicial appointments

Where the government is perceived to appoint deferential judges – or friends – to the bench, it damages trust in the judiciary, regardless of whether the judges are in fact biased in their rulings. In many countries the executive (is widely perceived to) decisively influence who are appointed as judges – even when there are rules and institutions in place to prevent this from happening. Judicial service commissions or other bodies designated a role in nominations, are often effectively circum-vented – or themselves 'packed' and politically biased. Rules of ratifica-tion or confirmation by parliament have often limited effect, particularly in dominant party contexts. In some cases the executive, like President Museveni in Uganda, has explicitly expressed intentions to 'appoint cadres to the bench' (Gloppen et al., 2004; Gloppen and Kazimbasi, 2008; Gloppen, 2010). In South Africa, some have interpreted ANC government officials as having a similar intention when they pursue the (otherwise legitimate) aim of 'transformation of the judiciary' (DA, 2007; Molele and Makinana, 2012).

Terms and conditions of tenure

Where judges are appointed for limited terms, and particularly where the terms of service are renewable and short, judges have an incentive to rule with an eye on the interests and preferences of those for whom they depend for reappointment (or new employment after they finish their judicial tenure). The same is true where judges' promotion/demotion depend on being favoured by their superiors, and where the security of tenure in practice is weak. Formal rules to protect tenure may not be sufficient to allay judges' fears if experience show that they in practice risk losing their seat if they fall out of favour with the government, or when administrations change, as has been the case for example with supreme court judges in Argentina (Gloppen, 2010).

Regulation of finances, including of salaries and benefits
Control over the purse strings gives many governments a stronghold – if not a stranglehold – over the courts, by enabling them to strategically regulate not only judges' salaries and benefits, but also the running costs of the judiciary. This may lead to (perceptions of) bias, as illustrated in Zambia and Malawi, where the timing of hikes in judges' salaries and benefits repeatedly coincided with pending court cases involving high stakes for the executive, most notably presidential election petitions (Gloppen, 2010). While in Africa, the judiciary commonly depends on parliament both for budgetary allocations and for regulation of salaries and benefits most Latin American judiciaries automatically receive a fixed share of the budget as part of the apparatus for insulating the judiciary from undue influence.

5.1.3   Undue Influence via the Internal Judicial Hierarchy

In many cases, undue influence on judicial rulings comes not from politicians directly, but via the judicial hierarchy (Gloppen, 2010). Such influence may be the result of direct pressure from superiors; more subtle incentives based on judges' anticipation that a 'wrong' decision in an important case could have career consequences; or selective allocation or cases to judges who are likely to rule in a particular manner. Besides, internal procedures can be misused to limit individual judges' ability to voice criticism, for example by refusing dissenting judgments. Hence, where the judicial leadership – and in particular the chief justice – is (seen to be) close to the sitting regime, this can taint the entire judiciary. Even where judicial appointments are otherwise effectively regulated in ways that place them beyond executive influence, the executive often has a much stronger say over the appointment of the chief justice and judge presidents (Gloppen, 2010).

   To sum up, corruption in the judiciary is undoubtedly widespread – and perceptions of judicial corruption even more so. There are many sources, both of bribery and undue political influence undermining judicial independence. Given the apparent scale and importance of this problem, it is essential to understand the mechanisms at play and examine efforts to address it. Efforts to reduce the challenges are many, but before turning to that, we will now consider how allegations of corruption among judges can be a powerful strategic tool. And disciplining systems ostensibly put in place to combat corruption may have the – intended – side effect of undermining judicial independence.

5.2 CORRUPTION CHARGES AND DISCIPLINING OF JUDGES AS A TOOL IN A POLITICAL POWER-GAME

Given that corruption in the judicial system is a problem in most countries, there is a need for systems to uncover irregularities, and discipline and dismiss corrupt officers. If misused, however, anti-corruption strategies become very effective tools for undermining judicial independence by ridding the judiciary of independent-minded judges that the authorities find bothersome, and scare others from following in their tracks. Examples are many. Below are some of the more recent investigations by the International Commission of Jurists (ICJ).

Due to concern for a high number of judicial dismissals in the Russian Federation, the ICJ, in May 2012, undertook a mission 'to assess the disciplinary procedure, grounds for disciplining and dismissals of judges and their potential effect on the security of tenure and the independence of the judiciary' (ICJ, 4 December 2012). They found that 'The threat of dismissal, and the uncertainty of the grounds on which a judge can be dismissed, affects the capacity of all judges to act independently', and that 'the threat of disciplinary action may hang over a judge for many years, since there is no limitation period for such action. This makes the judge susceptible to pressure from within the judicial hierarchy or from the executive.'

Similarly, the ICJ criticized Tunisia for summarily dismissing 70 judges: 'Instead of fulfilling the stated aim of eradicating corruption, the actions of the Minister of Justice undermine the independence of the judiciary in Tunisia and reinforce the previous practices of undue political interference in judicial matters' (ICJ, 6 August 2012). Criticism was also raised when Baltasar Garzón (the famous Spanish Judge who called for extradition of the Chilean dictator Pinochet) had criminal proceedings initiated against him for corruption and malfeasance as he was investigating the crimes committed by representatives of the Franco regime (ICJ, February 2012).

5.3 ADDRESSING JUDICIAL CORRUPTION

How can the risks of individual and systemic corruption in judicial systems be reduced without undermining judicial independence? As described, judicial system corruption is a diverse phenomenon and requires a range of responses. Simply put, the individual bribe or petty corruption, which is only one part of the problem, needs systemic responses whereby judges are made more accountable to the rules. Corruption stemming from undue political influence may, on the other hand, require reforms that make judges less accountable to the rulers, for example by weakening the mechanisms that political power-holders (and the judicial hierarchy) can use to influence judges' rulings. In either case, solutions must be developed based on deep knowledge of the particular society and informed by the broader normative, socio-political and economic context.

A large number of public institutions, donor agencies (most notably the World Bank) and independent organizations (such as TI, ICJ, Judicial Integrity Group (JIG), International Bar Association) are engaged in developing strategies for advancing judicial integrity. Setting common standards and fostering professional communities where these are not only known, but also matter for peer recognition has been one aspect of this. The Bangalore Principles for Judicial Conduct (2006), developed from within the profession, has become an international reference point with regard to what judicial independence requires (JIG, 2010, 2012). Despite the diversity of actors, and their different focus and priorities, there is relatively broad consensus on what is required to address corruption without undermining judicial independence.

5.3.1 Addressing Petty Corruption in the Judicial System

Petty corruption and bribery has generally been addressed along four lines, the first two seek to reduce the motivation to engage in corruption, the third seeks to reduce opportunities to do so, and the fourth seeks to put in place effective sanctions.

1. *Improvement in material conditions* for judicial personnel and support staff, particularly in the lower judiciary where the lack of a living or socially acceptable wage is seen to be a significant driving factor for corruption.
2. *Normative change* in the attitude towards bribery, primarily within the legal professions, but also in society more broadly. Measures include training, codes of conduct for judges, lawyers and judicial support staff, and efforts to build a culture where these norms matter for professional recognition and standing, through national and regional judicial forums.
3. *Preventive procedural measures* undertaken to reduce opportunities for corruption take many forms. Increased transparency around different types of transactions (filing of cases, allocation of cases to

judges, and so on) and improved case management systems and procedures that reduce the scope for individual discretion reduces the opportunities for both judges and support staff to 'levy fees' or conveniently lose files. Where judges are required to declare assets this may help uncover excessive income.

4. *Disciplinary/accountability systems* for judges normally include complaint mechanisms where members of the public can report knowledge or suspicion of corruption, investigative measures, as well as a hearing or 'trial' mechanism for disciplining and dismissal of judges. International standards require that the disciplining bodies should be independent from the government, and that disciplinary or removal proceedings against judges 'must be determined in accordance with well-established procedures that guarantee the rights of judges to a fair and transparent hearing and to an independent review' (ICJ, 6 August 2012).

Evidence suggests that, particularly where governance generally is weak and corruption levels high, traditional, anti-corruption reform measures that rely on reducing incentives for corrupt behaviour (higher wages, improved case-handling systems and disciplinary measures) have little effect unless accompanied by attitudinal change (Matei and Matei, 2011).

5.3.2 Addressing Undue Political Pressure on Judicial Personnel

Following the discussion on undue political influence above, we can distinguish between measures aimed at reducing political influence on the selection and appointment of judges; on judges' tenure; and through budgets and finances. In addition, there are efforts to strengthen judges' resistance to pressure by enhancing their competence and strengthening professional norms. It should be noted, however, that this is a controversial terrain and part of a much broader discussion about how politically unfettered unelected judges should be and how to check abuse of judicial power.

1. *Reducing political – and particularly executive – influence on judicial selection* has been the focus of much attention. Recommendations run along three lines: increase the number of actors (veto-players) involved in the selection process; establish clear criteria; and increase the transparency of the process. Following these principles, most countries now have a (more or less) independent body – a judicial council or judicial service commission – tasked with vetting and nominating candidates for judicial

offices. Their composition varies, some consist mainly of representatives from within the legal profession, others have a majority of politicians or are appointed by the executive, yet others have representation from civil society. The understanding is that to reduce executive influence, political appointees should not be in majority. Equally important is how the process is conducted and the degree of transparency. With vetting and nominations behind closed doors (sometimes not even the final list is public), the scope for executive influence is significant. More transparent processes, with open calls for nominations/applications, open hearings, public interviews of candidates, and open ranking lists, reduce the scope for undue executive influence. Clear and relatively demanding selection criteria (for example a minimum of 10 years of legal practice or more for the higher positions) reduces the pool of qualified candidates and makes political appointments more difficult, particularly in developing countries with a limited legal profession (Gloppen, 2010). Once nominations are made, the appointing body should be limited to select among the nominated candidates, not (as happens) have a free choice also outside the vetted nominees. Most countries also have different bodies involved in the actual selection, for example appointment by the executive and ratification by the legislature. Where the ruling party has a legislative majority, confirmation may have little effect, however, and special procedures and majority requirements are needed for an effective check.

2. *Minimizing political influence on judges' tenure and conditions* is arguably even more important. Once a judge is in place, who appointed him or her is less important than who holds the key to a future career and wellbeing. It is thus crucial to minimize the executive's ability to influence judges' tenure and conditions. Judges should thus be appointed for life, or for long non-renewable terms, and conditions of service should be constitutionally guaranteed, with strictly defined impeachment criteria and procedures.

3. *Eliminating undue influence on judicial budgets and administration.* Administrative autonomy and budget independence for the judiciary prevent the executive from 'starving' the judiciary – or rewarding judges when important decisions are pending. Such problems are avoided where the judiciary receives a guaranteed share of the national budget. A related issue concerns the jurisdiction of the courts. This should be clearly protected to avoid situations, like in Uganda, where the government has encroached on the jurisdiction and authority of the judiciary by moving politicised

cases into the military courts (Gloppen and Kazimbasi, 2008; Gloppen, 2010).

4. *Increasing resilience by strengthening judges' competence and professional norms* has been an important area of reform. Unlike most of the measures discussed earlier, this does not depend on new legislation or cooperation from the political authorities. Training and resources that make judges more professionally secure and skilled, reduces risks of submitting to pressure. By creating forums – within each country, as well as regionally and globally – where judges meet, share experiences, give support and exchange recognition, professional norms develop and reputations matter more. This raises the 'reputational costs' of succumbing to undue influence and may contribute towards a stronger sense of social purpose. It may also create material incentives, if judicial integrity and professional competence are seen as factors in appointments to attractive positions – including to international courts.

5.4 CONCLUDING COMMENTS

When setting the standard for judicial recusal, Lord Hewart famously stated that it 'is of fundamental importance that justice should not only be done, but should manifestly and undoubtedly be seen to be done' (*R v Sussex Justices, Ex parte McCarthy* ([1924] 1 KB 256, [1923] All ER Rep 233). This expresses why all forms of corruption and perceptions of such, whether in the form of bribery or bias, are so damaging to the judiciary. However, dilemmas arise in the work against judicial corruption since efforts to impose accountability may undermine the independence judges need to do their work. The discussion above shows how the two concerns interact, but also the challenges of getting from regulations to practice.

REFERENCES

Afrobarometer (2010/11), www.afrobarometer.org. Online data analysis: institutions and leaders → courts and security → corruption: judges and magistrates. Available at: www.afrobarometer-online-analysis.com/aj/AJBrowser AB.jsp.
Bangalore Principles (2006), Strengthening basic principles of judicial conduct (as endorsed through ECOSOC Resolution 2006/23). Available at: www.unodc.org/pdf/corruption/corruption_judicial_res_e.pdfwww.unodc.org/pdf/corruption/corruption_judicial_res_e.pdf.

DA (Democratic Alliance) (2007), The DAs judicial review: judicial independence. Available at: www.da.org.za/docs/621/judicialpercent20 review_document.pdf.

Eurobarometer (2012), Corruption (Special Eurobarometer 374). Available at: http://ec.europa.eu/public_opinion/archives/ebs/ebs_374_en.pdf.

GCR (2012), Global Competitiveness Report 2011–12. World Economic Forum, Geneva. Available at: http://www3.weforum.org/docs/WEF_Global CompetitivenessReport_2012-13.pdf.

Gloppen, S. (ed.) (2010), *Courts and Power in Latin America and Africa.* Basingstoke: Palgrave MacMillan.

Gloppen, S., R. Gargarella and E. Skaar (eds) (2004), *Democratization and the Judiciary: The Accountability Function of Courts in New Democracies.* London: Frank Cass.

Gloppen, S. and E. Kasimbazi (2008), Elections in court: the judiciary and Uganda's 2006 Election Process. In J. Kiiza, S. Mahara and L. Rakner (eds), *Electoral Democracy in Uganda*. Kampala: Fountain Publishers, pp. 53–89.

Golub, S. (2007), The 'other 90 per cent': how NGOs combat corruption in non-judicial justice systems. In TI (Transparency International), *Global Corruption Report 2007*. New York: Cambridge University Press, pp. 129–137.

ICJ (International Commission of Jurists) (10 February 2012), The International Commission of Jurists condemns the conviction of Judge Baltasar Garzón to an 11-year ban from the office. Available at: www.icj.org/the-international-commission-of-jurists-condemns-the-conviction-of-judge-baltasar-garzon-to-an-11-year-ban-from-the-office/.

ICJ (International Commission of Jurists) (6 August 2012), Executive control over judiciary persists in Tunisia. Available at: www.icj.org/executive-control-over-judiciary-persists-in-tunisia/.

ICJ (International Commission of Jurists) (4 December 2012), Russia: disciplinary measures must not hamper the independence of judges. Available at: www.icj.org/russia-disciplinary-measures-must-not-hamper-the-independence-of-judges/.

JIG (The Judicial Integrity Group) (2010), Measures for the effective implementation of the Bangalore principles of judicial conduct. JIG Meeting Lusaka, Zambia, January 2010. Available at: judicialintegritygroup.org/resources/documents/BP_Implementationpercent20Measures_Engl.pdf.

JIG (The Judicial Integrity Group) (2012), The Record of the Seventh Meeting of the Judicial Group on Strengthening Judicial Integrity. JIG meeting Garmisch-Partenkirchen, Germany, October 2012. Available at: http://www.judicialintegritygroup.org/resources/documents/JIG%202012%20MUNICH%20MEETING%20REPORT%202.pdf.

Latinobarometer (2010), at www.latinobarometro.org. Online data analysis: confidence in judiciary. Available at: www.latinobarometro.org/latino/LAT AnalizeQuestion.jsp.

Matei, A. and L. Matei (2011), Assessing the anti-corruption strategies. theoretical and empirical models. *Journal of Management and Strategy*, **2** (1), 23–40.

Molele, C. and A. Makinana (2012), ANC sets it sights on the judiciary. *Mail and Guardian*, 17 February 2012. Available at: http://mg.co.za/article/2012-02-17-anc-sets-its-sights-on-the-judiciary.

Nyamu-Musembi, C. (2007), Gender and corruption in the administration of justice. In TI (Transparency International) *Global Corruption Report 2007*. New York: Cambridge University Press, pp. 121–128.

TI (Transparency International) (2007), *Global Corruption Report 2007*. New York: Cambridge University Press.

TI (Transparency International) (2011), Global Corruption Barometer 2010/11. Available at: http://gcb.transparency.org/gcb201011/results/.

TI (Transparency International) (2012), Transparency International Annual Report 2011. Available at: www.transparency.org.

World Justice Project (2012), Rule of Law Index. Available at: http://worldjusticeproject.org/rule-of-law-index.

PART II

Grabbing at the level of sector and state
functions in a country context

6. Grabbing by strangers: crime and policing in Kenya[1]

Jens Chr. Andvig and Tiberius Barasa

The archetypical form of grabbing is stealing, plain and simple. This is where someone simply grabs some object without any form of compensation to the owner – who might have invested in the ownership or has, by other socially legitimate ways, established ownership rights over it. In crime statistics we may distinguish between different forms of stealing such as burglary, robbery, pick pocketing, car theft and so on. We can also usefully distinguish between theft accompanied with or without (threats of) violence. In large societies the scope of random theft through the use of violence is greater since mass mobility and large populations mean the risk of identification may be modest. Theft by known perpetrators may also be combined with violence either under a Hobbesian-like state of nature, where the strongest may steal: if the perpetrator and owner belong to different jurisdictions, or if the owner of the object has to submit to an organization that may apply violence on a regular basis, such as a local gang.

6.1 CRIME IN KENYA: EXTENSIVE, BUT HOW EXTENSIVE IS NOT KNOWN

The main method so far to gauge quantitatively the extent of citizen-to-citizen grabbing is by means of victimization studies where a sample of citizens are asked about their (or their household's) experiences with crime during a given period. The lowest crime incidence estimate reported for Kenya is 16 per cent: that is, about 16 per cent of households experience a crime during a year, most of which (87 per cent) imply some form of grabbing. The last two rounds of the Afrobarometer surveys report, however, that one-third of respondents have had 'something stolen from the house'. One must then also add grabbing outside the home to arrive at the final incidence of citizen-to-citizen grabbing. A victimization survey by the United Nations Office on Drugs and Crime (UNODC, 2010) implies that roughly 20 per cent of the adult population will experience that some of their valuables are snatched during a year. Some research indicates a much higher incidence of grabbing, however, towards 88 per cent for Nairobi (Stavrou, 2002).[2]

While the difference in outcomes is wide among these surveys, all of them indicate that Kenyans must expect to lose some of their property to individuals or small gangs who more or less randomly search for things to grab. More often than not, the victims do not know the perpetrators. Less common, but still significant, is a more systematic form of grabbing income where powerful groups of citizens wield the threat of force. Here we only have data from the last Afrobarometer round (round 5) where about 12 per cent of respondents reported having had such experiences during the past year.[3] Note that, in such cases, the grabbing is not performed by strangers.

6.2 GRABBING BY THIEVES AND ROBBERS AND GRABBING BY THE POWERFUL

Purely criminal forms of grabbing have some peculiar characteristics. Usually, the criminal grabber is not enabled to grab because of his particular societal position. More often than not, the individual or company that has lost the valuables grabbed will not be able to identify him. Unlike many other grabbers, he is not particularly powerful, except temporarily where he has access to a weapon and the victim does not. He is not locked into a pre-assigned position that allows him to grab, but moves freely around in space, and is likely to grab heterogeneous objects. When this happens, the individual victim is caught almost at random, although spatial characteristics and individual protection techniques influence the likelihood. Unlike grabbing performed by the powerful, the property rights to the objects or values grabbed are not contestable. There is no chance that criminal grabber can be seen as the true legitimate owner. Grabbing by groups of citizens or gangs is an intermediate form. In these situations, the grabbers are more powerful and their power is more lasting since they will often have at least partial physical control of an area for a period. The losers of the grabbed values know the identity of the grabbers, but like the freewheeling individual criminal, gang members may move around in a space, grabbing heterogeneous objects, although that space is now more clearly defined and circumscribed. Legally the ownership of the objects and values grabbed is not contested; they are stolen.

6.3 POLICE CORRUPTION IN KENYA IS EXTENSIVE, BUT HOW EXTENSIVE IS NOT KNOWN

The main public organization that contains crime is the police. In Kenya, as in many other low-income countries, the police are involved in more corrupt transactions than any other part of the bureaucracy and are widely despised (Andvig and Fjeldstad, 2008).[4] Different victim studies give widely different outcomes. Even the one with the lowest number of incidences informs us that about 6 per cent of respondents annually pay a bribe to the police.[5] The other studies report significantly higher incidences and, when they include comparative data, a larger share of respondents pay a bribe annually to the police than to other parts of the bureaucracy. In TI Kenya's yearly corruption survey the percentage of respondents having paid a bribe to the police varied between 26 per cent and 71 per cent for the years 2001–08 (Andvig and Barasa, 2011: 34). According to the Afrobarometer surveys (rounds 2, 3 and 4), about a quarter of respondents paid bribes annually to avoid the police.

According to UNODC (2010), about 7 per cent of the population is likely to pay a bribe to the police each year. This result seems close to the one cited in Republic of Kenya (2006). The UNODC authors observe, however, that around half of the respondents are inspected by the police and about half of those again experience extortion where they must pay a fee. That is, about 22.6 per cent are extorted, more than three times as many who had to pay bribe, and a third of the population must illegitimately pay the police. Our own research confirms that police grabbing due to their arresting powers is more frequent than grabbing due to their powers of criminal investigation. Roughly, about 14 per cent of 242 respondents paid a bribe in order to register a crime, while 60 per cent paid the police to prevent an arrest or to be released from incarceration (Andvig and Barasa, 2011: 68–70).

6.4 POLICE AND REGULAR BUREAUCRATIC GRABBING COMPARED

Different civil servants' opportunity to grab may depend on the economics and politics of their assigned space. In principle, police officers are as mobile geographically as the thieves and robbers they are supposed to control, a mobility that is essential for their crime control efforts. The police has formal authority, but unlike other bureaucrats they are not locked *ex ante* into interactions with a narrow pre-assigned set of citizens or enterprises. The police may initiate interactions with anyone. Some grabbing opportunities for the police are similar to opportunities that arise elsewhere in the bureaucracy, though stimulated by the extent of citizen-to-citizen grabbing. This determines the flow of crime events, each offering grabbing opportunities for the police who may: (1) ask for bribes in order to register the theft (robbery or burglary), (2) ask the likely perpetrator for a bribe to avoid sanctions, or (3) threaten a known innocent with accusation for the crime and ask for a bribe for not pursuing the matter. This flow of possible events is in many respects similar to, for example, that relating to driving licenses.

Through active monitoring of their assigned area the police may discover crime events of their own accord. Their inclination to do so might be particularly strong in cases of so-called victimless forms of crime, such as drug dealing, prostitution and gambling, where no one has an interest in reporting. Here quantitative data is completely missing, and we have very limited fact-based information about the incidence of such grabbing or the magnitude of assets stolen. In addition, by using their right to wield force and the corresponding power of arrest, the mobility of the police also allows it to initiate a large number of acts of pure extortion where the victims are either threatened with incarceration and pay *ex ante*, or are incarcerated and must pay *ex post*. As shown above, this is the most common form of grabbing by the police in Kenya. It is based on the *combination* of both legal and physical means of force that neither robbers nor regular bureaucrats possess.

6.5 RULED BY STRANGERS

Before Kenya was colonialized by the British there were no towns or cities inland, and, except during famines, the cross-community circulation of people – which often allows grabbing by strangers – was rare. Moreover, there were no regular jails or police, which are institutions introduced by the European colonialists.[6] Still, important features of present policing in Kenya reflect its colonial origins, as analysed by Anderson (1991, 2000). One important maxim of British rule was not to recruit the apparatus of violence from the area to be controlled. It should be ruled by strangers. The main motivation was political: to make violent rebellions more difficult to organize; to keep the tools of control in the hands of people who would not sympathize with rebellious locals. Rotation of officers was seen as necessary to prevent lasting solidarity with the groups to be ruled. All parts of the police forces should be ruled by the centre of authority.

Rotation of officers was also seen as a means to prevent corruption. The idea was that it would be easier for officers to engage in bargaining for and collecting bribes where they grew social roots in the area to be policed. Unlike India, where extensive cross-cultural rotation of officers only takes place at higher ranks, Kenya applied – and still applies – a rotation system which implies frequent rotation also at the lower ranks of the police hierarchy.[7] However, while an anti-corruption effect may defend rotation of other public officials, its effects may be questionable for the police. The reason is that pure extortion – the most common form of police corruption in Kenya (as described) – is easier to perform on strangers. In a situation where the police are strangers, there is less need for side-agreements with consenting parties in order to facilitate the extortion. On the contrary, it is easier to arbitrarily incarcerate a citizen who is not a member of your tribe, a friend of a friend, or a neighbour. It is also easier to wield unpopular power if you live in police camps and away from your family: both historical leftovers from British rule.[8] Revenge for acts of extortion, conducted by the police, will then become more difficult, and as a result, the police can make use of force, not only for control but also for personal profit.

A third aspect of colonial rule has left its mark on present police extortion processes. During the colonial period, the police were instructed to regulate the internal mobility of the local population due to the geographic spread of European settlers. This was done to shape labour markets and to control any local violence or grabbing directed against Europeans. Early on, Kenya established advanced identification cards for locals that the police controlled. Particularly when entering a European area, these cards were eagerly controlled. While European areas no longer exist, the police have retained great freedom to control the mobility of citizens and incarcerate them if they behave suspiciously. In some of the rural areas visited by our research team summer 2010, the police extortion (in addition to general fears of crime) resulted in a de facto curfew starting at 8 p. m. for pedestrians and cyclists. After 8 p. m., the risk of being threatened by incarceration or actually jailed without legitimate reason was high.[9]

6.6 CITIZEN GRABBING, POLICE GRABBING AND ECONOMIC DEVELOPMENT

We have suggested that the rise of crime in Kenya may be understood in light of societal changes that are associated with development, in particular more frequent encounters among people not known to each other. This is not an original idea, but was launched in classical sociology by Emile Durkheim (1935; around his notions of anomie) and more recently by Samuel Huntington (1968). No police grabbing could of course exist before the police itself, which was introduced as part of the institutional development in Kenya. Nor could the police misuse its authority for extortion before enforcement mechanisms and jails were established. In economic research, there are several results on how crime rates can be explained by the more general economic development, including levels of poverty and economic inequality as explanatory factors (cf. Fajnzylber et al., 2002).

Some economists have also turned the direction of causality around: Acemoglu et al. (2001) explored the importance of property rights for economic growth rates. Since crime is an obvious violation of property rights, a number of studies have assessed the extent to which crime and corruption can explain growth rates. Andvig and Barasa (2011), for example, studied the combined effects of crime and police corruption on economic development.[10] Unlike other victimization studies, we asked directly about the size of bribes and the severity of the economic effects of respondents' crime experiences. Among the around 50 per cent who reported a crime experience, 65 per cent said that the crime had hit them either 'very' or 'quite badly', and about one-third told us they either had to close a shop or change their lifestyle as a result. These are consequences which may have a direct negative impact on economic growth, particularly when crime levels are as high as reported in Kenya. Moreover, informal probing revealed cases where whole families' lives had been shattered and well-off families had sunk into poverty. Rough calculations suggest that the direct economic cost of police corruption for Kenya could reach USD 120 million (Andvig and Barasa, 2011: 41), while losses associated with citizen-to-citizen grabbing could be as much as USD 750 million (*ibid.*: 71). In addition, citizen-to-citizen grabbing could cause even more substantial consequences which are difficult to estimate, long-term economic losses such as for example the shattering of families referred to above. When asked, Kenyans appear more worried about crime than corruption, including grabbing from the police. Only 2 per cent of Kenyan respondents considered corruption the most important issue for the government to address while 6 per cent considered crime to be so (Afrobarometer Network, 2008).[11]

6.7 IMPLICATIONS

This chapter has focused primarily on the *direct* effects of citizen-to-citizen and police grabbing. A number of *indirect* mechanisms are likely to be more important, some of them reflected by the following facts:

- A total of 33 per cent of Kenyan enterprises considered crime to be a 'major or very severe constraint', while 38 per cent considered corruption (Iarossi, 2009) to be so (of which police corruption is found significant but not major factor). The distortive effects on foreign direct investment are likely to be significant.
- Demands for bribes cause a significant cost in rural–urban transport.
- Police corruption increases the risk of road accidents, particularly if corrupt police allow drunk driving, substandard vehicles, non-qualified drivers, etc.
- In some urban areas crime recruits talented youths (Andvig and Attila, 2010), while it discourages others, mainly girls, from schooling (Mudege et al., 2008).
- Crime-preventing investments, such as protective fences, electronic equipment and other forms of private security, are costly, and thus too rarely applied.
- The combined effects of police and citizen grabbing may slow down otherwise productive rural economic activities.

Typically, the effects of citizen and police grabbing are many and multi-faceted since they impact the population frequently and in many different situations. While each may be a minor incident on its own, the total effect is likely to be significant. This total effect is, however, not precisely known.

6.8 CONCLUSIONS AND POLICIES

A little more than a century ago, a colonial ruling structure was imposed on what is now Kenya. In order to do so a large share of agricultural land was grabbed by the new rulers and transferred to European settlers. This process was basically continued by the local elite after independence. To protect opportunities for grabbing at the centre and the resulting economic inequalities, a considerable degree of force had to be applied. This has left its traces both on the behaviour of the police and citizens.

In our study, we analysed the behaviour of frontline police officers along with citizens' exposure to police corruption and to their fellow citizens' grabbing. We criticized the present *rotation* policy of lower-ranked officers as potentially counter-productive, since most bribes are in fact collected through extortion, a form of misuse of authority that can be conducted more easily for those who are strangers in a community. This alienation effect is intensified by the arrangement of having the police forces living in separate camps, away from their families and their own communities. The practice of using police forces who are strangers in the areas they patrol, may have contributed to the now frequent use of police brutality. The wide authority allocated to the police in *controlling citizen mobility* may have made citizen-to-citizen grabbing more difficult but at the same time, it has given extensive scope for police grabbing.

Some policy improvements have been made to reduce police corruption: roadblocks are more difficult to erect and the formal powers to incarcerate at will are now slightly reduced. A simple but effective policy instrument that should be considered, is the increased use of *street lighting,* which is likely to reduce both citizen-to-citizen crime and police grabbing. Such efforts have been introduced in slum areas like Mathare with clear impacts on crime levels.

The effects of the policy changes discussed in this chapter are likely to be modest. Modifying rotation rules, restraining arbitrary ID inspection rights, closing down police camps and adding street lights are all feasible. However, they all address acts and decisions at the bottom of the law-enforcement hierarchy. Major changes in frontline police corruption will require upheavals at the apex of the pyramid as well. Rwanda's achievements of dramatic decline in police corruption (Transparency International-Kenya, 2010) came as a result of changes initiated at the level of the country's president. These modest policy proposals, however, are the most compatible with the scope of the results of our research.

NOTES

1. The authors thank the Research Council of Norway Poverty and Peace/ NORGLOBAL programs for financial support. The chapter is based on empirical information presented in Andvig and Barasa (2011) and collected by a research team during summer 2010. The team visited 10 police stations at various locations in Kenya, interviewing 5 police officers in each and 25 citizens in each police neighbourhood, using separate questionnaires for the police and their communities. No claim to statistical representativeness can be made since practical circumstances did not permit random sampling.
2. A presentation and discussion of the various results of the crime victimisation research from Kenya, including our own is to be found in Andvig and Barasa (2011:

16–30). About half of the respondents in our own mini-exploration said that they had experienced a crime during the last 2 years.

3. Results using Afrobarometer online analysis, 25 March 2013. The question was formulated: 'In the last year, how often have powerful people or groups other than government, such as criminals or gangs, made people in your community or neighbourhood pay them money in return for protecting them, their property or their businesses?'.

4. Various explanations may be launched. First, frontline police officers are notoriously difficult to monitor given to their mobility across location and situations. The officers have the right to initiate engagements with the public. Therefore, as a second explanation, the corrupt officers have stronger incentives to engage in transactions with citizens than honest ones. The third explanation considers the nature of the matchings between corrupt officials and citizens: more matchings are likely to result in a corrupt deal when one side may use force to conclude it. However, the willingness to pay bribes increases with the use of threats (in other words, corrupt police with guns). Likewise, the police may initiate extortion acts on their own.

5. Republic of Kenya (2006, Appendix 7, Table 1). When adding the reported experiences with corruption in police administration (police and the chiefs) we get about 6 per cent, which is half of all reported corruption experiences.

6. Before the British rule, regular trade expeditions from the coast took place, involving slave catching. Temporary incarceration was of course necessary to perform this form of grabbing.

7. In the small selection of officers – skewed towards the lower ranks – we surveyed in summer 2010 the average number of transfers was 5.5 during an average employment length of 8 years. Of the 49 officers who responded to the question, 35 said that they lived in a 'government' house which indicates that they lived away from their home area and had to operate with two households –another vestige from the military style of colonial policing (Andvig and Barasa, 2011: 50–52). Many officers were not able to speak the local language needed to communicate with the older and least educated citizens.

8. In our small study 35 of 49 officers lived in government houses. None of the others had brought their families, although it has now become legal to do so.

9. Since our observations were made just in the aftermath of the World Cup of football in South Africa, a larger number than usual risked the walk to the pub, were threatened and had to pay the police, one source of error in our project.

10. Official crime statistics is not useful for this purpose at all since economic improvement will normally also increase judicial efficiency, so increasing official crime rates will go together with economic growth. In the case of Kenya the official crime numbers records only one-sixteenth of the lowest victimization estimates and imply that each police officer is able to handle one crime a year (Andvig and Barasa, 2010). To explain this, the multiplicative structure of crime reporting should be noted: if only a quarter of victims report the crime, only half of those are accepted by front line officers and only half of those are to be acted upon and registered by the head of the station, only one sixteenth of the crimes are registered.

11. Part of the reason for the low concern shown for either crime or corruption compared to unemployment and poverty may have been that they were listed late among the alternatives.

REFERENCES

Acemoglu, D., S. Johnson and J. A. Robinson (2001), The colonial origins of comparative development: an empirical investigation. *American Economic Review*, **91** (5), 1369–1401.

Afrobarometer Network (2008), The quality of democracy and governance in Africa: new results from Afrobarometer round 4. Afrobarometer Working Papers, no. 108.

Anderson, D. M (1991), Policing, prosecution and the law in colonial Kenya, c. 1905–1939. In D. M. Anderson and D. Killingray (eds), *Policing the Empire*. Manchester: Manchester University Press, pp. 1183–1201.

Anderson, D. M. (2000), Master and servant in colonial Kenya. *Journal of African History*, **41** (3), 459–485.

Andvig, J. C. and G. Attila (2010), Crime, police corruption and development. NUPI Working Paper, no. 772. Oslo.

Andvig, J. C. and T. Barasa (2011), Cops and crime in Kenya. A research report. NUPI Working Paper, no. 794. Oslo.

Andvig, J. C. and O.-H. Fjeldstad (2008), Crime, poverty and police corruption in non-rich countries. NUPI Working Paper, no. 738, Oslo.

Durkheim, E. (1935), *The Division of Labour in Society*. Glencoe, IL: Free Press.

Fajnzylber, P., D. Lederman and N. Loayza (2002), Inequality and violent crime. *Journal of Law and Economics*, **45** (1), 1–39.

Huntington, S. P. (1968), *Political Order in Changing Societies*. New Haven, CT: Yale University Press.

Iarossi, G. (2009), *An Assessment of the Investment Climate in Kenya*. Washington DC: The World Bank.

Mudege, N. N., E. M. Zulu and C. Izugbara (2008), How insecurity impacts on school attendance and school dropout among urban slum children in Nairobi. *International Journal of Conflict and Violence*, **2** (1), 98–112.

Republic of Kenya (2006), Governance, Justice, law and order sector reform programme; National integrated household baseline report, Appendix 7, selected data tables. Nairobi: GJLOS, September.

Stavrou, A (2002), Crime in Nairobi. Results of a citywide victim survey. UN-Habitat, Safer Cities: Series# 4, Nairobi, September.

Transparency International-Kenya (2010), The East Africa bribery index 2010. Transparency International-Kenya, Nairobi.

UNODC (United Nations Office on Drugs and Crime) (2010), Crime victimization survey in Kenya. Final report. Kenya Institute for Public Policy Research and Analysis, June.

7. Grabbing land in Malawi

Blessings Chinsinga and Liam Wren-Lewis

The distribution of land in Malawi is highly unequal and frequently inefficient. Large areas of land are underutilized in a context where many Malawian farmers would be able to put such land to productive use. In this context, the Malawian government has been slow and ineffective in undertaking land reforms, despite large demand for change both from investors and the local population. This chapter explores the role that *grabbing* of land in Malawi plays in contributing to this situation. We focus on various forms of malpractice, corruption or opportunistic behaviours associated with land transfers. We begin by briefly setting out the history and context of land in Malawi, and then discuss various types of land grabbing that occur currently. We highlight the problems that this form of corruption leads to, before moving to consider policy suggestions for both the government and donors. Finally, we conclude by attempting to draw out any lessons that this example may teach us about corruption more generally.

7.1 BACKGROUND AND CONTEXT

The grabbing of land is not a new phenomenon in Malawi. Much of the current context around land is a result of previous land transfers that took place under colonial rule. The expropriation of land by white settlers was not as large as in Zimbabwe or South Africa, but, by the time Malawi had acquired independence in 1964, Europeans had acquired 'some of the most fertile and well-watered lands' (PCILPR, 1998: 29). These lands had typically been acquired through some form of agreement with local chiefs, but, in parallel with present day land grabs, it was contentious as to whether these traditional authorities had the right to alienate the land in this way (Holden et al., 2006). A set of land reforms was implemented in 1967, but these did not represent any significant break from the past, instead reflecting almost wholesale continuity with the colonial frame-work governing land tenure patterns and ownership that resulted in massive alienation of customary land to the estate sector owned largely by the local elites (Ng'ong'ola, 1986; Kanyongolo, 2004).

The coming of multiparty democracy in 1994 was closely linked to a rise in land up the policy agenda. Advocates of the new political system argued that embracing the political transition offered opportunities to address a whole range of inequities and injustices, including inequitable land redistribution patterns (Kanyongolo, 2004; Chinsinga, 2011). The question of land reform was generally flagged as an immediate course of action to address the problem of poverty should Malawians choose to embrace a democratic political dispensation. However, despite this promise, little has been achieved with regard to land reform to date. A land policy concluded in July 2002 still remains largely unimplemented, with parts of the supportive legislative framework for the policy yet to be approved by cabinet or parliament.

The current land framework in Malawi therefore strongly resembles that which existed under colonial rule. Land in Malawi is divided into three types: public, private and customary. Public land is owned and managed by the government, while owners of private land have similar rights to those in other countries. The vast majority of land is customary land, which falls under the jurisdiction of traditional authorities and is administered under customary law – powers for the distribution and control of this land rests in the hands of traditional leaders. While there is pressure to move to a market system of privatized land, this is somewhat at odds with traditional cultures, and Malawi's institutions are not necessarily set up to deal with such a system (Mkandawire, 1983). Under the current legislative framework, customary land can be converted to private land (though not vice versa), but the exact process for doing so is somewhat unclear except when it is for development purposes (the existing law allows the government through the Minister of Lands and Physical Planning to appropriate customary land if it is intended for development such as roads and public buildings).

7.2   LAND GRABBING IN MALAWI

Within this land policy context, there are a range of malpractices that occur that could be described as land grabbing. Perhaps the form of land grabbing closest to traditional forms of bureaucratic petty corruption occurs in the allocation of publicly owned land. In some urban centres, for example, land is supposed to be allocated by the government based on need and the date of applications. However, in practice, corruption occurs such that public officials will allocate the land based on other criteria. For example, the Lilongwe Land Allocation Committee is supposed to allocate land within the city, but in practice the committee is bypassed and its efficiency suppressed by the actions of ministers, principal secretaries, business magnates and other influential persons in society who pressurize government officials to favour particular applications (Mwakasungula, 2009). Having purchased Makande Tea Estate in 2001 from one the European settler farmers, the government decided to donate it Thyolo District Council for distribution to the people in the district. The beneficiaries were supposed to be land-poor and landless households with property value of less than MK 20 000, but it later turned out that many richer persons acquired land on the estates (Holden et al., 2006).

More commonly, allegations of land grabbing originate from customary land. The root of such malpractice normally centres on traditional chiefs and other authorities mishandling their duties in exchange for private gain. At the smallest level, this can include petty bribes given to leaders by members of the community to settle inter-communal land conflicts (Peters and Kambewa, 2007). Here, however, it may be difficult to draw the line as to what is labelled corruption and what is instead part of an established system of tribute giving. A clearer cut case comes in a recent World Bank sponsored pilot of land reform, where local authorities gave land to family, friends and those who bribed at the expense of households genuinely in need of land (Chinsinga, 2011). Moreover, the government is empowered to convert customary land into public land for development purposes, but only after a due process that includes proper compensation to the dispossessed communities.

At a larger scale, much controversy also revolves around traditional authorities 'selling' customary land to those from outside the community, typically allowing it to become private land in the process. Frequently it is felt that chiefs do not reflect the will of the community in such transactions, and indeed residents of the land in question typically do not receive compensation for loss of land (since technically the land was never owned by them). At times, this may be relatively informal and without the consent of higher authorities. At other times, however, government has been demarcating areas of customary land for development purposes, and may be involved in incentivizing the traditional authorities to consent to its transfer (Mwakasungula, 2009).

Several recent examples of this type of land transfer involve the development of land for growing sugarcane. Since sugarcane growth is most profitable when done over a large scale with capital investment, it is difficult for smallholder farmers to take advantage of growing the crop. The government is therefore encouraging the development of land by private companies willing to invest in sugarcane. Recent cases include land near Dwangwa in Nkhotakhota district, and Nchalo in Chikawa district (Chingaipe et al., 2013). In both cases, private companies have acquired land to grow sugar despite opposition from local smallholders.

Recent studies have shown that the land deals pertaining to the sugar plantations have been concluded by traditional authorities despite resistance by communities because they have been offered some inducements by the investors. This has led to traditional authorities sealing land deals with prospective investors without the knowledge of the owners or users of the land (Chingaipe et al., 2013; Chinsinga et al., 2013). The communities have only discovered that their land has been sold when they see the new owners working on it. While on paper these transactions are supposed to be transparent and accountable, and concluded only after communities' consent and acceptable forms of compensation have been worked out, communities have been completely sidelined in these deals. The resistance by communities has been countered by force using the police and, where communities have taken the disputes to the courts, lawyers that have represented them have often dropped out of the cases on rather dubious grounds after initial rounds of success. Allegedly, they are induced to do so by favours from both the investors and the government. The involvement of the government in these land grabs suggests that they view customary land as an 'unlimited reservoir that can be targeted for conversion for privatization' (Chingaipe et al., 2013: 7).

In other instances, land transfers have taken place in ways that completely bypass the local authorities. In the southern district of Mulanje, Mulli Brothers, a local conglomerate with links to the previous president, demanded land belonging to an orphanage that bordered a plantation they owned. Despite a decision by the High Court that the land belonged to the orphanage, Mulli put armed guards on the site while waiting for appeal, and the lawyer representing the orphanage suffered from two petrol bomb attacks. When the Supreme Court of Appeal upheld the earlier decision, the then Minister of Lands declared that the land should be given to a businessman close to Mulli Brothers. The land has only now been returned to the former owners due to a change in regime that is less favourable to the Mulli Brothers conglomerate.[1]

Overall, a lack of transparency and efficacy in the formal land management process leave the system ripe for a range of abuses. The existing law requires that traditional leaders consult community members for their consent to proposed land transfers before the deals can be effectively concluded. However, reports circulate of local chiefs selling the same piece of land to more than one buyer.[2] Meanwhile, details of a potential lease of land to the government of Djibouti remain unclear.[3] Indeed, a reflection of the lack of transparency and potential for corruption can be seen in the banning of land transactions for 2 weeks in 2012. This occurred just after the death of President Binguwa Mutharika, when the lack of an effective minister meant there was considered to be a power vacuum in the Ministry of Lands. The banning of transfers was apparently put in place for the situation 'not to be taken advantage of'. This can be seen as an implicit admission of the potential for corruption within the transfer of land.

7.3 CONSEQUENCES AND DISTORTIONS CAUSED BY LAND GRABBING

The most immediate impact of land grabs is a worsening inequality in the ownership of land as it is mostly the better off and foreigners who are able to get land at the time when per capita land ownership in Malawi has greatly diminished. The combined effects of the postcolonial development strategy and the rapid increase in population growth have led to the dramatic decline in per capita landholding sizes to as low as 0.8 ha in the 2000s from 1.53 ha in the late 1960s (Chirwa, 2004). Within this context, the distribution of land is highly unequal – it is estimated that between 1.8 and 2 million smallholder farmers cultivate on average 1 ha, whereas 30 000 estates cultivate 10–500 ha (Kanyongolo, 2004).

This inequality, combined with the non-consensual nature of many land grabs, has led to a rising resentment of the redistribution of land, particularly focused on foreigners. A recent report by Mwakasungula (2009) states: 'many people have observed that only foreigners can manage to purchase land because of their economic muscles while ordinary Malawians cannot. The general feeling is that the current policy or existing laws favour foreigners in accessing and distribution of land' (Mwakasungula, 2009). While such anti-foreigner feeling may be justified on occasion, it may make it even more difficult for foreign investors to acquire and invest in land in a legitimate and transparent fashion.

At times, resentment over land transfers has spilled over into damaging conflict. In the case of the Makande Estate distribution described above, neighbouring villages were not satisfied with the resettlement plan and started encroaching into the area. This led to the involvement of police, several violent clashes and two persons being killed. Settlers' houses were demolished, crops destroyed and women harassed. There were also accusations that neighbouring villages attempted to contaminate the water sources of the settlers and stole building materials. This conflict arose partly due to 'the perception that there were many rich civil servants, politicians and business people that had obtained land through corruption' (Holden et al., 2006).

The indirect effects of corruption in land are also highly damaging. In addition to the resulting distribution being inequitable, corruption has also resulted in an inefficient allocation of land. Since corruption may enable purchasers to obtain land quickly and with greater ease than usual, there is an incentive to gain as much as possible, even if this is more than one could use. Indeed, there is widespread feeling that many of the large estates are underutilized (Longley et al., 2003). Moreover, corruption means that land is allocated to those who might be best politically connected at the moment, rather than those that make best use of it, and land under contention due to suspected corruption may lie fallow for many years while matters are concluded in court (Mwakasungula, 2009). Corruption in land transfers also creates severe problems for the environment. Since corruption prevents land regulations from being effectively enforced, areas may become overpopulated, leading to deforestation.

Finally, one major result of corruption in land transfers is that it leads to a reduced political appetite to carry out appropriate land reform. This reduction in desire for reform comes from three main sources.

First, since elites who would like to obtain land can do so corruptly, they do not need to change the system in order to purchase land. Indeed, a more transparent and well-understood system may actually worsen the terms on which they obtain land. Corruption in the obtaining of land therefore separates the elite away from other members of society, and shields them from the inefficiencies and problems of the current land framework.

The second reason that corruption in land transfers reduces the desire for reform is that it creates resistance amongst those that benefit from this corruption. For example, a number of traditional authorities were opposing the recent Land Bill even though they – or their representatives – had earlier commented on the report and considered its proposals at least positively through a Special Commission's consultative process. Their resistance was, however, based on the conception that this Bill would eventually undermine their traditional and legitimate power over land at the local community level because it suggested that the role that traditional authorities currently play should be performed by a committee of four people with traditional authorities as *ex-officio* members. This would enhance transparency and accountability in land transaction matters but more critically take away the opportunity space for traditional leaders to extract personal benefits from the processes as is currently the case (Mwakasungula, 2009).

A third reason why corruption reduces elites' desire to reform land is that land reform potentially opens up the possibility of previous corrupt gains being reversed. For example, a commission appointed to consider land reform in the 1990s stated that is was persuaded that 'the acceptance of Certificates of Claim and the consequent legitimisation of title to land to which they relate, was a serious historical wrong to indigenous communities especially in the Southern Region of Malawi' (PCILPR, 1998: 53). The severe land pressure in the southern districts of Mulanje, Thyolo and Chiradzulu was thus, in part, seen as a result of this 'historical wrong', and the Commission stated that 'it is not unreasonable that demands for some form of land readjustment are being asserted in those areas'. While in theory it would be possible to separate redistribution of land from reform of the current regime, in practice the two aspects come as a bundle. For instance, implementation of the new land policy is likely to involve a clearer demarcation as to the ownership of current landholdings, and hence intensify conflicts where they exist.

7.4 POLICY SUGGESTIONS

7.4.1 For Government

At one level, recommendations for government fit within a more general anti-corruption agenda. Greater detection and prosecution of public officials involved in corruption should reduce the propensity of bureaucrats to take bribes in exchange for approving land transfers. Equally, increasing the transparency of land ownership and transfers is likely to make it harder for corrupt purchases to be hidden. Greater resources channelled towards institutions that play roles within the sector, such as the judiciary involved in land disputes, may also facilitate the processing of legal transfers and the resolution of land conflicts.

At a higher level, however, the previous sections have underlined that corruption in land transfers is fundamentally linked to a poorly enforced and inadequate land policy. Thus a key priority for the government in tackling land grabs should be to move towards enforcing a clear and consistent land policy. In order for corruption to be minimized, such a land policy will have to take into account the interest of both government and private actors to transfer some land into private ownership. However, for it to be enforced, it must also build upon and be strongly compatible with the ways in which land has been managed historically. By facilitating legal and consensual transfers, this should reduce some of the pressure that results in corrupt land transfers. At the same time, land reform should ensure that previous corrupt transfers are rectified in some way. Not only would such a policy partially compensate those who previously suffered from land grabs, but it may also discourage future land grabbing.

Pursuing land reform is likely to be rife with controversies that cannot be shied away from. For example, foreign investment in land can clearly bring economic benefits to the country, but it also carries risks of expropriation and people losing their traditional way of life. Currently, the government is attempting to have the best of both worlds through advocating an anti-foreign ownership policy while encouraging certain purchases when they perceive there to be large economic gains. In order for land transfers to be legitimate, there is a need for public debate on which transfers should and should not be allowed. A key component of this debate will be the role of traditional authorities. While these authorities have clearly traditionally been the arbiter of land rights, it is not clear they are so suitable to manage wholesale alienation of land rights.

7.4.2 For Civil Society and International Donors

One of the major problems caused by land grabbing is that it dulls the incentives of elites to undertake land reform and reduce corruption. There is therefore an important role for civil society and international donors to push forward this agenda. An obvious aspect of this role is to push for the kinds of reforms outlined above. In doing so, there may, however, be a conflict between pushing for the types of reform that would be optimal, and encouraging the enforcement of a set of policies that improves upon the existing regime.

In addition to this advocacy role, both civil society and international donors may have a role to play in increasing the transparency of potential land grabs. The use of land is generally visible on the ground, and therefore local NGOs can play an important role in transmitting information on land use as well as telling the stories of those dispossessed. International donors, on the other hand, may have a comparative advantage at investigating large-scale international deals, particularly if they involve international companies. At the extreme, it should be possible for organizations to regulate international companies to ensure that land obtained is acquired in a clean manner, in a similar way to the Extractive Industries Transparencies Initiative. By providing further information about corrupt land transfers, there may be increased pressure on government to carry out the type of corruption-reducing reforms described above.

7.5 CONCLUSION

Overall, the grabbing of land described in this chapter has brought out a number of points that are likely to be true of corruption across different sectors and countries. In particular, one stark element is the connection between corrupt acts and reform of the sector. Corruption in land transfers is partly a result of gaps within the implementation of an effective land policy. Moreover, we see a vicious circle, whereby greater corruption reduces the incentive of the government to carry out exactly the type of reform that would reduce corruption. In this way, it aids our understanding of why corruption persists and may be so difficult to fight, despite the obvious inefficiency it causes.

The description of land grabbing above also brings out points that are more particular to land in Malawi. Some of the cases above have illustrated the difficulty of defining acts as corruption when there is a clash between Western-style laws and historical practices. This comes out particularly strongly when we examine the role of traditional authorities in land transfers. Can giving benefits to chiefs in exchange for land be described as corruption when it is a traditional part of the way societies have been organized? Similarly, to what extent are traditional authorities unaccountable in their decisions to transfer land when accountability mechanisms have not been formally defined? These questions force us to think beyond standard legal definitions of corruption.

NOTES

1. http://www.nyasatimes.com/malawi/2012/07/17/mulanje-orphans-get-their-land-back-from-mulli/.
2. http://www.nyasatimes.com/malawi/2012/08/25/chiefs-aiding-land-laundering-crime-in-lilongwe/.
3. http://farmlandgrab.org/2908.

REFERENCES

Chingaipe, H., M. Chasukwa, B. Chinsinga and E. Chirwa (2013), The political economy of land grabs and land reforms in Malawi. *Journal of Agricultural and Environmental Ethics*, March 2013.

Chinsinga, B. (2011), The politics of land reforms in Malawi: the case of the Community Based Rural Land Development Programme (CBRLDP). *Journal of International Development*, **23**, 380–393.

Chinsinga, B., M. Chasukwa and S. Zuka (2013), When possession of land becomes a misfortune: the political economy of land grabs and rural development in the sugar industry in Malawi. A Draft Report submitted to the Organization for Social Science Research in East and Southern Africa (OSSREA), Addis Ababa, Ethiopia.

Chirwa, E. W. (2004), Access to land, growth and poverty reduction in Malawi. Consult Working Paper WC/03/04, University of Malawi, Chancellor College, Wadonda August 2004, Available at: http://www.wadonda.com/land0304.pdf.

Holden, S., R. Kaarhus and R. Lunduka (2006), Land policy reform: the role of land markets and women's land rights in Malawi. Noragric Report No. 36.

Kanyongolo, F. E. (2004), Land occupations in Malawi: challenging the neoliberal legal order. In S. Moyo and P. Yeros (eds), *Reclaiming the Land: The Resurgence of Rural Movements in Africa, Asia and Latin America*. London: Zed Publishers, pp. 118–141.

Longley, C., R. Kachule, M. Madola, I. Maposse, B. Araujo, T. Kalinda and H. Sikwibele (2003), *Agricultural Input Vouchers: Synthesis of Research Findings from Malawi*. Mozambique and Zambia: FANRPAN.

Mkandawire, R. M. (1983), Customary land, the state and Agrarian change in Malawi: the case of the Chewa peasantry in the Lilongwe rural development project. *Journal of Contemporary African Studies*, **3**, 109–128.

Mwakasungula, U. (2009), Land access, distribution and the role of parliament in fostering land justice. Mimeo.

Ng'ong'ola, C. (1986), Rural development and the reorganization of customary land in Malawi: some lessons from the Lilongwe Land Development Programme. *University of Malawi Journal of Social Science*, **13**, 39–56.

Peters P. and D. Kambewa (2007), Whose security? Deepening social conflict over customary land in the shadow of land tenure reform in Malawi. *The Journal of Modern African Studies*, **45**, 447–472.

PCILPR (Presidential Commission of Inquiry on Land Policy Reform) (1998), Preliminary Report of the Presidential Commission of Inquiry on Land Policy Reform. Lilongwe, Commission of Inquiry on Land Policy Reform, 8.

8. Using salaries as a deterrent to informal payments in the health sector

Ida Lindkvist

Informal payments for public services are widespread in many low-income countries (Killingsworth et al., 1999; Balabanova and McKee, 2002; Barber et al., 2004). Such payments can reduce trust in health-care providers (Vian et al., 2006), switch health-worker attention from patients' health to ability to pay (Lindkvist, 2012) and reduce demand for health care (Falkingham, 2004). Costs related to maternal health care is a likely explanation for the current failure in many countries to reach the health-related millennium development goals (MDGs), in particular when it comes to a reduction of maternal mortality (Borghi et al., 2006). The potential effects on health and poverty could be dire, and we must consider all forms of explanatory factors behind weak performance, including how to reduce the presence of informal payments. Suggestions typically range from formalizing such payments to making it less attractive to accept them.

In this chapter I will use data I collected in Tanzania to shed light on the relationship between salary and informal payments: specifically I will discuss the extent to which wage differentials and salary packages can deter corrupt practices among public officials. Tanzania is one of the countries not on track to reduce maternal mortality sufficiently to reach MDG5 (Hogan et al., 2010). Part of the explanation for the slow progress could be the additional costs women incur related to maternal health services. A third of the population have been asked for informal payments (REPOA, 2006), and qualitative data suggest that such payments also occur in the labour ward (Kruk et al., 2008; Mæstad and Mwisongo, 2011). The data set from Tanzania collected in 2007 has data on both gifts offered by patients and the skills of each health worker, as well as data on salaries, management and local labour market conditions. In an earlier study, I used these data to develop a new measure of informal payments: the probability that a single health worker accepts such payments.[1] Using this measure of informal payments, I find that higher salaries are indeed related to a lower probability of accepting informal payments. Interestingly, other aspects of the salary package, such as the way promotions are offered, appear to be more strongly related to the probability of accepting informal payments. Merit-based promotions and the quality of management appear to be more important than salary levels as deterrents to the acceptance of informal payments. It is uncertain whether merit-based promotions can be employed as a tool to combat informal payments without strengthened management at health clinics.

8.1 LITERATURE ON SALARIES AND INFORMAL PAYMENTS

The assumption that salaries can influence an official's decision to engage in corrupt practices dates back to the work of Becker and Stiegler (1974) and Shapiro and Stieglitz (1984). The theory postulates that salary levels can deter illegal activities if officials risk losing their job as a result of the illegal activities. According to this theory, a civil servant will engage in corrupt practices if the expected cost is lower than the expected benefit. The expected cost is a function of the probability of detection and costs associated with detection. Empirically, studies of the low-salary hypothesis have, however, resulted in mixed results. Van Rijckeghem and Weder (2001) tested the hypothesis on a large cross-country data set and found that higher salaries in the public sector are indeed associated with lower levels of corruption. However, their data suggest that a substantial raise is needed for salaries to work as a deterrent for corruption. Other studies have found little or no effect of salaries on corruption (Rauch and Evans, 2000; Treisman, 2000; Jaén and Paravisini, 2001; Gong and Wu, 2012).

One explanation for the low support for the low-salary hypothesis could be that the probability for detection and punishment is low, as argued by Besley and McLaren (1993). Another explanation might be that previous studies have underestimated the effect of salaries on corruption. To the extent that employers can assess workers' skills, these studies fail to take into account that workers have different chances of success in the labour market. Health workers who are highly skilled may have lower costs associated with engaging in corruption because they are more sought after on the job-market. These health workers may also receive higher salaries blurring the relationship between salaries and corruption. If we do not take into account worker skills when we test the low-salary hypothesis empirically this may bias the estimate downwards leading us to underestimate the influence of high salaries.

The low-salary hypothesis has been tested on salary levels, however, as salary levels affect the probability of accepting informal payments, we should observe the same for merit-based promotions. Promotions can be used to deter informal payments if employers are aware of the practice, oppose it and are able and willing to withhold promotions to deter informal payments. Using promotions as a deterrent to informal practices may be more effective than increasing salary levels as it may be easier to withhold a promotion than it is to fire an employee. So far, there is hardly any quantitative evidence on the effects of merit-based promotions

8.2   DATA

Data on health-worker skills, probability of corruption and salaries were collected in 2007 by a team of 12 medical degree graduates from Tanzania in all rural districts in Dodoma and Morogoro. Altogether the team visited 126 clinics. More than 3000 patients and 158 health workers were interviewed. Information on salaries and informal payments were obtained from 145 workers.[2] For a detailed description of data collection and a description of health workers and facilities, see Mæstad et al. (2010) and Lindkvist (2012).

In short, the probability of accepting informal payments, labelled *infpay* in the statistical results below, is calculated using patient interviews, utilizing the number of patients seen by a doctor and the number of patients who say that the health worker will offer better services if provided a gift. Lindkvist (2012) uses this information to calculate the probability that individual health workers accept informal payments. The variable *salary* is measured in Tsh 100 000, about USD 344 at the time (see Lindkvist, 2012).

Worker skills are measured using vignettes. Every health worker was presented with a case, where one of our research assistants pretended to be a patient. The pretend patient presented one symptom and the health worker was invited to conduct a consultation to the best of his ability. The variable measuring the skill level of the health worker is labelled *skills*[3] and is calculated as the sum of all items conducted correctly by the health worker, divided by three (we employed three different vignettes).[4]

We asked health workers about the most important factors that influenced their chance of being promoted, and the two most common replies were the number of years worked (tenure) and doing a good job.[5]

The variable *tenure* takes the value 1 if the health worker mentioned this and 0 otherwise. The variable *good job* is coded in the same way.

During the health worker interviews we also took note of the gender of the health worker (*male*) as well as the *age*. Recall that the alternative wage is assumed to depend positively on skills, gender (men receive a higher wage) and age (experience).

Besides, our research assistants undertook an extensive interview with the managers of each clinic and assessed how capable they believed the health worker was as a manager. The manager is presumed to be capable if he is rated to be of above or very much above average capability, this variable is labelled *manage*.

One reason why we may observe a negative correlation between salary levels and informal payments is if the manager of a clinic accepts informal payments because salaries are low. To take into account whether this was in fact the case we asked health workers whether the management accepted informal payments because salaries were low. I have created a dummy variable *accept* to pick up this attitude. If health workers did not disagree with the statement[6] the variable takes the value 1, and 0 otherwise.

To assess the influence of salaries on informal payments accurately, it is important to control for local labour market characteristics. The variable *noemploy* captures one aspect of the local labour market; whether there are alternative jobs outside the clinic. Salaries that may be too low to deter informal payments in one area may be high enough in other areas if no other employment opportunities exist.

Other control variables included are whether the health worker works at a hospital (*hospital*), a health centre (*h_c*), at a faith-based facility (*faith*). Table 8.1 presents descriptive statistics for the 145 health workers in the sample.[7]

On average 28.6 per cent of the health workers accept informal payments (*infpay*, Table 8.1), the average take home salary after tax is approximately Tsh 1 808 000 (approximately USD 620 at the time of the study) and there is quite a lot of variation in salary levels. Salaries vary from 0 to Tsh 4 850 000. Most of the workers working for free are employed by faith-based organizations. On average health workers are familiar with 47 per cent of the items we tested for. Again there is variation in the skill level of the health workers. The skill level ranges from 6 per cent to over 80 per cent of the items they should conduct according to guidelines. Although all health workers in our sample worked as doctors and consulted patients in the outpatient department (OPD), not all had formal medical training, which can perhaps explain the variation in skills. Approximately 36 per cent of the health workers

Table 8.1   Descriptive statistics

VARIABLES	(1) mean a	(2) mean b	(3) std.dev b	(4) min b	(5) max b
infpay	0.286 (0.0438)	0.355 (0.0337)	0.395	2.40e-05	1
salary	1.808 (0.110)	1.648 (0.0702)	0.895	0	4.850
skills	0.468 (0.0260)	0.454 (0.0124)	0.150	0.0612	0.816
skills_salary	0.919 (0.0833)	0.796 (0.0430)	0.534	0	2.727
manage	0.362 (0.0660)	0.352 (0.0398)	0.477	0	1
accept	0.0551 (0.0219)	0.0690 (0.0211)	0.257	0	1
noemploy	0.0889 (0.0405)	0.0897 (0.0238)	0.291	0	1
good_job	0.266 (0.0649)	0.221 (0.0346)	0.429	0	1
tenure	0.216 (0.0526)	0.276 (0.0372)	0.448	0	1
hospital	0.0761 (0.0279)	0.117 (0.0268)	0.327	0	1
h_c	0.128 (0.0346)	0.234 (0.0353)	0.422	0	1
faith	0.182 (0.0382)	0.276 (0.0372)	0.459	0	1
age	41.59 (1.328)	41.38 (0.866)	10.48	22	70
male	0.403 (0.0625)	0.469 (0.0416)	0.501	0	1
Observations	145	145	145	145	145

Notes:

Standard errors in parentheses
a: with survey weights
b: without survey weights
sd = standard deviation

worked in clinics with managers thought to be of above-average capability. Only 5.5 per cent of health workers believed that the management of the clinic would accept informal payments because of low salaries. Around 8.9 per cent of health workers worked in clinics where they believed no outside job opportunity existed.

The average health worker is 42 years old, a woman (40 per cent are male), works in a dispensary (8 per cent work in hospitals, 12.8 per cent work in health centres) and in public clinics (only 18 per cent work in faith-based clinics).

8.3 RESULTS

Table 8.2 displays the results of the simple regression analysis.

Table 8.2   Regression results

VARIABLES	(1) *infpay*	(2) *infpay*
salary	–0.0656 (0.0417)	–0.0972** (0.0467)
skills		0.367** (0.163)
age	0.00455 (0.00288)	0.00687** (0.00305)
good_job	–0.143** (0.0719)	–0.150** (0.0688)
tenure	0.232*** (0.0873)	0.224*** (0.0856)
noemploy	–0.124* (0.0635)	–0.180** (0.0696)
accept	0.461*** (0.108)	0.459*** (0.0976)
manage	–0.246*** (0.0729)	–0.259*** (0.0692)
hospital	0.229** (0.111)	0.255** (0.107)
h_c	0.0431 (0.0815)	0.0368 (0.0807)

VARIABLES	(1) *infpay*	(2) *infpay*
faith	−0.0476 (0.0775)	−0.0419 (0.0758)
male	−0.104 (0.0876)	−0.103 (0.0843)
co	−0.00870 (0.109)	−0.0275 (0.105)
Constant	0.311* (0.173)	0.123 (0.176)
Observations	145	145
R-squared	0.363	0.380

Notes:

Standard errors in parentheses
*** p<0.01, ** p<0.05, * p<0.1
Survey weights used
PSU = 126
weights = *fac_weight*hw_weight*
Tsh measured in 100 000

In the first regression I have not controlled for *skills* (Table 8.2, (1)), and as hypothesized in Section 8.2 the model fails to pick up any correlation between informal payments and salaries. As expected, when *skills* are included, the correlation between salaries and the probability that a health worker accepts informal payments is negative. In line with previous studies the effect is however not very large: a one hundred thousand Tsh increase in salary is associated with a 10 percentage points reduction in the probability of accepting informal payments (Table 8.2, (2), *salary*). Recall that the average salary is Tsh 1.808 hundred thousand, which means that one hundred thousand is more than a 50 per cent increase for the average health worker. Furthermore, observe that the variable skills should now be interpreted as a proxy for the salary the health worker can obtain in a different job. As hypothesized, *skills* is positive. An increase in skills by one standard deviation is associated with an increased probability of accepting informal payments of 6 percentage points (0.150×0.367; *skills*, Table 8.1 and Table 8.2 (2)).

If doing a good job (*good_job*, Table 8.2 (2)) is important for promotions, the probability of accepting informal payments is 15 percentage points lower than if this is not the case. By contrast, if health workers said that years worked (*tenure*) is important for promotions, the probability that the health worker accepts payments is 22 percentage points higher (*tenure*, Table 8.2 (2)).

Clearly the extent to which the health worker has local external job opportunities can also affect the cost of job loss. In this sense the external job market should have a negative effect on the probability of accepting informal payments. The variable *noemploy* is negative and associated with 18 percent lower probability of accepting informal payments (*noemploy*, Table 8.2 (2)).

Other aspects of management that can affect the probability of accepting informal payments is the quality of the management more generally, and the management's attitude on compensation in particular. If our research assistants believed that the manager was above-average quality, in other words, the variable *manage* takes value 1, the probability of accepting informal payments is 0.259 percentage points lower (*manage*, Table 8.2 (2)). However if the management accepts payments, in other words, if health workers do not disagree with the statement that the management accepts gifts from patients because salaries are so low, the probability that they accept payments is 46 percentage points higher (*accept*, Table 8.2 (2)).

Other aspects associated with a higher probability of accepting informal payments are age and whether the health worker works at a hospital relative to a smaller health facility. Health workers in a hospital have a 0.255 percentage point higher probability of accepting informal payments (*hospital*, Table 8.2 (2)). An increase in age by 10 years (one standard deviation), is however only associated with a less than 1 percentage point increase in the probability of accepting informal payments (*age* × 10, Table 8.2 (2)).

Ownership or gender seems to have no influence on the decision as to whether to accept informal payments.

8.4 DISCUSSION AND CONCLUDING REMARKS

Although the simple regression analysis in the previous section cannot differentiate between various explanations for the observed relationship, it certainly supports the low-salary hypothesis. However, it is less evident whether the data also support the idea that salaries and salary packages can be used strategically to reduce informal payments.

Health workers with higher salaries than health workers with the same skill level are less inclined to accept informal payments. A likely explanation is that they are reluctant to risk losing a relatively well-paid job. Similarly, when salaries depend on doing a good job, the probability of accepting informal payments is lower, while when salaries depend on years worked, this inclination to accept informal payments increases. Unsurprisingly, when the management is lenient with respect to informal payments, the probability of accepting payments is also higher, and likewise, good management is associated with a lower probability of accepting informal payments.

These results do not necessarily imply that higher starting salaries should be offered to all highly skilled workers as a deterrent to informal payments. The simple regression analysis does not make it possible to differentiate between the reasons for observed interlinkages between salaries and informal payments. If the observed relationship between informal payments and salaries is due to the low-salary hypothesis, then offering all highly skilled health workers high salaries would mean that no one received a relatively higher salary (if they had the same skills). Hence, high salaries would no longer work as a deterrent since salaries would not longer be relatively higher for some of the health workers. However, if the relationship is due to fairness concerns; in other words, highly skilled health workers who receive a relatively low wage recipro- cate by accepting informal payments,[8] then increasing low salaries to the same level as other highly skilled health workers may in fact act as a deterrent.

Rather than increasing starting salaries, policymakers could consider promoting policies that link promotions (and wage increases) to job performance. This is challenging though, since it requires that the manager can observe the workers' effort levels. The Tanzanian govern- ment has attempted to make promotions merit-based through the Open Performance Review Appraisal Systems (OPRAS). A qualitative study by Songstad et al. (2012) suggests, however, that this reform has not been successful so far, one reason being that information on job performance is not sufficiently fed back into the system, and thus, not used for promotion decisions.

In general, it may be difficult to use merit-based promotions strategic- ally since it is difficult to quantify job performance since we easily face the challenge of *multitasking*, as described in (Holmstrom and Milgrom, 1991). In this context, multitasking refers to the tendency of job- performance schemes to reward what can be measured, while workers stop focusing on what cannot be measured. A prerequisite for the effectiveness of merit-based promotions may thus be the capacity of management to see through these challenges, and design the performance-based payment accordingly.

Since good management at the clinic level is associated with a lower probability of accepting informal payments, we could draw the implication that improving management at clinic level could work also as a deterrent to informal payments.

As a general lesson, policymakers should be careful using salary differential as a tool for targeting informal payments, particularly until we can differentiate between the various explanations for the observed relationship between salaries and informal payments. Furthermore, even if merit-based promotions introduced to target informal payments may prove effective, it is unlikely to be a quick-fix since it may, as discussed, have to be followed by longer-term investment in competence-training for management.

NOTES

1. Patient data on informal payments are used to assess the likelihood that a particular health worker accepts informal payment. For each health worker, we asked several patients about their experience with demand for informal payments. We used the different replies to calculate the conditional probability that a single health worker accepted gifts, while taking into account that some patients would not be willing to say that the health worker accepted gifts when this was the case, some would be mistaken, while others would correctly state that the health worker accepted gifts. See Lindkvist (2012) for a detailed description.
2. Data is missing for the following reasons: some health workers had to leave because of emergencies and some health workers did not yet know their salary levels because they had just started working. For some we had missing data on one of the other variables.
3. A less precise measure of skills would be cadre; not all the health workers in our sample were qualified to consult with patients. In Tanzania, clinical officers, assistant medical officers and medical officers are cadres educated to consult with patients. Medical officers are equivalent to what is normally called a physician in the US/Europe, while assistant medical doctors and clinical officers have less education but are qualified to consult with patients in Tanzania. Skills will also vary with cadre, however we assume that skills is a more precise measure of labour market attractiveness.
4. See Lindkvist (2012) for a more detailed description.
5. Health workers were asked which of the following were most important for being promoted; (1) tenure, (2) doing a good job, (3) having friends in local/central government, (4) education and (5) other.
6. 'Because the salaries of health workers are low, accepting a gift from patients is usually tolerated by the management'.
7. Originally we interviewed 158 health workers; however, the sample analysed is smaller. See note 2.
8. See, for example, Akerlof (1982) who discusses wages as a partial gift exchange.

REFERENCES

Akerlof, G. A. (1982), Labor contracts as partial gift exchange. *Quarterly Journal of Economics*, **97**, 543–569.

Balabanova, D. and M. Mckee (2002), Understanding informal payments for health care: the example of Bulgaria. *Health Policy*, **62**, 243–273.

Barber, S., F. Bonnet and H. Bekedam (2004), Formalizing under-the-table payments to control out-of-pocket hospital expenditures in Cambodia. *Health Policy and Planning*, **19**, 199–208.

Becker, G. S. and G. J. Stigler (1974), Law enforcement, malfeasance, and compensation of enforcers. *The Journal of Legal Studies*, **3**, 1–18.

Besley, T. and J. Mclaren (1993), Taxes and bribery: the role of wage incentives. *The Economic Journal*, **103**, 119–141.

Borghi, J., T. Ensor, A. Somanathan, C. Lissner and A. Mills (2006), Mobilising financial resources for maternal health. *The Lancet*, **368**, 1457–1465.

Falkingham, J. (2004), Poverty, out-of-pocket payments and access to health care: evidence from Tajikistan. *Social Science and Medicine*, **58**, 247–258.

Gong, T. and A. M. Wu (2012), Does increased civil service pay deter corruption? Evidence from China. *Review of Public Personnel Administration*, **32**, 192–204.

Hogan, M., K. Foreman, M. Naghavi, S. Ahn, M. Wang, S. Makela, A. Lopez, R. Lozano and C. Murray (2010), Maternal mortality for 181 countries, 1980–2008: a systematic analysis of progress towards Millennium Development Goal 5. *The Lancet*, **375**, 1609–1623.

Holmstrom, B. and P. Milgrom (1991), Multitask principal-agent analyses: incentive contracts, asset ownership, and job design. *Journal of Law, Economics, and Organization*, **7**, 24–52.

Jaén, M. H. and D. Paravisini (2001), Wages, capture and penalties in Venezuela's public hospitals. In: R. Di Tella and W. D. Savedoff (eds), *Diagnosis Corruption: Fraud in Latin America's Public Hospitals.* Washington DC: Latin American Research Network, Inter-American Development Bank.

Killingsworth, J. R., N. Hossain, Y. Hedrick-Wong, S. D. Thomas, A. Rahman and T. Begum (1999), Unofficial fees in Bangladesh: price, equity and institutional issues. *Health Policy and Planning*, **14**, 152–163.

Kruk, M. E., G. Mbaruku, P. C. Rockers and S. Galea (2008), User fee exemptions are not enough: out of pocket payments for 'free' delivery services in rural Tanzania. *Tropical Medicine and International Health*, **13**, 1442–1451.

Lindkvist, I. (2012), Informal payments and health worker effort: a quantitative study from Tanzania. *Health Economics*, DOI: 10.1002/hec.2881.

Mæstad, O. and A. Mwisongo (2011), Informal payments and the quality of health care: mechanisms revealed by Tanzanian health workers. *Health Policy*, **99**, 107–115.

Mæstad, O., G. Torsvik and A. Aakvik (2010), Overworked? On the relationship between workload and health worker performance. *Journal of Health Economics*, **29**, 686–698.

Rauch, J. E. and P. B. Evans (2000), Bureaucratic structure and bureaucratic performance in less developed countries. *Journal of Public Economics*, **75**, 49–71.

REPOA (2006), Combating corruption in Tanzania, perception and experience. Afrobarometer briefing paper no 33. REPOA, Dar es Salaam.

Shapiro, C. and J. E. Stiglitz (1984), Equilibrium unemployment as a worker discipline device. *The American Economic Review*, **74**, 433–444.

Songstad, N. G., I. Lindkvist, I., K. M. Moland, V. Chimhutu and A. Blystad (2012), Assessing performance enhancing tools: experiences with the open performance review and appraisal system (OPRAS) and expectations towards payment for performance (P4P) in the public health sector in Tanzania. *Globalization and Health*, **8**, 1–13.

Treisman, D. (2000), The causes of corruption: a cross-national study. *Journal of Public Economics*, **76**, 399-457.

Van Rijckeghem, C. and B. Weder (2001), Bureaucratic corruption and the rate of temptation: do wages in the civil service affect corruption, and by how much? *Journal of Development Economics*, **65**, 307–331.

Vian, T., K. Gryboskb, Z. Sinoimeric and R. Halld (2006), Informal payments in government health facilities in Albania: results of a qualitative study. *Social Science and Medicine*, **62**, 877–887.

9. Financial 'blood-letting' in the Colombian health system: rent-seeking in a public health insurance fund

Karen Hussmann and Juan Carlos Rivillas

The Colombian health-care system has experienced a systems crisis due to large-scale schemes of corruption combined with mismanagement and lack of control. In May 2011 news broke of major corruption allegations in the use of the public health insurance fund, FOSYGA (*Fondo de Solidaridad y Garantía del Sistema General de Seguridad Social en Salud*). Since then it has become clear that virtually all actors of the health system have participated in and/or tolerated growing levels of corruption or *grabbing* leading to a profound crisis of financial sustainability as well as of legitimacy.

To understand the case, we need to briefly explain the complex insurance-based Colombian health system, which was established in its current form (of regulated competition between health insurers) through a major reform in 1993. The Colombian health system aims at universal health insurance coverage and consists of three sub-systems: (1) the public health insurance system, which covers around 90 per cent of the population and is divided into two sub-systems, the contributive system for people with capacity to pay for health insurance (approximately 40 per cent) and the subsidized system for the poor and marginalized (approximately 50 per cent); (2) the public system for the poor without health insurance coverage; and (3) private health insurance which offers complementary coverage. In the public health insurance system there are health insurance companies, EPS (*Empresas Promotoras de Salud*) and health service providers (health service providers, which can either be public or private in nature (Pinto and Hsaio, 2007). The contributive system, a main part of the public health insurance system, is financed through a parastatal tax of 12.5 per cent of the beneficiaries' income, while the subsidized system is mainly financed through national and regional taxes.[1] Both the contributive and subsidized systems consist of a benefit package, POS (*Paquete de Beneficios de Salud*)[2] that defines the medical treatments and drugs that beneficiaries are entitled to. All treatments and drugs not covered by the POS are called NO-POS services. Given that health insurers, the EPS, do not get funding for NO-POS services through the system, funding for these services can be claimed at the FOSYGA which, if approved, reimburses the EPS for the costs incurred. It is precisely this mechanism that has been widely abused for private gain (Hussmann, 2011).

In Colombia the right to health is enshrined in the Constitution of 1991 (República de Colombia, 1993). Given that the health packages, in other words, the POS, by definition limits the treatments and drugs beneficiaries are entitled to, mainly due to reasons of financial sustainability of the system[3], citizens may use legal action (petitions or '*tutela*' in Spanish) to claim funding for the constitutional right to health, no matter which service or drug is needed.

FOSYGA is an independently managed fiduciary fund under the Ministry of Health. The role of the FOSYGA in the NO-POS reimbursement scheme is to conduct a medical, legal and financial analysis of the reimbursement claims presented to it by the EPS (Ministerio de Salud, 2010) as well as to reimburse the requested costs to either the EPS or citizens if these use legal procedures described below. Within the EPS a Technical–Scientific Committee will medically and legally approve the request of a patient for a NO-POS drug or treatment. In many cases, the Technical–Scientific Committee of the EPS do not approve the request so that patients may then resort to the use of legal procedures (*tutelas*) to get access to the needed drugs. Both mechanisms, the process with the Technical–Scientific Committee and the *tutelas*, have grown rapidly in use partly due to the rent-seeking opportunities as a result of a lack of control.

Given that the original scandal broke only in early 2011, not much has been written yet about the case. This chapter aims to explain what happened and describe some of the first responses to the disclosure of loopholes that allowed corruption and mismanagement. While focusing specifically on the uses and abuses of FOSYGA, we will now list some of the main irregularities and corrupt practices, point at how early warning signals failed to result in timely action, illustrate some of the emergency actions taken by the current government, and discuss further options for pending action.

9.1 FOSYGA: A FIDUCIARY FUND WITH PUBLIC FUNCTIONS OPEN FOR RENT-SEEKING

The use of NO-POS reimbursements through FOSYGA grew exponentially from 2002 onwards and against initial projections of the Colombian health authorities. Alerts regarding fraud, other types of irregularities and outright corruption emerged fairly early on. As shown in Figure 9.1, reimbursements of NO-POS drugs and medical services amounted to COP 5.311 million (*Colombian pesos*) in 2001, multiplied ten times in only one year, and continued to grow on average 68 per cent per year between 2003 and 2009 reaching an amount close to COP 2.5 billion in 2010 (21 times as much as in 2003). This was about half a point of GDP or USD 1.317 million (Federación Médica Colombiana, 2011). While the mechanism was designed for exceptional situations, it quickly became a regularly used tool.

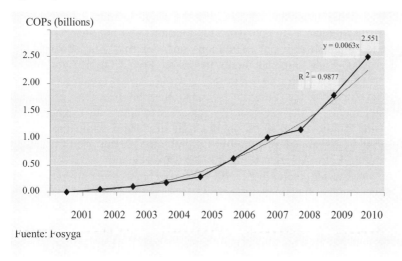

Fuente: Fosyga

Sources: FOSYGA: Reimbursements of NO-POS drug supplies (30 November 2010).

Figure 9.1   Evolution of reimbursements of NO-POS drugs and medical services in Colombia, 2001–2010

In 2010, the health sector oversight institution Supersalud (Superintendencia de Salud) reported that 25 per cent of these reimbursements from FOSYGA to the EPSs were fraudulent, as they involved drugs and health services that are included in the health insurance package POS (*El Tiempo*, 2011). Furthermore, drugs were reimbursed at prices much higher than those in the market, some of them at 1000 per cent of their market value, with the profitable difference going to corrupt pockets (*El Universal*, 2011). In 2006, the Federación Médica Colombiana (FMC) denounced the way these legal arrangements allowed FOSYGA to make reimbursements without any control, leading to severe financial blood-letting of the health-care system. Additionally, it is important to note that reimbursements were concentrated in drugs for high-cost diseases such as cancer, rheumatoid arthritis, transplant management and rare diseases (Ministerio de Salud, 2011).

These developments coincided with several related public policy changes. In 2002, the then minister of health, foreseeing the potential risks of this reimbursement scheme for the financial viability of the health system, sanctioned 32 drug laboratories for price fixing and other irregularities, and included crucial drugs in the regime of direct price control. However, in 2003 the Ministry of Health began to promote a drug market deregulation which was formalized through a Circular issued in 2004 by the National Drug Price Commission (Comisión Nacional de Precios de Medicamentos, 2010). This measure was not successful as it failed to establish efficient regulations and controls. Subsequently the value of NO-POS reimbursements increased from COP 113 million in 2003 to COP 2.5 billion in 2010.

The volume of the drug costs constituted 82 per cent of overall reimbursements in the previous 2 years. The country also experienced increasing public discussions on the right to health while the use of *tutelas* was encouraged, resulting in Colombia becoming one of the main countries in Latin America using this legal instrument.

The unexpected increase of NO-POS reimbursements over the past 10 years can be explained by several factors. One main reason is the growing number of patients using the right to petition (*tutela*) to claim financial coverage of needed drugs not included in the POS. Using *tutelas* is legal and legitimate. However, the apparent lack of oversight and control by and within FOSYGA and other health sector actors seem to have resulted in considerable fraud and corruption. In addition, it led to a growing tendency of the Scientific–Technical Committees assessing the case of patients requesting a specific drug or medical treatment not included in the POS to recommend that the patients are granted the requested drug or service on medical reasons. In case of approval the EPS is obliged to provide the drug or service and can claim back the funds from FOSYGA. This latter mechanism is equally legal and legitimate but has also been prone to increasing abuse. Third, the lack of external control has made possible outright abuse of the above-mentioned mechanisms through the following means: (1) claims for reimbursement of drugs that are included in the POS resulting in charging the system twice for the same drugs and treatments; (2) claims for reimbursements of drugs way above the market prices; (3) illicit arrangements among officials of the Ministry of Health and FOSYGA to authorize drug reimbursements to ghost health-care institutions (*El País*, 2011; *El Espectador*, 2012).

In sum, corruption in ensuring access to and supply of drugs seems to have become a common practice in the Colombian health system exacerbating an overall system crisis and depleting the health system of already scarce resources. Figure 9.2 illustrates the different practices of grabbing, abuse and mismanagement involving virtually all actors in the Colombian health system.

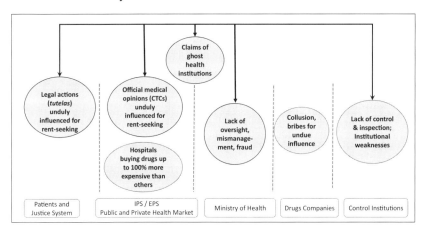

Source: Hussmann and Rivillas (2013).

*Figure 9.2   Practices of abuse and mismanagement in drug
                reimbursements in Colombia, 2012*

9.2   EARLY WARNING SIGNALS DID NOT LEAD TO TIMELY ACTION BY RESPONSIBLE ACTORS

The explosion of drug reimbursements over the last decade, consisting of nearly 1 million administrative processes per year, certainly exceeds the administrative capacity of the control and oversight system. It should be noted that to date there is no agreed methodology among health sector actors that allows us to establish the incidence and volumes of corrupt practices in drug reimbursements accurately. In many cases, investigations are still under way. Nevertheless, early warning signals that have emerged over the years from different quarters have not been taken up by the respective and relevant public and private actors to exert timely control and to remedy irregularities and corruption allegations.

These early warning signals, as well as publicly reported corruption allegations, include:

- In 2006, the FMC criticized the inconsistencies in legal decisions relating to reimbursement claims and their catastrophic effects on the financial viability of the health system. Also, several publications from the Observatory of Medicines showed that the drug price deregulation policy had a huge impact on the drug reimbursements by FOSYGA (Federación Médica Colombiana, 2011).
- From 2009 onwards, several reports have noted that drug reimbursements made by FOSYGA to the EPS have been fraudulent and inconsistent, many of them, as noted above, covering drugs and services included in the POS. Analyses found significant price differences between the reimbursements paid to EPS and health service providers and normal sales values of the drugs in question, as reported by pharmaceutical companies (*El Tiempo*, 2011; *El País*, 2011).
- In 2010, the FMC itself had to resort to a *tutela* (in other words, legal action) to get access to the database of FOSYGA in order to monitor drug reimbursements and drug pricing. The *tutela* obliged FOSYGA to provide access to reimbursement records from 2007–09. While the FMC pointed to the gross abnormalities in drug prices, the incumbent government initially did not take decisive action. The FMC continued to report evidence on high drug prices that eventually led to reactions by the new government (Federación Médica Colombiana, 2011).
- In 2012, investigations by the national auditor general's office (Contraloría) discovered disproportionate increases in drug costs reported by the EPS and revealed that some hospitals were acquiring drugs at double the price of others (Contraloría General de la Nación, 2012). These irregularities had a significant impact in terms of increasing the capitation payment that EPS receive per beneficiary.

There are open questions as to why these early warning signals were not reacted upon in a timely manner, leading to the collapse of the system.

Part of the answer can be attributed to system weaknesses and loopholes, but part of the answer must also be sought in the realm of political will for action.

9.3 WHAT HAS BEEN DONE TO COUNTERACT IRREGULARITIES AND TO INCREASE CONTROL?

Colombia has begun developing strategies to counteract the irregularities and corrupt practices discussed here. The following actions to encourage the rational use of drugs and remedy pharmaceutical market imperfections that have generated opportunities for rent-seeking are in particular:

1. The Colombian Constitutional Court demanded that the executive strengthens controls in the health system. High-level multi-institutional investigations have so far resulted in: arrested public officials (6 cases), officials investigated on charges of forming a drug cartel (25 cases), hospital managers sanctioned (34 cases), EPS intervened administratively by the Health Superintendency (15 cases) while no less than COP 4.5 billion are at risk of being lost (La Nación, 2012; Noticias Caracol, 2011).[4]
2. Unification and updating of the POS insurance package: This has been an important step as it allows for (a) discouraging the perverse practices linked to NO-POS reimbursements by FOSYGA, and (b) including high-cost drugs often solicited under the *tutela* or Technical–Scientific Committee of the EPS to eliminate the incentives for abuse by EPS.
3. Design of a strategy for the reduction and control of reimbursements. The Ministry of Health has designed a strategy that intends to standardize criteria for the decisions of the appeal judges when assessing a *tutela* and ordering the delivery of a drug: (a) Judges should order the active ingredient instead of deciding on the trademark; (b) in case they decide to order a specific trademark drug, the judges should substantiate with evidence the inadequacy of the corresponding generic drug; and (c) an active information exchange will be ensured regarding the technical evaluation criteria and claims management. In this endeavour, the protection of the right to health will be upheld.
4. Definition of maximum values for reimbursements. In 2010, Colombia aimed to establish maximum values for drug reimbursements, with data available from SISMED (*Sistema Nacional de Precios de Medicamentos*) (Comisión Nacional de Precios de

Medicamentos, 2010). However, for this to be effective SISMED, as a national drug pricing database, needs to be considerably strengthened according to the FMC (Federación Médica Colombiana, 2011).

5. Approval of the first National Pharmaceutical Policy. This policy provides an important opportunity to strengthen national drug governance and one of its most relevant elements is related to information systems (Departamento Nacional de Planeación, 2012). It foresees the establishment of a public information system, available in real time, that basically integrates a database of the national food and drug regulatory agency, and provides economic information on drug prices (through the SISMED) after data has been checked for inconsistences and facts.

Overall these examples of different actors taking action illustrate that in Colombia, public pressure and political commitment to remedy the damage caused by fraudulent drug reimbursements has increased.

9.4 POLICY RECOMMENDATIONS

The health system in Colombia is experiencing a historic crisis. A culture of fraud and corruption in drug reimbursements appears embedded in the system and millions of dollars appear to have been diverted for illegal and illicit purposes. Colombia needs to focus political efforts on implementing measures to increase transparency, integrity, efficiency and control in the realm of drug reimbursements. Doing so requires involving the coordination and cooperation of relevant public and private actors at national and local levels. Improving mechanisms for risk assessment and monitoring is also crucial (Hussmann, 2011). Special attention needs to be paid to strengthen the regulatory system and regulations themselves. Remedial actions should aim at: (1) generating baselines for measurement, (2) characterizing the forms of corrupt behaviour associated with the drug reimbursement scheme, (3) identifying risk areas and processes that create opportunities for abuse, and (4) introducing strategic actions to prevent, detect and punish the corrupt. Eliminating the perverse incentives for the business of drug reimbursements through the FOSYGA needs to include the strengthening of EPS in their role of health insurance administrators and controllers, ending their role as beneficiaries of drug reimbursements. The reviewed health insurance package is an important step in this direction as it is expected to discourage the now too frequent use of *tutelas*. This needs to be complemented by efforts to train appeal judges and the members of the Technical–Scientific Committee in legal and ethical decision-making.

Some fundamental trade-offs have to be addressed. The dichotomy between the right to health through the reimbursement scheme and the need to ensure financial viability of the system through a clearly delimited health insurance package needs to be addressed. Potential solutions need to be sought through participatory mechanisms including the current public and private actors as well as academia, trade unions and civil society. A new Institute for Technical Evaluations of Medical Supplies[5] will have a crucial role in this process, although its institutional design and operations need to be strengthened against undue influence. Moreover, the dichotomy between free competition and the need to strongly regulate certain aspects of the pharmaceutical market due to its many imperfections requires decisive, clear and transparent action on the side of the government regulator. This case study illustrates how the deregulation of the pharmaceutical market coincided with significant regulatory gaps and weak mechanisms of inspection, monitoring and control, leading to systematic rent-seeking by the health industry that severely destabilized the financial basis of the health system and contributed to its delegitimization.

Several of the factors that may change rent-seeking opportunities, must be attended to quickly, although they will require not only coordination between institutions from the health and law-enforcement sector, but also political will. For example, following the scandal and public allegations in 2011, the high-level multi-institutional investigations were stopped seemingly through political interference. Since then, no further public officials accused of corruption have been arrested, and neither is there information on additional investigations conducted.

Additionally, the lack of integrated and inter-operational information systems for the country makes it hard to get reliable, up-to-date information on how resources have been used regarding drug reimbursements. It is important to issue clear guidance so that information is made available based on principles of transparency and accountability. Only in this way can practices of abuse and corruption be detected, pursued and prevented.

Finally, this case shows how systematic corruption and rent-seeking that has spiraled out of control can lead to a system-wide crisis, weakening trust in state administration and delegitimizing the current system model, which despite serious problems, has also seen important achievements. There are now important and loud political voices demanding system reform on the grounds that this would allow combating corruption in the health sector. However, in this case, complete reform is not necessarily the right way forward. It is not the current drug and treatment reimbursement system or the regulated competition per se that is weakly designed. Instead, the levels of corruption seem to have developed because of weak implementation of adequate controls, information systems, transparency and effective oversight.

NOTES

1. See Ministerio de Salud y Protección Social, National Report of Coverage Health and Social Assistance Indicators (2005).
2. The POS of the subsidized system is still less comprehensive but harmonization with the contributive POS has been mandated by the Constitutional Court and is gradually being pursued.
3. No health system can pay all technically possible health interventions with public funds for its entire population, therefore countries pursue different ways to guarantee certain health services for all, while excluding others from public funding.
4. The Superintendencia de Salud has the faculty to 'take over' the administration of EPS in cases where gross mismanagement is detected.
5. IETS – *Instituto de Evaluación de Tecnologías en Salud*.

REFERENCES

Comisión Nacional de Precios de Medicamentos (National Drug Price Commission) (2010), Maximun values for drugs reimbursement in Colombia. Circular no. 004 of 2010. Comisión Nacional de Precios de Medicamentos, Bogotá, Colombia.

Contraloría General de la Nación (National Audit Office) (2012), Health report by the National Audit Office. Contraloría General de la Nación, Bogotá, Colombia. Available at: http://www.contraloriagen.gov.co/.

Departamento Nacional de Planeación (National Planning Department) (2012), CONPES 155 National Pharmaceutical Policy. Departamento Nacional de Planeación, Bogotá, Colombia.

El Espectador (h April 2012), The favors of the Colombian minister of health to the company Roche. Available at: http://m.elespectador.com/noticias/investigacion/articulo-336662-el-favor-de-palacio-roche.

El País (3 May 2011), Corruption scandal seemingly affects the health sector in Colombia. Available at: http://www.elpais.com.co/elpais/colombia/escandalo-corrupcion-afectaria-minproteccion.

El Tiempo (7 May 2011), Basic guide to understand the health scandal in Colombia. Available at: http://www.eltiempo.com/justicia/guia-basica-para-entender-el-escandalo-en-el-sector-de-la-salud_9304308-4.

El Universal (3 May 2011), Health sector scandal causes losses up to 30 000 Millions COP. Available at: http://www.eluniversal.com.co/cartagena/nacional/escandalo-en-sector-salud-por-desfalco-de-30-mil-millones-de-pesos-22174.

Federación Médica Colombiana (Colombian Medical Federation) (2011), The National auditor office will investigate 'cartel in medicines' in the health sector. Available at: http://www.federacionmedicacolombiana.com/index.php?option=com_content&view=article&id=229:contraloria-investiga.

Hussmann, K. (2011), Vulnerabilities to corruption in the health sector: perspectives from Latin American sub-systems for the poor (with a special focus on the sub-national level. UNDP Regional Centre, Panama. Available at: http://www.regionalcentrelac-undp.org/en/our-knowledge-products.

Ministerio de Salud y Protección Social (Ministry of Health) (2005), *National Report of Coverage health and Social Assitance Indicators.* Bogota, Colombia: Ministerio de Salud y Protección Social.

Ministerio de Salud y Protección Social (Ministry of Health) (2010), *Fondo de Solidaridad y Garantía FOSYGA.* Available at: http://www.fosyga.gov.co/AcercadelFOSYGA/QupercentC3percentA9eselFOSYGA/tabid/103/Default.aspx.

Ministerio de Salud y Protección Social (Ministry of Health) (2011), Final report on general drug system supplies in Colombia: design of policies in oncologic drugs provision. Ministerio de Salud y Protección Social, Bogotá, Colombia.

Noticias Caracol (15 May 2011), The EPS in the hurricane's eye facing 326 investigations by Supersalud. Available at: http://www.caracol.com.co/blogs/las-eps-en-el-ojo-del-huracan-enfrentan-326-investigaciones-en-supersalud/blog/1472416. aspx.

Pinto, D., and W. Hsaio (2007), Colombia: social health insurance with managed competition to improve health care delivery. In W. C. Hsaio and R. P. Shaw (eds), *Social Health Insurance for Developing Nations.* Boston, MA: The World Bank Institute and Harvard University, pp. 137–182.

República de Colombia (1993), *Law 100 of 1993. Creation of the National Health System in Colombia.* Bogotá, Colombia: República de Colombia, Chapter III: Overall national fund of solidarity and guarantee FOSYGA.

PART III

When political grabbing prevents the
performance of a sector or state function

10. Transport infrastructure failures in Spain: mismanagement and incompetence, or political capture?

Germà Bel, Antonio Estache and Renaud Foucart

Although Spain ranks remarkably well in international comparisons in terms of access to transport infrastructures, it does not seem to meet demand, leading to well-documented mismatches between demand and supply. This is a recurring hot political theme in Spain as in many other countries, developed and developing. The consequences are costly, unfair and unsustainable in the current context of economic crisis. So what's the problem?

This chapter argues that bad governance, capture and political interests, rather than incompetence, are the main drivers of supply–demand mismatches. The current state of transport infrastructure is above all the result of a strong political will to maintain Madrid as the centre of distribution of the economic benefits of all decisions on transport infrastructure investment.[1]

While it is fair for elected politicians to use their mandate to make tough decisions, it would be just as fair to make sure that they do not ignore the high economic and social costs for the country (Albalate and Bel, 2011; Bel, 2011, 2012; Bel and Fageda, 2011; De Rus, 2011). Moreover, there are reasons to suspect that key private actors have captured some policy decisions. The high concentration and strong political leverage of construction companies specializing in infrastructure have fuelled the sector's overinvestment and high fiscal costs. This interference with the planning and implementation of key decisions in the sector has not reached the outrageous levels of corruption cases documented in urban development projects, but the consequences are no less dramatic for Spain.[2]

10.1   THE BIG PICTURE

The Great Recession is an economic and social challenge to Spain, Europe's fifth largest economy. Income per capita has been dropping steadily since the early days of the crisis, income differences are worsening, unemployment increasing, the informal market growing fast, skilled labour is migrating and capital is sneaking out. This downward spiral has been happening at the same time as Spain has been steadily dropping in its corruption ratings for almost 10 years.[3] According to Transparency International (TI), in 2011, Spain's perceived corruption level ranked 31st from 183 in the world, with an average grade of 6.2. This may help explain why it only ranks 36th in terms of competitiveness in the 2012–13 Global Competitiveness Report (GCR, henceforth).

Political parties are seen as the country's most corrupt institution.[4] It does not help that the judicial power is not considered to be very independent. It only ranks 65th of 142 in the GCR. Corruption cases have been documented at all levels of government across political colours, a lot more than one would expect for countries at this level of development. Media on all sides of the political spectrum have been covering the issue quite aggressively (Lapuente, 2011; Rivero and Fernández-Vázquez, 2011; Villoria et al., 2011; Costas-Pérez et al., 2012; Jiménez and Carbona, 2012; Jiménez and García, 2012; Villoria and Jiménez, 2012). Corruption, incompetence and politics are blamed for everything that is going wrong. Somehow, it feels like Spain is on its way to underdevelopment unless it gets its act together.

Until the recent explosion of its real estate bubble, things looked good. It is easy to forget that not that long ago, at the end of the 1970s, Spain was still eligible for loans from the World Bank (WB) – in other words, it was still regarded as a developing economy. Much of the WB's support to Spain between 1963 and 1977 was used to finance transport infrastructure. In particular, a 1963 loan was instrumental in upgrading and redesigning Spain's road network to increase the competitiveness of all regions. A poor and insufficient road capacity was seen as an impediment to diversified growth. Similar issues were raised for rail and ports. The message for all of these projects was that transport supply did not match demand.

About 35 years after the last WB loan to Spain and after many more loans and grants provided by the European Union, Spain's supply of infrastructure has increased a lot. The GCR ranks Spain's infrastructure fifth in the EU, tenth in the world, and better than the United States and Japan. Only China has a longer high-speed train network (Albalate and

Bel, 2011). According to Eurostat, Spain counts twice as many international airports as Germany and 30 per cent more than the UK. Spain has almost 10 per cent more highways than Germany, almost 20 per cent more than France and four times as many as the UK (Bel, 2012). It has about 15 per cent more large ports than the UK or Germany and three times as many as France. At the technical level, at least, incompetence does not seem to be a problem.

This should be good news since transport infrastructure is an essential input for any strategy to get Spain out of the crisis and into a new growth path through a diversification of the economy and increased exports – just like in the 1960s! But the key weaknesses can easily be overlooked when focusing on quantity. When considering quality indicators in the GCR, Spain drops 10 points in the world ranking (to 18th; although the drop is dominated by quality issues in the electricity sector, it also hits airports (17th), ports (14th) and roads (13th)). This indicates 'over-or mis-engineering'. Furthermore, there are problems in that: (1) the use of this impressive capacity is largely concentrated in some specific hubs (and largely underused otherwise), (2) it ignores necessary cost-effective international interconnections for specific regions, (3) it imposes modal choices that ignore key users' preferences, and (4) it costs a lot more to taxpayers than it was supposed to.

In sum, 50 years after the thorough WB evaluation, the diagnostic of Spain's transport problems has hardly changed in its core substance. Something is wrong since 50 years of transport planning has not yet delivered a match between supply and demand in quantity and in quality, at a high cost to Spanish and European taxpayers. The outcome could be explained by incompetence, governance problems (corruption or something equivalent but more subtle) or conventional pork barrel politics, or a combination of factors as discussed later.

10.2 INSTITUTIONS AND SPAIN'S TRANSPORT POLICY

The conclusions of a plethora of recent highly publicized corruption trials, a number of academic studies (for example, Kaufmann et al., 2011) and a 2012 diagnostic conducted by Transparency International (TI) converge to show that institutional design is certainly part of what has gone wrong. Villoria et al. (2011) explain why the problem is more related to corruption than to incompetence.

Objective evidence is unfortunately hard to come by – as is usually the case with corrupt activities. And Spain does indeed have a problem when it comes to publishing key data. On financial secrecy, it ranks very low, 53rd of 71. One way around the data gap is to look at specific undesirable outcomes and figure out what drives them. There are four basic outcomes of interest to assess the effectiveness of transport policy: (1) quantity, (2) quality defined broadly, including the evolution of modal market shares, (3) costs, and (4) prices and subsidies. It is also useful to look at processes. There are three broad groups of processes that are relevant to the diagnostic of the sector: (1) the extent to which procurement rules are likely to lead to cost and quality efficient outcomes, (2) the extent to which competition and regulation policy stimulates incentives for supply to adjust to demand, and (3) the extent to which the agencies responsible for monitoring performance do what they are expected to do.

On quantity and quality, the consensus among the experts is that the evidence justifies the concern for the mismatch and recent policies have not done much to fix it. For instance, freight rail is slow in speed (15–20 km/h on average) and in handling. It is also unreliable and poorly connected to other modes, which determines a very low modal share. Spain's peripheral location and poor policy add up to explain the low traffic density and a high 'empty' traffic. Roads are not faring much better. All the concessions awarded since the late 1990s, are on the border of bankruptcy.[5] The Spanish Road Association (AEC, 2012) shows that roads have never been so poorly maintained in Spain. Moreover, it is now well-documented that traffic forecasts used to justify toll roads were overestimated by the public sector and private operators – and much more so than world average for the sector (Baeza and Vassallo, 2010).

On costs, processes to cut costs and agencies to monitor costs, academics provide ample evidence on the inefficiency of Spanish regional airports, ports and rail.[6] This evidence on inefficiency complements well the familiar anecdotes on regional airports, train stations and roads with hardly any traffic. The Spanish TV channels have enjoyed documenting the existence of what they call 'ghost airports and HSR (high-speed rail) stations'.[7] It is unlikely that current procurement practices will do much to cut costs in the sector. Indirect but powerful evidence is provided by the fact that most of the empirical research assessing the performance of transport infrastructures needs to rely on partial physical information rather than on the sort of reliable data that could be generated from sound cost accounting. The fact that this detail seems to escape the Spanish Audit Court (Tribunal de Cuentas), unlike what happens in the UK, France or Australia or even in emerging economies such as Brazil or Mexico, illustrates the core weaknesses of the institutions, a fact recently voiced by TI (Mulcahy, 2012). This is a problem in a sector without an independent regulatory agency, with a history of bilateral negotiation and renegotiation of contracts, and a record of political interference with transport planning.

On prices and subsidies, total infrastructure expenditures will be around EUR 10 billion in 2013 (around 0.9 per cent of GDP). About 90 per cent will go to transport, including 40 per cent to railways, focusing on high demand traffic, 29 per cent to roads and 6 per cent to support private investment in roads, 10 per cent to ports and 5 per cent to airports. The rest will finance various types of transport subsidies. Subsidy rates in the transport sector are among the highest in Europe.[8] This would be fine if the subsidies were cost-efficiently serving public service obligations. But the extremely low demand for a large share of the traffic supply would lead to the deduction that public money goes more to subsidize the supply side of the market.

Despite repeated calls from high profile actors of the sector,[9] the government has picked a strategy that is likely to reinforce the role of supply signals rather than address demand signals. Indeed, whenever possible, the government also wants to rely on public–private partnerships (PPPs) to reduce the short-term public financing requirements imposed by its involvement in the sector.[10] This seems unreal. Indeed, the case for PPPs in Spain's transport is happening in a context in which all the major private partners are going to be able to renegotiate their contracts to benefit from even more subsidies (through minimum income guaranteed schemes), longer contractual terms or other forms of endorsement which ensures that the risk component of the public-private partnerships is absorbed by the users or the taxpayers, without much concern for costs levels or effectiveness. Initially, the current Conservative administration wanted the few firms in the sector to merge to reap any scale economies – ignoring the weak demand and without a fair assessment of the degree of scale economies in the sector!

It is really hard not to suspect capture, collusion or other types of distortions in the market when the evidence of perverse behaviour is so strong. Too many top researchers have pointed to the weaknesses of current policies for anyone to be able to argue lack of knowledge or incompetence. Or then, incompetence has no limits.

10.3   THE POLITICS AND THE CONSTRUCTION BEHIND INFRASTRUCTURE

To get a sense of the realism of the assumption of a strong risk of capture, it is useful to step back and have a look at the history of the intense and somewhat incestuous relationship between the political power (of all colours) and the construction industry. This history is quite long. For instance, during the 1940–50s, the Francoist regime provided political prisoners as cheap labour to companies involved in the construction of key infrastructures, in particular railways. Many of these workers were quite qualified and hence more productive than workers available on the regular labour market, yet their salaries were significantly lower (Olaizola Elordi, 2006). It also had a non-negligible impact on the launching of a strong, high-return, Spanish construction industry. It is sometimes easy to forget how strong industries are born. But we'll come back to that.

Since the beginning of democracy and the fast acceleration of infrastructure investment during the 1980s – partially thanks to EU funding – there are many more illustrations of the unhealthy interactions between politics and construction. The increased political and regulatory control and hence the higher level of transparency of the interactions between the public and the private sector provides more recent examples of poor governance and corruption in the design and implementation of infrastructure policy in Spain.

The first major documented case of corruption that led to jail sentences took place in the early 1990s in the transport sector. It involved congressmen and administrators of the Spanish Socialist Party who had been in power from 1982 to 1996. It was based on 'fake' firms used to ensure the financing of the party's expenditures through overbilling of public contracts for the construction and operating of the first Spanish high-speed train between Madrid and Seville. The latest significant case was in March 2012. It sentenced Jaime Matas, the previous president of the Baleares region, a member of the Conservative Party (Partido Popular) for corruption in the construction of a multi-sports arena. In between, there have been many more open corruption cases in Spain, about 400 pending corruption cases as of mid-2012, most of them involving real estate and public service contracts at the regional and local level.

Overall, what seems clear is that many of these cases involve construction companies, large and small. This is not to say that the vast majority of construction companies are not clean. But the somewhat conspicuous relationship between politics and construction seems always to be present. Moreover even if legality is usually respected, it is often at the limit of what is considered to be good governance in terms of transparency. Many key policy decisions and laws in transport are concerned with the supply side of the market, which is dominated by the transport companies.

In practice, many of the large companies have the necessary economic weight to have political leverage on all government levels, including the national level. In 2012, among the 35 firms tracked by the Spanish stock market index (IBEX-35), eight were construction and public works companies: Abengoa, Acciona, ACS, FCC, Ferrovial, OHL, Sacyr and Técnicas Reunidas. This means that the performance of these companies drives 25 per cent of the index. In all of them, except Ferrovial and Sacyr, the board includes individuals who occupied high-level political positions. Even if this is not that uncommon in Spain for large companies (Castells and Trillas, 2013), it is noteworthy. Indeed, Faccio (2010) has shown that the firms with the strongest political connections tend to obtain larger market shares than unconnected firms. More consistent with the average evidence on performance reported earlier, these connected firms also tend to show lower productivity. This productivity deficit of connected firms is stronger the higher the corruption level in the country.

But incentive issues do not only arise from their relative importance in the IBEX-35. They can also be seen in the not-so-subtle management of human resources by the construction companies. An interesting illustration is offered by the Association of Construction Companies at the National Level (SEOPAN). It was created in 1957 during the Franco era to represent the large firms in interaction with public administration. Since the 2008 election, which maintained the Socialists and the prime minister in power, SEOPAN designated David Taguas as its president. Taguas was director of the Economic Office of the Prime Minister until his nomination. In spite of the controversy raised by the nomination, it was eventually approved under the pretext that this lobbying association was a non-profit organization. There was thus legally no conflict of interest since there were no financial interests. This episode ended with the firing of Taguas by SEOPAN, 2 months after the return of the Conservatives to power.

This close relationship between political parties and the construction sector offers the sector a strong national leverage, but also an important international leverage. In 2010, five Spanish companies (ACS, FCC, Sacyr, Ferrovial and Acciona) ranked among the top 50 construction firms in the world in terms of sales. This is where politics and policy converge again. Spain, like other countries with international geopolitical ambitions, wants to have national champions with an international standing. This is one of the drivers of its industrial policy that justifies what boils down to poor governance. It also explains the incentive to focus on the supply side of the market and on the need to overinvest in transport infrastructure to showcase Spanish capacity. The Spanish excess supply of transport networks is consistent with a marketing strategy to the benefit of Spanish companies and its owners, but financed with taxpayers money with little benefit to its users. This is, at best, poor governance or poor judgment. At worst, it is a matter for competent independent institutions responsible for the promotion of a fair, efficient and accountable economy.

10.4 CONCLUSION

In a nutshell, the Spanish government and its taxpayers are paying too much for an excess supply of transport infrastructure that offers the wrong mix of capacity and the wrong modal choice. It mostly benefits the construction industry and some political actors while hurting taxpayers and users, including those willing to pay for services they do not get. This case study yields many practical lessons for Spain. But for a wider audience, the main lessons are as follows.

The first lesson is that politics matter. Bad politics continue because politicians can afford it; in other words, they are not necessarily replaced as a result. Political accountability seems quite limited in Spain. Political scientists, sociologists, historians and economists have all shown with their own tools that the risks associated with bad policies and even corruption are low in terms of voter sanctions in Spain. The majority of the voters in this relatively young democracy do not seem to grasp the fact that political interference does not come cheaply. Getting transport planning wrong, or allowing it to support an excessive centralization of transport investments, has both efficiency and equity costs. Much of this cost has been too easy for the central government to blame on excessive regional ambition.

The second lesson is that the risks of capture are serious and make industrial policy quite tricky. National champions do not come cheaply to local users and taxpayers, in particular in sectors with small productivity gains such as transport. This is because, unchecked, these champions tend to fare well in collusive environments in which rents are high and hence incentives to block change are strong. For over 50 years, the same key actors, the same procurement rules and the same political interferences within the key regulatory and policy processes seem to be willing to sacrifice Spanish users of transport infrastructures and taxpayers for the private benefit of expansion in international markets.

The third lesson is that more transparent, more accountable and more technical institutions are not a luxury. They are the anchor of competent policy. They are a sign of progress in the respect of voters, taxpayers and users. Without them, any form of governance deviance is likely to be blamed on a lack of knowledge and maybe lack of competence. It is necessary to make this game harder to play by ensuring the institutional system sends clear signals to isolate the cheaters. This step cannot afford to be only anchored in legalistic jargon. It needs to have clear accounting, procurement and competition rules as well as regulation. So far, the system has failed on all counts in Spain.

Collusion and capture do not come cheaply. And taxpayers will continue to pay, *for long*, and a few will continue to benefit, *a lot*. Failing to build the right institutions increases the risks of capture and politics to de-link transport planning from economic opportunities for society. Ultimately, getting governance and institutions right may be the most cost-effective way of getting politics right and minimizing the odds of capture and other corrupt practices. It takes time. It also takes political will and committed voters. Spanish people love to say they 'do not care (about anything)'.[11] And that is where the problem may lie for now in Spain. Maybe, they should care more. Politics is too serious to be left to politicians alone.

NOTES

1. The Spanish road network has been radial from Madrid for over two centuries to ensure the control of the country by the capital city, following the French central-ization model (Bel, 2011, 2012; Holl 2011). This does not mean that regional infrastructure policy has been more efficient than the central one. However, according to the distribution of powers and resources in Spain, all major infrastructures are centrally managed, so the dimension of the problem is much higher in the central end.
2. The most frequent form of local corruption stems from a 1998 national law allowing a high degree of autonomy to local government to reclassify land and zone parcels of land as building sites. It eased real estate development and fuelled a 10 year construction boom, but unfortunately, there are many instances in which bribes were the trigger for the reclassification that allowed the development.
3. http://info.worldbank.org/governance/wgi/sc_chart.asp#
4. See for instance Eurobarometer (2012) or Villoria and Jiménez (2012). Spain is also currently the only EU country without a law granting the public a right to access state information.
5. The older and more important concessions (AP7 Mediterráneo, AP2 Valle del Ebro and AP9 Atlántico) are doing quite well.
6. For example, on ports, see Trujillo and Tovar (2007) or Rodriguez and Tovar (2010); on rail, Cantos et al. (2010); on airports, Bel and Fageda (2011).
7. See for instance, http://www.antena3.com/noticias/economia/aeropuertos-fantasma-espana-derroche-antes-crisis_2012012200027.html or http://deconomiablog.blogspot.com/2012/10/cuando-eramos-ricos-salvados.html.
8. The total cost to operate and upgrade the sector in a country with Spain's characteristics is usually around 1.5 per cent of GDP. The 2013 budgetary allocations are around 0.8 per cent of GDP. This implies that subsidies could very well be over

   50 per cent. Some may be necessary, but accounting for the high levels of inefficiency in the sector, their costs could probably be cut.
 9. Colegio de Ingenieros de Caminos, Canales y Puertos (2010).
10. The experience of the radial toll ways in Madrid shows that this may be a long shot. Three have indeed already filed for bankruptcy, and the public budget is likely to have to pick up the bill.
11. 'Paso (de todo)' in Spanish.

REFERENCES

Albalate, D. and G. Bel (2011), Cuando la economía no importa: auge y esplendor de la alta velocidad en España. *Revista de Economía Aplicada*, **55** (XIX), 171–190.

Asociación Española de Carreteras (AEC) (2012), *Estudio sobre Necesidades de Inversión en Conservación.* Madrid: AEC.

Baeza, M. A. and J. M. Vassallo (2010), Private concession contracts for toll roads in Spain: analysis and recommendations. *Public Money and Management*, **30** (5), 299–304.

Bel, G. (2011), Infrastructure and nation building: the regulation and financing of network transport infrastructures in Spain (1720–2010). *Business History*, **53** (5), 688–705.

Bel, G. (2012), *Infrastructure and the Political Economy of Nation Building in Spain* – 1720–2010. Sussex: Academic Press.

Bel, G. and X. Fageda (2011), La reforma del modelo de gestión de aeropuertos en España: Gestión conjunta o individual? *Hacienda Pública Española/Revista de Economía Pública*, **196** (1-2011), 109–130.

Cantos, Pedro, J. M. Pastor and L. Serrano (2010), Vertical and horizontal separation in the European railway sector and its effects on productivity. *Journal of Transport Economics and Policy*, **44** (2), 139–160.

Castells, P. and F. Trillas (2013), The effects of surprise political events on quoted firms: the March 2004 election in Spain. *SERIES, Journal of the Spanish Economic Association*, **4** (1), 83–112.

Colegio de Ingenieros de Caminos, Canales y Puertos (2010), Tarificación de infraestructuras de transporte en la UE: Adecuación del sistema español y su aplicación en la red viaria. June.

Costas-Pérez, E., A. Solé-Ollé and P. Sorribas-Navarro (2012), Corruption scandals, voter information, and accountability. *European Journal Political Economy*, **28** (4), 469–484.

De Rus, G. (2011), The BCA of HSR: should the government invest in high speed rail infrastructure? *Journal of Benefit–Cost Analysis*, **2** (1). Available at: http://www.bepress.com/jbca/vol2/iss1/2.

Eurobarometer (2012), Corruption – Report. Special Eurobarometer 374.

Faccio, M. (2010), Differences between politically connected and non-connected firms: a cross country analysis. *Financial Management*, **39** (3), 905–927.

Holl, A. (2011), Factors influencing the location of new motorways: large scale motorway building in Spain. *Journal of Transport Geography*, **19**, 1282–1293.

Jiménez, F. and V. Carbona (2012), Anatomía de la corrupción en España. *Letras Libres*, February.

Jiménez, L. and C. García (2012), Corruption and local politics: does it pay to be a crook? IREA Working Papers 2012.12, University of Barcelona, Research Institute of Applied Economics.

Kaufmann, D., A. Kraay and M. Mastruzzi (2011), The Worldwide Governance Indicators: 1996–2010. Available at: www.govindicators.org (September).

Lapuente, V. (2011), ¿Por qué la corrupción no se castiga? *Colección Política Comparada*, 02/2011, Fundación Alternativas.

Mulcahy, S. (2012), *Money, Politics, Power: Corruption Risks in Europe,* Transparency International: Berlin.

Olaizola Elordi, J. (2006), *Destacamentos Penales y construcción de infraestructuras ferroviarias.* Paper presented at IV Congreso de Historia Ferroviaria, Málaga, 20–22 September 2006.

Rivero, G. and Fernández-Vázquez, P. (2011), 'Consecuencias electorales de la corrupción, 2003-2007', Estudios de Progreso 59. Madrid: Fundación Alternativas.

Transparency International (TI) (2011), Corruption perceptions index 2011. Transparency International. Available at: http://cpi.transparency.org/cpi2012/.

Trujillo, L. and B. Tovar (2007), The European port industry: an analysis of its economic efficiency. *Maritime Economics and Logistics*, **9**, 148–171.

Villoria, M. and F. Jiménez (2012), La corrupción en España (2004–2010), datos, percepción y efectos (Corruption in Spain (2004–2010), Data, perception and consequences), *Revista Española de Investigaciones Sociológicas*, April–June, 109–134.

Villoria, M., G. Van Ryzin and C. Lavena (2011), Consequences of corruption: a study of political attitudes in Spain. Mimeo, 7th Transatlantic Dialogue on Strategic Management of Public Organization, Rutgers University, Newark, New Jersey.

World Bank (1963), Spain – Highway Improvement and Maintenance Project, Washington, DC. Available at: http://www.worldbank.org/projects/P037483/highway-improvement-project?lang=en.

11. 'Pay up and off you go!' Buying political positions in Bangladesh

Inge Amundsen

11.1 POSITIONS FOR SALE

'You can now buy yourself an MP nomination the same way as you buy an air ticket to Singapore: pay up and off you go!' This statement by a Member of Parliament of Bangladesh illustrates a pertinent predicament in current Bangladeshi politics; public positions are up for sale. The expression came in an in-depth interview with an opposition Member of Parliament (MP) of the Jatiya Sangsad (House of the Nation). We were a group of researchers making inquiries for a study on accountability and representation of the parliament[1] when the phrase came up in informal discussions on the roles of MPs in Bangladesh.

That individuals can 'buy' parliamentary positions is also described in a study by International IDEA: 'The main sources of income for parties [in South Asia] are donations by companies and individuals, and membership fees. Money raised by an application fee from aspiring candidates for party tickets [can] be substantial during an election year. The Bangladesh Awami League reported most of its income by this method. In the 2001 elections it could gather a substantial sum of 24 million BDT (around 430 000 USD)' (International IDEA, 2007: 101–102 and footnote 23). In other words, the ruling Awami League, along with some other parties, has now developed a practice of receiving applications from aspiring candidates. The applications are scrutinized by a core group of leaders of various party organs, but the party president makes the final nominations (Amundsen, 2013). What is important is that the applicants have a considerable popular following in their respective areas, or a long association with the party, or are confidants or advisors to the leader.

The practice has led to an influx of businessmen into Bangladeshi politics, and specifically into the parliament. There is now a big change in the professional background of the MPs. Whereas less than 30 per cent of the MPs elected in the 1970s were businessmen or industrialists, more than 50 per cent of the MPs in the fifth, eighth and ninth parliaments belong to this category (Jahan and Amundsen, 2012: 32). Businessmen and industrialists now count for 56 per cent of the current parliament members, and this fact is of increasing concern among observers and intellectuals.

11.2 POLITICS AS A PROFIT-MAKING INVESTMENT

One of the problems of this practice is that people with money are progressively getting party nomination. With the rising costs of running election campaigns (in Bangladesh as elsewhere), the practice is pushing people with fewer means out of the competition, and the parliament is becoming a rich men's club. In a country like Bangladesh, with an overwhelming majority of poor people, the practice makes social representation even more biased towards the rich (and especially towards rich men).

Another problem is that many of them are newcomers with no experience in parliamentary work. This is a serious problem, as the Parliament of Bangladesh is already weak in terms of exercising controls and checks and balances on the executive. One book described the political system of Bangladesh as a 'prime-ministerial' system with a parliament 'seriously disadvantaged vis-à-vis the executive' (Ahmed, 2000: 137). Another called it 'dormant' with a 'dominant' executive branch (Khan, 2006). This practice also adds to the corruption problem in Bangladesh. The country ranked at the top of the Corruption Perception Index (CPI) list for five successive years (2001–05), and the political parties continue to be perceived as among those institutions most affected by corruption.

More importantly, however, the businessmen are accused of seeking positions and personal benefits; they are not promoting the business sector as such. We found no evidence that they have advanced initiatives in terms of promoting a better business climate, making law propositions on the tax regime, discussing labour unions, or otherwise advancing the collective interests of the business sector. It rather seems that they are in parliament to protect and expand their private interests, and that they are striving for access to government contracts and protection for their private businesses.

According to the Bangladesh Parliament's House Rule 188 (2), an MP with a personal/pecuniary interest in a matter is barred from becoming a member of a committee. However, this rule is not adhered to in practice, and there is no mechanism to screen out committee members who may have conflicts of interest (Jahan and Amundsen, 2012: 26). Unlike many other parliaments, the Parliament of Bangladesh has no register of the financial interests and/or assets of MPs to determine whether any area of their work may potentially cause a conflict of interest. The issue of conflict of interest is often raised in various media reports in Bangladesh, and there are frequent allegations of parliamentarians using their influence to advance personal financial gains (ibid.: 38).

According to a recent report from TI Bangladesh, over 70 per cent of the MPs are registered business owners or operators, and among these the large majority have government contracts. Besides, around 97 per cent (of the 149 surveyed) Bangladeshi lawmakers were involved in 'some form of negative activities' and more than half were directly engaged in criminal or corrupt acts such as killings, land grabs, extortion, cheating, and bid rigging. Among those involved in 'negative practices', only a quarter were charged with a crime (Akram, 2012). Also, among these MPs involved in 'negative activities', some were engaged in activities related to influencing local administrative decisions, like job-placements. Others use local development project funds for their own benefit. This included abusing their supervisory authority over projects for personal gain, providing family members with undue advantage, awarding project contracts to members of their own political party, and taking bribes (often termed a 'commission') when distributing development funds (ibid.).

Most MPs were found to have opportunity to influence government procurement decisions. According to the report by Akram (2012): 'In almost 89 per cent of cases government party MPs got the contract of development activities in their own constituencies, and the rest were also manipulated by taking commissions from the individuals/companies getting the contracts.' Furthermore, the MPs frequently influenced local government elections, through bribery, providing party support for a candidate, openly declaring support for a specific person, and manipulating election results (ibid.).

Many MPs have been accused of seeking a seat in parliament because it gives them judicial impunity for as long as they serve. Some are also collecting status indicators; a business card with business, academic, religious and/or political titles is an impressive social asset, and an MP title is an economic boon. A further indication of the businessmen using MP positions for personal advantage is the rising number of conflicts of interest. Several parliamentary committees have, for instance, been constrained because some of the committee members have personal and business interests in the area of the committee (Jahan and Amundsen, 2012: 26). The committee on energy is reported as a preferred committee to serve in, probably because of the good opportunities to get information and access to up-coming government contracts. According to Al Masud Hasanuzzaman (2011: 16):

> People with money and muscle power have therefore made inroads into the major political parties … Party nominations are influenced by money and muscle power. Owing to the considerable entry of political opportunists in the nominations of the parties', old party loyalists without financial strength and muscle power are ignored.

11.3   A WEAK REGULATORY FRAMEWORK

According to Article 90F (1) of the Bangladesh law Representation of the People (Amendment) Order Act of 2009, 'a registered political party shall be entitled to receive donation or grants from any person, company, group of companies or non-government organization' (with the exceptions stipulated in other clauses of the law, for instance a ban on foreign donations and a limit on donations from individuals to BDT 500 000, ca. USD 6500, per year) (Global Integrity, 2012). Thus, donations to political parties from individuals and companies are not prohibited in Bangladesh. Foreign donations are not a problem, but it is doubtful if the limit on donations from individuals is at all respected. The law, consequently, does not ban the selling of parliamentary tickets, or more precisely, the fees taken by the party from aspiring candidates. (Interestingly, if the 500 000 limit had been respected – which is doubtful – the Awami League party 'sold' around 50 parliamentary 'tickets' in 2001).

This method of financing parties is not even corrupt, according to legal definitions, and may not be seen as too bad when compared to the parties' illegal collections and unreported sources. There is no provision for direct public funding of political parties in Bangladesh, and consequently no public funding available for parties. The parties have to fend for themselves. Mostly, the political parties in Bangladesh fund their day-to-day activities and election campaigns from these application fees from aspiring candidates, and to a lesser degree from members' dues, donations, and the like. It 'commercialises' politics when so much of a party's finances stem from selling tickets to aspiring candidates, and not from member fees or the public.

However, parties have allegedly also resorted to obtaining funds through improper and unethical means. Political parties in Bangladesh (and in particular the ruling party, at any given time) manipulate their powerful positions to extort bribes, to offer their 'contributors' and 'benefactors' rewards in terms of positions in the public sector, and to channel public resources into the hands of the party leaders and supporters (Hasanuzzaman, 2011: 18). With an Election Commission that fails to enforce the election and party laws, a Commission and a judiciary that fails to take the necessary steps against political parties and candidates, corruption and black money continues to play the determining role in politics and elections (TI Bangladesh, 2009: 2).

Recently, the laws and regulations on party financing have been somewhat strengthened. Parties have been required to register with the Election Commission and have to submit their audit reports annually. According to IDEA's Political Finance Database (International IDEA, 2012) there is no ban on corporate donations or donations from trade unions to political parties or candidates, not even on donations from public or partially government owned companies. There is only a limit on anonymous donations (BDT 5000) and on corporate donations (BDT 2.5 million) per year to political parties (but no limit on donations to candidates), and a ban on foreign donations and a spending limit. The latter depends on the number of candidates a party files; the two large parties are in practice each limited to BDT 45 million (approximately USD 550 000), and a limit of BDT 1.5 million (USD 20 000) per candidate per constituency.

However, the rules and laws on campaign expense ceilings and on accounting and auditing of parties funds and candidate spending are not put properly into operation. Reports should be filed before and after elections, but often they have flaws, and sometimes they are not filed at all. The bookkeeping, reporting, reliability of reporting, public disclosure and related sanctions are poor (Hasanuzzaman, 2011: 19). For instance, in the parliamentary election of 2008, candidates seeking nominations spent three times more than the permissible spending limit, but the EC neither took measures to prevent it, nor took any action against the perpetrators of such violations (TI Bangladesh, 2009: 2). Hasanuzzaman, 2011: 17) explains:

> In Bangladesh political funding is not transparent … No audited balance sheets are available and until now the reporting on finance within the party or the Election Commission is quite inadequate. Such reports, when submitted, are far from comprehensive and lack in depth. Disclosure by parties or candidates in election is inconsistent and thus not reliable. Sanctions … are hardly employed. The system of monitoring, including state oversight and civil society oversight, is yet to become practical.

11.4 POLICY DISCUSSION

Political parties seldom practice the desired level of transparency, disclosure and accountability in terms of managing their finances. This is especially evident in developing countries such as Bangladesh, where the issue is neither among the priorities of the parties themselves nor of the government, and where public interest in the issue is limited. According to TI Bangladesh (2009: iii):

> One of the key reasons why political finance remains almost a taboo in Bangladesh is that politics has become a 'winner-takes-all' game and indeed a profit-making investment, where parties and candidates taking part in elections invest huge funds to gain power, and therefore, transparency and disclosures are the last thing in the agenda of political parties.

Other factors contributing negatively to this process are the existing confrontational political culture, and a gross lack of agreement on the general rules of the game (Hasanuzzaman, 2011: 16). The confrontational political climate is played out between the two political parties in a 'zero-sum game', the Awami League (AL) and the Bangladesh Nationalist Party (BNP). These two parties have dominated Bangladeshi politics since formal, multiparty democracy and the parliamentary system were restored with free and fair elections in 1991. Since then, the two parties have successively won every other election, and ruled one after the other. When in power, the ruling party (no matter which) has always used the incumbency advantage to the full, and tried to establish hegemonic control over the political agenda and over the use of public resources (Jahan and Amundsen, 2012: 55).

On the other hand, when in opposition (no matter the party) each claim to be marginalized and that parliamentary work is without purpose. In opposition, they have therefore repeatedly boycotted the parliament and taken to the streets. Street manifestations and *hartals* have become the preferred mode of political action. Hartals are a form of mass protest, including a shutdown of many workplaces, offices, shops and schools, but also public agitation, street demonstrations and sometimes civil disobedience. The opposition can muster millions of protesters throughout the country, and shut it down for a day or two (Amundsen, 2012: 1–3).

There is still no agreement between the two dominant parties or their leaders on the basic rules of the game of electoral democracy (Jahan and Amundsen, 2012: 14). A strengthening of the rules and regulations on party finance is indeed necessary. In particular, the possibility of direct public funding for political parties should be considered, with stronger conditions attached. And transparency in political finance is necessary; transparency can be a powerful tool to reduce the corruption risk arising from monetary and in-kind contributions to parties or individual candidates. But this is not enough. The sanctions regime must be boosted. Stronger rules and regulations need to be followed up with enforcement and efficient penalties, swifter punishment, more quickly and systematically delivered than is currently the case. A repeated and sustained debate on these matters can also be beneficial. The ruling AL has made a (symbolic and vague) commitment in its election manifesto to introduce a 'transparent system of political finance', but this is only a start; the follow-up remains.

As long as politics is seen as a profit-making investment, there will be few incentives to strengthen and enforce the rules. The only hope rests with the voters; only when they punish the profit-seekers through the ballot box and elect clean candidates with a political agenda that benefits the electorate in the long run, can the vicious circle be broken. Although too many examples exist in Bangladesh of political positions that have been up for sale, there are at the same time a few exceptions. The most recent example is when the voters refuted the sweet proposal of a lavish spender (the official AL candidate) and voted-in a less resourced candidate (an unofficial AL candidate) in the 2012 Dhaka mayoral by-election.

NOTES

1.   Published as Jahan and Amundsen (2012).

REFERENCES

Ahmed, N. (2000), *Parliament and Public Spending in Bangladesh: Limits of Control*. Dhaka: Bangladesh Institute of Parliamentary Studies (BIPS).
Akram, S. M. (2012), *Positive and Negative Roles of the Members of the 9th Parliament: A Review*. Dhaka: Transparency International Bangladesh.
Amundsen, I. (2012), Parliament of Bangladesh. Boycotts, business, and change for the better. CMI Brief vol. 11, no. 2. Chr. Michelsen Institute, Bergen.
Amundsen, I. (2013), Democratic dynasties? Internal party democracy in Bangladesh. Forthcoming in *Party Politics*.
Global Integrity (2012), Bangladesh Integrity Scorecard. Available at www.globalintegrity.org/report/Bangladesh/2010/scorecard (accessed 9 October 2012).
Hasanuzzaman, A. M. (2011), *Political Party Funding in Bangladesh*. Islamabad: IRS Institute Of Regional Studies (Spotlight on Regional Affairs).

International IDEA (2007), *Political Parties in South Asia: The Challenge of Change*. Stockholm: International IDEA (The International Institute for Democracy and Electoral Assistance).

International IDEA (2012), Political Finance Database: Political finance data for Bangladesh. Available at: http://www.idea.int/political-finance/country.cfm?id=20 (accessed 30 October 2012).

Jahan, R. and I. Amundsen (2012), The Parliament of Bangladesh. Representation and Accountability. CPD-CMI Working Paper no. 2, April, Centre for Policy Dialogue and Chr. Michelsen Institute, Dhaka and Bergen.

Khan, M. M. (2006), *Dominant Executive and Dormant Legislature: Executive-Legislative Relations in Bangladesh*. New Delhi: South Asian Publishers.

TI Bangladesh (2009), *Transparency in Political Finance in Bangladesh*. Dhaka: Transparency International Bangladesh.

12. Monopolising reconstruction: Angolan elites and Chinese credit lines[1]

Lucy Corkin

12.1 SETTING THE SCENE

In 2004, China Export–Import (China Exim) Bank extended a USD 2 billion oil-backed loan to the Angolan government for the purpose of post-war national reconstruction. This dismayed the international donor community, which viewed the loan agreement as having allowed the Angolan government to have escaped the stringent conditionalities regarding transparency and macroeconomic policy that would have been attached to an International Monetary Fund (IMF) loan, the negotiations for which had collapsed just prior to the China Exim Bank agreement (Brautigam, 2009: 275; Global Witness, 2011). The China Exim Bank loan facility has been extended several times and as of 2012 total pledges reportedly stood at USD 10.5 billion. The loan is repayable at 3-month Libor[2] + 1.5 per cent over 17 years, including a grace period of 5 years.[3] According to Alves (2010: 12) the interest was reduced to Libor + 1.25 per cent for successive tranches after the first USD 4.5 billion in credit lines. In the Angolan case, added to these terms is the management fee of 0.3 per cent of the loan amount, and a 0.3 per cent 'commitment fee' (Dubosse, 2010: 75). The Angolan government must provide a down-payment of 10 per cent of the project value of each financed project.

Such an arrangement has been the centre of controversy for a number of years, for two main reasons. First, the nature of the mechanism; being a bilateral transaction reduces its transparency. The loan, Angola's largest ever, is off-budget and while there is a limited amount of information available from the Angolan Ministry of Finance, which officially co-ordinates the fund disbursement with China Exim Bank, such data is incomplete and out of date. Second, and of equal concern, is the fact that the construction and infrastructure projects that the Chinese funds are financing must be undertaken principally by Chinese construction companies, whose propensity to collaborate with local companies is notoriously low, despite a commitment to reserve up to 30 per cent of the contracts' value for Angolan subcontractors.[4] Furthermore, at least 50 per cent of project procurement must be sourced from China.

As a researcher of China–Angola interactions for the past 8 years, I have focused for my doctoral studies on the mechanism and implementation process of the China Exim Bank credit line in Angola. This has provided me with a unique opportunity to observe not only how Luanda interacts with Beijing, but also to discover that the nature of such relations were in fact a function of the Angolan government's approach to governance. As I will argue here, the Angolan political elite has used the China Exim Bank credit line to strengthen its hold on power, effectively adapting a strategy of extraversion[5] to take into account Angola's shifting political context in the post-war era. It is important to note here that I am not arguing that the China Exim Bank loans are exclusively propping up the current regime. Rather I am using the example of the China Exim Bank credit line to illustrate how the Angolan political elite has the agency to seize and subvert access to economic rents, such as those presented by the credit line, to strengthen and reinforce mechanisms through which it retains power.

12.2 SUBVERTING THE 'NATIONAL RECONSTRUCTION' POLICY FRAMEWORK

It must be borne in mind that China is by no means the only country that has extended financing to the Angolan government in recent years for construction projects. Indeed, the various oil-backed credit lines that the Angolan government has access to generally operate in the same way. Thus my focus is not on the fact that the credit line is Chinese nor the mechanism of the credit line itself, but the way in which it is systematically manipulated by the Angolan political elite. I have used the Chinese Exim Bank loans as an example, purely because their size dwarfs other credit lines (see Table 12.1).

National reconstruction, funded in a large part by the China Exim Bank credit line, has been advanced rhetorically as an urgent priority by the Angolan government, not only as a short-term election campaign promise, but also in order to bolster long-term regime legitimacy. However, the mechanism through which this reconstruction is pursued focuses only on the projects themselves as constitutive of the physical rebuilding of the country's infrastructure, rather than the active participation of Angolans

Table 12.1   China Exim Bank compared to Angola's other creditors (June 2009)

DATE	LENDER	VALUE	PURPOSE	TERMS AND CONDITIONS		Guarantee
				Interest Rate	Commissions and Fees	
Nov 2003	Deutsche Bank – Spain	USD 500 million	Public investment projects	Libor + 1~5%	1% (flat) arrangement fee 1% (flat) management fee	Angolan Finance Ministry
Mar 2004	China Exim Bank	USD 2 billion (1st tranche)	Public investment projects	3-month Libor + 1.5%	0.3% management fee 1% arrangement fee (N/A)[a] 0.3% commitment fee	Contract of Petroleum Supply
Aug 2004	India Exim Bank	USD 40 million	5 contracts for the supply of equipment for Moçamedes Railway	1.75%		Angolan Ministry of Finance
Nov 2004	Portugal Cosec	EUR 300 million	Public investment projects	Euribor + 0.4~0.6%	0.1% management fee	Angolan Ministry of Finance
2005	China International Fund	USD 9.8 billion	Projects managed by government	3-month Libor + 1.5%	0.3% management fee 0.3% commitment fee	Contract of Petroleum Supply
Mar 2005	Santander Bank – Spain	EUR 100 million	Public investment projects	6-month Libor + 1~1.5%	0.5% (flat) management fee 0.25% (flat) commitment fee Variable insurance fee	Angolan Finance Ministry
Sept 2005	Fortis Bank – Spain	EUR 250 million	Public investment projects	6-month Libor + 0.75~1%	2% (flat) management fee 0.5% (flat) commitment fee Variable insurance fee	Angolan Ministry of Finance
Dec 2005	Korea Exim Bank	USD 31.4 million	Rehabilitation of cotton project in Sumbe	0.6%	0.1% (above each disbursement) management fee	Angolan Ministry of Finance

Date	Lender	Amount	Purpose	Interest rate	Fees	Guarantee
2006	Proex[b]	USD 580 million	Public investment projects	Libor	0.5 % (flat) management fee 0.5% (flat) arrangement fee	Contract of Petroleum Supply
2006	Brazilian Development Bank	USD 750 million	Public investment projects	Libor +1%	1% (flat) management fee 0.5% (flat) arrangement fee	Contract of Petroleum Supply
Jul 2006	India Exim Bank	USD 10 million	Acquisition contract of 599 tractors	6-month Libor +2.5%	0.5% (per year) management commission 0.5% (flat) arrangement commission	Ministry of Finance
Jul 2007	China Exim Bank	USD 500 million (supplement to 1st tranche)	Public investment projects	3-month Libor +1.5%	0.3% management fee 1% arrangement fee (N/A) 0.3% commitment fee	Contract of Petroleum Supply
Sep 2007	China Exim Bank	USD 2 billion (2nd tranche)	Public investment projects	3-month Libor +1.5%	0.3% management fee 1% arrangement fee (N/A) 0.3% commitment fee	Contract of Petroleum Supply
Apr 2008	Deutsche Bank – Spain	USD 225 million	Public investment projects	Libor+ 1–5%	1% (flat) arrangement fee 1% (flat) management fee	Angolan Finance Ministry

Notes:

[a]This *arrangement fee* is payable only if the loan is syndicated.
[b]*Programa de Financiamento às Exportações* – This was a programme of the Brazilian government designed to facilitate Brazilian exports, deemed illegal under WTO statutes.

Source: Author's own research; Croese (2011: 28).

generally in the reconstruction of their country. Only a select group have access to the economic gains to be made from reconstruction itself.

Journalist and anti-corruption activist Marques de Morais (2010a–c) has conducted a series of investigations which detail how state assets, through the ostensibly legal process of privatization, are sold to high-ranking government officials in their private capacity. In a similar way, government officials have been allowed to subcontract public tenders financed by the Chinese credit lines to their own companies, using their official position to benefit commercially. Often, these politically con-nected Angolan companies are the only such local firms to gain access to sub-contracting for the credit-line financed projects. Key among these beneficiaries are high-ranking generals. We can assume this is in order to retain their loyalty in a highly militarized society and to prevent dos Santos' removal by coup (Le Billon, 2001: 70). This practice is not only contrary to several long-standing laws in Angola, but is expressly forbidden in the Law of Public Probity passed in November 2009. Nevertheless, as pointed out by Marques de Morais (2009, 2010c), some of the most blatant instances of this kind of rent-seeking have occurred simultaneously or immediately following the passing of this law. He argues that this institutionalized form of corruption is condoned because: 'They [the power-holders] plunder, but also allow others [principal clients of the regime] to plunder their share' (Marques de Morais, 2010b).

As a result of these patronage networks, political and economic power is concentrated into the hands of a select few. Economic opportunity is a function of political access and the elites thus fundamentally rely on dos Santos, in whom the majority of political power is centralized. He relies on them for support to remain in power, rendering a classic example of the neo-patrimonial state.[6] Dos Santos' most intimate cabal of advisors is known colloquially as *Futungistas* after one of the President's palaces, *Futungo de Belas* (Shaxson, 2007: 51; Sogge, 2009: 14).

The Angolan government, while portraying the Chinese credit line as crucial for national reconstruction has not focused on the (re)building of 'soft infrastructure', such as institution- and capacity-building through local participation. This refers not only to the specific potential of the construction projects to facilitate skills transferal to Angolans, but also a much broader nation-building project, in allowing Angolans to participate in the physical reconstruction of their own country. While the official reason is that such localization processes slow projects' completion schedules, it is evident that political elites have a vested interest in retaining a monopoly over existing economic activity and preventing the formation of alternative 'power centres' that might challenge their control (Migdal, 1988: 211). This averts the rise of independent entrepreneurs operating outside of the central patronage networks and ensures the current regime's maintenance of the status quo (Bayart, 1993: 91).[7] In the balancing act between regime stability and economic growth, it is clear that in the case of Angola, regime stability has been prioritized. However, the durability of an essentially predatory regime that monopolizes access to economic rents ultimately undermines sustainable and broad-based economic growth.[8] A contradictory policy environment ensures that only the politically connected may benefit from the reconstruction process, thus reinforcing the political and economic status quo maintained by patronage. In this way, the political elite have adapted the patronage system to serve in peace time, or instrumentalized the post-war environment (De Beer and Gamba, 2000). Put differently, the Angolan political elite has 'adapted its grip to a peace-time gear', according to Soares de Oliveira (2007a: 148).

12.3 CONTEXTUALISING THE POLICY ENVIRONMENT

Concurrently to the control of economic rents created by the credit lines, the Angolan regime has allowed the official government structures to decay, essentially facilitating what Chabal and Daloz (1999: 103) call 'instrumentalising disorder' for its own ends. Angola is indeed a prime example of this. During the period 1987–2004, the central government promulgated no less than 11 different over-arching economic plans, lasting between a fortnight and a few years. Furthermore, between 1990 and 2003, President dos Santos appointed and subsequently dismissed ten Ministers of Finance and six Governors of the Reserve Bank (Pinto De Andrade, 2007: 17). This rendered it impossible to maintain even a semblance of policy continuity, much less allow any political figure to build up a domestic support base through a competing patronage system. This level of dysfunctionality has been 'to a degree self-serving' (Herbst and Mills, 2006: 128) as the Angolan executive actually has a high level of functional capacity, should it be moved to use it.

President dos Santos is also adept at balancing the institutions tasked with managing national reconstruction, thus preventing the institutionalization of figures in places of power. This is a recognized strategy that intentionally weakens bodies within the state so that they pose no threat to the executive (Migdal, 1988: 214). Access to the Chinese credit lines, although nominally managed by the Ministry of Finance, is closely monitored by the president. The president has been quick to reshuffle the line of command if any political figure is suspected of gaining too much influence by their proximity to the credit lines, ensuring that he alone as the head of state is the sole source of political continuity. Indeed, he has gone a step further and re-arranged the institutional structures as well. The power to be able to enact such bureaucratic changes rests with the president's powers of appointment, enshrined in the 2010 Constitution, which extend to all high-level positions in government as well as the judiciary (Orre, 2010: 13).[9] President dos Santos also exercises these powers to identify a scapegoat when political failure is evident[10] while simultaneously distancing his office from the issue in question, despite the fact that most national policies require his personal approval.[11]

It is clear that the process of national reconstruction facilitated by China Exim Bank's credit lines is in principle a positive process for both countries, espousing the concept of *win-win*. However, in practice, the implementation has shown that not all parties are equal winners; in fact some are not benefitting from the process at all. Consequently, it is visible that gains on the part of the Angolan government do not necessarily represent gains for the Angolan population, albeit that this is a function of the implementation of the credit lines rather than the financing itself.

The Angolan elite has accrued significant benefits in several ways. On a practical level, the Chinese credit line represents a new source of economic rents, centrally controlled by the Presidency in order to preserve political dominance as the gatekeeper to such wealth. The president and his closest associates have managed to instrumentalize the credit lines for a wider set of objectives and subverted the China Exim Bank loan process in order to consolidate and retain both economic and political power.

Concurrently, the Angolan government has been at pains to widen and improve its access to international funding in order to reduce its reliance on a single partner. Despite a rocky relationship in previous years, the IMF made provisions for a standby loan of USD 1.4 billion for Angola in 2009. This was linked to a number of required reforms in fiscal governance. The Angolan government is however adept at making incremental changes that do not fundamentally alter the structure of the economy. Instead, these 'easy' reforms act as a release valve for potential dissension and obfuscate the actual lack of reform occurring (Van de Walle, 2001: 37); what Migdal (1988: 242) calls *tokenism*. Indeed, as Global Witness notes (2011), increased information does not always lead to increased transparency. Tellingly, certain key conditions of the IMF loan, such as a ceiling on additional borrowing, were waived.

12.4   THE SOCIO-ECONOMIC AND POLITICAL DIMENSIONS OF NATIONAL RECONSTRUCTION

Some of the infrastructure projects have had genuine developmental benefits for Angolan citizens. With an eye on the inevitability of national elections, which took place in 2008, the ruling party saw the political dividends of public investment in infrastructure. Many of the public works were presented as MPLA (Movimento Popular de Libertação de Angola, or People's Movement for the Liberation of Angola) achievements, rather than government achievements, once again blurring the distinction between the party and the state. This calculated merging of ruling party and state institutions allowed the MPLA to benefit from the successful delivery of such public works. These were particularly important in rural areas where infrastructure was not only sorely needed, but the MPLA image required bolstering.

The MPLA, Pawson (2008) argues, has used its political dominance to subvert the electoral process of September 2008 in order to gain international sanction for the consolidation of the ruling party's hold on power. This resonates with Messiant's (2007: 106) description of MPLA manipulation of the previous elections in 1992 in what she terms the 'consolidation of hegemonic power'. The 2008 elections, during which MPLA secured 87 per cent of parliamentary seats, provided much needed legitimacy to MPLA rule, not only for international observers, who declared the ballot free and fair (Orre, 2010: 8) but for their domestic constituencies. Furthermore, the landslide parliamentary victory facilitated a new constitution which further consolidated incumbent power, albeit it in legitimate procedure.[12] This indicates the importance of the legitimacy conferred by the 2008 elections. A similar strategy was employed in the 2012 national elections.

With regard to the Angolan government's domestic role in the economy, it is clear the MPLA government has rhetorically upheld national reconstruction as a priority since the end of the civil war. This is designed to consolidate President dos Santos' role as the 'peace-maker', having vanquished UNITA (*União Nacional para a Independência Total de Angola* or National Union for the Total Independence of Angola) to bring an end to the country's protracted armed conflict in 2002. It is also targeted at bolstering the Angolan government's internal legitimacy, particularly in the run-up to legislative elections that were finally held in 2008. However, despite claiming to promote national reconstruction 'for the people', Angola's population has been kept largely separated from the reconstruction process. Marques de Morais (2010a) views the Chinese credit line as a new avenue for elite enrichment under the guise of national reconstruction.

The lack of broad-based participation in the China Exim Bank process means that the implementation of the construction projects is not rendering as much benefit to local industries as it could. The regime is approaching national reconstruction rather as a patrimonial provision of services by a paternalistic government in order to reinforce itself as the source of all public goods. National reconstruction is thus portrayed as the delivery of a turn-key product rather than an interactive process required to re-establish a connection between the rulers and the ruled. Furthermore, it is increasingly a paid-for service, outsourced to foreigners with no provision for Angolans to maintain or even organically expand on what external contractors provide.

12.5 PROSPECTS FOR THE FUTURE

Given the ease with which the Futungo elite has incorporated Chinese funding into the consolidation of domestic political power, it is unlikely that Angola's development or lack thereof is a result of genuine lack of capacity. It is far more due to a lack of political will and institutions weakened by design. Moreover, I argue that the lack of support for broader-based local participation in the national reconstruction process is a conscious strategy to prevent the creation of economic growth independent of the patronage linkages of the political elite. This is to deter political challenges to the ruling party's control from an alternative economic base of power, which could contest the regime's internal legitimacy.

However, since early 2011, the MPLA, and more importantly the president's attempts to monopolise Angolan political life have started to backfire. Because of their long-established monopoly over reconstruction decision-making, the president and his government have been directly responsible for the country's political economy. The president sought in his 2010 State of the Nation address to dismiss tensions arising from sustained income disparities between Angola's small political elite and the rest of the population, as well as widespread corruption.

The passage of time has nevertheless given rise to a generation of jobless and disaffected youth with no memory of the civil war or Soviet-style purges. MPLA will face continuing and increasing challenges unless the incumbent regime can facilitate increased access to meaningful political participation.

12.6 POLICY IMPLICATIONS AND RECOMMENDATIONS

A fundamental contradiction exists in the Angolan policy space. Although a robust set of legislation governing foreign investment and local participation exists to encourage broad-based economic development, it is not effectively implemented and is actually undermined by a lack of political will and vested interests. There is a sense that political elites have an interest in thwarting any local business development in order to prevent the development of an alternative economic locus which might in time lead to competition for their economic interests and ultimately a political threat.[13]

This short-termism needs to be replaced by a broader developmental vision. The Angolan government needs to streamline policies and realign them to encourage local industrial development sustainably and in the long term, rather than opting for quick fixes. This could include creating economic incentives for foreign companies, among them Chinese, to invest in their local supply chain and reformulating policies to reflect the importance of skills and technology transfer rather than simply the reconstruction of the national infrastructure.

Ultimately, there is a real opportunity provided by the China Exim Bank credit line, among others, to act as a catalyst for the kind of economic development and job-creation desperately needed by Angolans. Indeed, the democratization of access to economic means would go a long way in assuaging the grievances of an increasingly restless and jobless youth, the very section of society that, if unheeded, may in time present a real challenge to the incumbent's political power.

NOTES

1. This chapter has been adapted from a longer text by the author – Corkin, L. (2013) *Uncovering African Agency: Angola's management of Chinese Credit lines.* Surrey: Ashgate.
2. Interest rate is quoted according to the Angolan Ministry of Finance. Libor, according to the British Banker's Association, is the most widely used benchmark or reference rate for short-term interest rates.
3. Interview, GAT, Angolan Ministry of Finance, Luanda, 30 May 2007.
4. For a more detailed analysis of the supply chain of the Chinese construction projects in Angola, please see Corkin (2011).
5. 'Extraversion' was first coined by Bayart (1993) who describes the process whereby the monopoly of access to foreign influence and capital is used as a tool to maintain internal power. Fundamentally, African agency rests on the fact that African elites can manipulate the external world and adapt it to their needs (Clapham, 1985: 5).

6. A full analysis of the nature of the neo-patrimonial oil-state is beyond the scope of this work. For in-depth analysis see Soares de Oliveira (2007b), Shaxson (2007) and Hodges (2004).
7. Soares de Oliveira (2007a: 91) details how Sonangol's expansion into non-oil sectors and services has 'crowded out other entrepreneurs' as Sonangol not only commands greater resources, but also demands that international firms form joint ventures with its own subsidiaries, thus making market entry and/or technological transfer opportunities for other fledging Angolan businesses hard to access.
8. For a full discussion, see Corkin (2013).
9. Although presidential decrees can be overruled by parliament, in the unlikely event of this occurring, the president can veto parliamentary laws (Orre, 2010: 13).
10. An example is the dismissal of Housing Minister Diekumpuna Sita José in April 2009, as political pressure mounted over an MPLA campaign promise to provide 1 million houses for the poor.
11. Elite advisors are often 'recycled'. Several prominent figures have fallen from grace only to be re-instated or promoted in later years. Examples are current Minister of State (Civilian House) Carlos Feijó, disgraced several years previously, and General Miala, imprisoned for insubordination, but pardoned several years later.
12. For an in-depth discussion of this, see Orre (2010).
13. Interview, foreign diplomat, Luanda, 22 July 2010; interview, oil major employee, 12 July 2010.

REFERENCES

Alves, A. C. (2010), The Oil factor in Sino-Angolan relations at the start of the 21st century. South African Institute for International Affairs, Occasional Paper No. 55, February.

Bayart, J. (1993), *The State of Africa: The Politics of the Belly*. London: Longman Group UK Limited.

Brautigam, D. (2009), *The Dragon's Gift: The Real Story of China in Africa*. Oxford: Oxford University Press.

Chabal, P. and J. Daloz (1999), *Africa Works: Disorder as a Political Instrument*. Oxford: James Curry.

Clapham, C. (1985), *Third World Politics: An Introduction*. London: Croom and Helm.

Corkin, L. (2011), Chinese Construction Companies in Angola: a local linkages perspective Discussion paper No. 2. Online: Making the Most of Commodities Programme (MMCP), March: http://www.cssr.uct.ac.za/publications/incidental-paper/2011/750 (accessed 1 June 2012).

Corkin, L. (2013), *Uncovering African Agency: Angola's Management of China's Credit Lines*. Surrey: Ashgate.

Croese, S. (2011), One million houses? Angola's national reconstruction and China and Brazil's engagement. In *Strengthening the Civil Society Perspective Series II: China and Other Emerging Powers in Africa*. Oxford: Fahamu, pp. 7–29.

De Beer, H. and V. Gamba (2000), The arms dilemma: resources for arms or arms for resources. In J. Cilliers and C. Dietrich (eds), *Angola's War*

Economy: The Role of Oil and Diamonds. Pretoria: Institute for Security Studies, pp. 69–94.

Dubosse, N. (2010), Chinese development assistance to Africa: aid, trade and debt. In A. Harneit-Sievers, S. Marks and S. Naidu (eds), *Chinese and African Perspectives on China in Africa*. Oxford: Pambazuka Press, pp. 70–81.

Global Witness (2011), *Oil Revenues in Angola: Much More Information, But Not Enough Transparency*, London: Global Witness, pp. 1–50.

Herbst, J. and G. Mills (2006), Africa's big dysfunctional states: an introductory overview, In C. Clapham et al. (eds), *Big African States*. Johannesburg: Wits University Press, pp. 1–16.

Hodges, T. (2004), *Angola: Anatomy of an Oil State*. London: James Currey.

Le Billon, P. (2001), Angola's political economy of war: the role of oil and diamonds 1975–2000. *African Affairs*, **100**, 55–80.

Marques de Morais, R. (2009), Angola's presidential promiscuity has corrupted society. *Pambazuka*, **460**, 3 December. Available at: http://pambazuka.org/en/category/features/60707 (accessed 7 December 2011).

Marques de Morais, R. (2010a), Angola's MPs and business dealings. *Pambazuka News*, **464**, 6 January. Available at: http://www.pambazuka.org/en/category/features/61246 (accessed 25 March 2011).

Marques de Morais, R. (2010b), MPLA Ltd: The business interests of Angola's ruling elite. *Pambazuka*, **469**, 11 February. Available at: http://pambazuka.org/en/category/features/62194 (accessed 7 December 2011).

Marques de Morais, R. (2010c), The self-dealings of Sonangol's CEO. *Pambazuka News*, **487**, 24 June. Available at: http://www.pambazuka.org/en/category/features/65422 (accessed 25 March 2011).

Messiant, C. (2007), The mutation of hegemonic domination. In P. Chabal and N. Vidal (eds), *Angola: The Weight of History*. London: Hurst and Company, pp. 93–123.

Migdal, J. (1988), *Strong Societies and Weak States*. Princeton, NJ: Princeton University Press.

Orre, A. (2010), Who's to challenge the party-state in Angola? Political space and opposition in parties and civil society. Paper presented at CMI and IESE conference Election processes, liberation movements and democratic change in Africa, Maputo, 8–11 April, pp. 1–20.

Pawson, L. (2008), The Angolan Elections: Politics of no change. Online: Open Democracy, 25 September. Available at: http://www.isn.ethz.ch/isn/Current-Affairs/Security-Watch/Detail/?ots591=4888CAA0-B3DB-1461-98B9-E20E7 B9C13D4&lng=en&id=91981 (accessed 12 December 2008).

Pinto de Andrade, V. (2007), A China e a assistência ao desenvolvimento de Angola. Unpublished paper, Universidade Católica de Angola.

Shaxson, N. (2007), *Poisoned Wells: The Dirty Politics of African Oil*. New York: Palgrave Macmillan.

Soares de Oliveira, R. (2007a), Business success, Angola-style: post-colonial politics and the rise and rise of Sonangol. *Journal of Modern African Studies*, **45** (4), 595–619.

Soares de Oliveira, R. (2007b), *Oil and Politics in the Gulf of Guinea*. London: Hurst and Company.

Sogge, D. (2009), Angola: 'failed' yet 'successful'. Working Paper 81, Fundación par alas Relaciones Internacionales y el Diálogo Exterior (FRIDE), 1–28 April.

Van de Walle, N. (2001), *African Economies and the Politics of Permanent Crisis.* Cambridge: Cambridge University Press.

13. Grabbing an election: abuse of state resources in the 2011 elections in Uganda

Svein-Erik Helle and Lise Rakner

Elections are an integral part of representative democracies. Well-functioning elections contribute to democratic accountability and democratic institutions, which in turn contributes to economic and human development too (Acemoglu and Robinson, 2012; Gerring et al., 2012). But the integrity and quality of the electoral process is in many countries threatened by the growing importance of money in politics: vote buying and the use of state and other illegal resources for partisan purposes (Annan et al., 2012). Electoral fraud has both economic and political consequences, as illustrated by the 2011 parliamentary, presidential and local elections in Uganda. They ended, as many observers expected, with a landslide victory for incumbent President Yoweri K. Museveni and his National Resistance Movement (NRM). The victory was Museveni's fourth consecutive election victory, after winning in 1996 and 2001 under the 'Movement-system' when no opposition parties were allowed, and the first multiparty electoral competition in 2006.

The legitimacy of the election processes and election results in all elections under NRM-rule have been questioned. Criticism has related to what we perceive to be a form of grabbing: use of public (state) resources in election campaigns for the ruling party. The importance of money and resources has been a recurring issue in the 1996, 2001 and 2006 elections (William, 1997; Tripp, 2004; Kiiza, 2008). As this chapter highlights, these problems were even more prevalent in 2011. The NRM candidates, and especially President Museveni, had distinct resource advantages compared to the opposition parties and candidates, much of it fuelled by access to the state apparatus and state finances. This contributed to the opposition facing an uneven playing field in the 2011 elections that again contributed to the elections being deemed 'not fair' by international standards (COG, 2011; EUEOM, 2011).

In this chapter we argue that grabbing not only affected electoral accountability through tilting the electoral playing field in favour of the ruling party, but also that it affected financial stability and contributed to rising inflation and subsequent unrest. We draw on interviews with members of political parties, stakeholders and political commentators collected during the run-up to the election as well as published material. Our analysis of the role of money in Ugandan electoral politics suggests that this form of grabbing is detrimental to development because it creates an uneven electoral playing field, distorts the true reflection of the people's will, and undermines the purpose of holding elections. The economic implications of election-related grabbing must be understood in light of the high costs of elections in sub-Saharan Africa. Using inflation data, we highlight the inflation effects during and after the 2011 elections in Uganda. We argue that in order to improve accountability and development, stakeholders should focus on electoral quality in order to avoid 'election grabbing'.

13.1 THE IMPORTANCE OF MONEY IN UGANDAN ELECTORAL POLITICS

Comparative research indicates that money is relatively *more* important in electoral politics in poor countries with a challenging geography and infrastructure compared to more developed countries (Saffu, 2003). Money and resources play an important role in Ugandan politics. When asked what the main challenges facing their party were before the 2011 elections, representatives of all the major opposition parties responded that attracting enough funding to run a campaign effectively was one of their biggest challenges.[1] For the ruling NRM, however, the challenges were slightly different. According to NRM Party Spokesperson Ofwono Opondo, their main challenge was: 'the incumbency – the people believe that because the NRM is the ruling party, we have so many resources. So people are not willing to do anything without direct payment'. Maintaining a financial advantage over the opposition is a key concern for the NRM. The ruling party financially supports their national candidates during electoral campaigns, in contrast to the situation for opposition candidates where only the presidential candidate gets financial support from the party.[2] The financial wealth of the NRM is to some extent linked to support from the business community.[3] However, the bulk of the resources are linked to the NRM's control of state resources.

13.2 GRABBING FROM THE STATE: NRM FUNDING FOR ELECTORAL CAMPAIGNS

It is necessary to distinguish between two types of funding advantages related to access to the state that the NRM enjoy. First, a direct advantage is the use of public resources and money in the campaigns of the ruling party. Second, an indirect advantage is linked to a sophisticated patronage system that permeates the political and bureaucratic sphere in Uganda. Although the direct and indirect use of public resources is interlinked, the dynamics at play are different.

The incumbent party and president in Uganda have several legal advantages that enable them to use state resources to mobilize the voters before and during the campaign, both in parliamentary and presidential elections. The first clause in Article 25 in the Parliamentary Elections Act of 2005 specifies that candidates shall not use government or public resources for the purpose of campaigning for election. Nevertheless, clause 2 specifies that ministers and any holder of official office can use official facilities ordinarily attached to his or her office as long it is used to facilitate 'the execution of his or her office'(GoU, 2005a). What this execution entails is not defined and leaves considerable room for the respective official to use public resources for campaigning purposes. Given the significant number of junior and senior ministers in the NRM government, as well as the often partisan nature of other officials (Helle, 2011), many NRM candidates are given important resource advantages compared to opposition candidates. These advantages were utilized during the 2011 election campaigns, and it was often hard to separate official ceremonies from campaign rallies of the NRM (COG, 2011; EUEOM, 2011). The Presidential Elections Act of 2005 provides the incumbent president with even stronger resource advantages. According to the law, 'a candidate who holds the office of president, may continue to use government facilities during the campaign' (GoU, 2005b). The president is only supposed to utilize the facilities that are ordinarily attached to the office, but this is not a very restrictive measure. In effect, it puts the whole State House apparatus at the president's disposal during the campaign. The 2010 Presidential Elections (Amendment) Act amends and strengthens the penalty for violating these regulations, but it does not specify or restrict the facilities at the president's disposal. In practice, those who are in position of public office can utilize state resources legally during their campaign. The NRM party spokesperson acknowledged in interviews that these facilities are utilized and that it has advantages. However, he argued that it is an incumbency advantage that you find in many established democracies as well.[4] The scale of the facilities provided the government with an unfair advantage though, something that was commented on by several electoral monitoring missions (COG, 2011; EUEOM, 2011).

In addition to using government facilities, there are clear indications that money from the state revenue was used directly for partisan purposes, both before and during the campaign period. First of all, the president has a considerable budget for making what are known as 'presidential donations'. During 2010, the president had approximately USD 10.2 million available for such donations through the State House budget. These funds are handed out at the president's discretion to individuals. Donations are not allowed during the official 3-month campaign period, but they were nevertheless frequently used in the period leading up to the official campaign.[5] President Museveni highlighted his use of these pledges in his 2010 State of the Union Address, stating that by March 2010 he had made 166 Presidential Pledges at approximately USD 1 million (Museveni, 2010).

Financial activities during the electoral campaign indicate that state resources were in high demand. Six weeks before the election the NRM-dominated Ugandan Parliament passed a supplementary budget. This USD 257 million budget came barely 6 months after the original budget was posted and only 2 months after it was approved. Among the expenditure was a USD 33.6 million allocation to State House.[6] The expenditure items in this allocation were left open. For example, USD 4.2 million was given to 'facilitate jobless youth'. A few days after the supplementary budget was passed all MPs in parliament were given USD 8500. Since NRM party representatives dominated the eighth parliament, NRM candidates received the bulk of the money.

The NRM does not hand in audited accounts to the Electoral Commission as required by law.[7] It is therefore difficult to know the exact source of their financing and what happened to the public money spent during the campaign period. A month after the supplementary budget was passed and a few days before the election, Finance Minister Syda Bbumba claimed that the government had already spent its budget. The money from the supplementary budget had gone into administrative processes related to the election, and other sectors such as health and education were therefore not receiving their allocation.[8] Still, significant parts of the budget were also allocated to State House and the army, who were not supposed to be engaged in the electoral process.

The issue of the indirect funding advantage relates to the patronage-network of the ruling party. According to the NRM, they receive large portions of their income from contributions from elected and unelected government officials: All NRM party officials with public positions are expected to contribute a percentage of their salary to the party. The party in turn uses this money to support its flag-bearers financially during election campaigns.[9] In other words, the more NRM party-officials that hold public positions, the more resources the party has available to distribute. The NRM government has increased gradually over the past 20 years (Tumushabe, 2009). By 2012 the cabinet counted 76 senior and junior ministers in addition to the president and vice president. Both the elected and unelected local government network is substantial. In the 2011 elections there were 18 629 posts for which a nomination fee was attached to the contest, and this is only down to the LC3 level: there are even more positions at lower levels.[10] All these positions are paid an honorarium, and elected positions in Uganda are well-paid in comparison to the average salary in the country (DEMGroup, 2011). The number of positions has increased significantly over the last 10 years as a result of the growing number of electoral and administrative districts in Uganda (Tumushabe, 2009; Helle, 2011). Thus, the expansion of the state in Uganda carries an indirect financial benefit for the ruling party.

13.3   ELECTIONS WITHOUT ACCOUNTABILITY

A recent report on how to improve the integrity of elections worldwide found that 'uncontrolled, undisclosed and opaque political finance poses a fundamental threat to the integrity of elections'(Annan et al., 2012: 7). As outlined by Casas-Zamora, there are several reasons why an election with uneven distribution of financial resources among the competing parties is bad for holding a free and fair election: it provides undue influence to a small group of individuals and a lack of focus on the common good, as well as creating uneven competition (Casas-Zamora, 2005: 2).

The resource advantages of the NRM had an impact on the election outcome in the 2011 election, as shown in multiple articles and reports that have highlighted the important role of money and state resources in the campaign (COG, 2011; DEMGroup, 2011, EUEOM, 2011; Izama and Wilkerson, 2011). Contrast this with Conroy-Krutz and Logan, who claim that the impact of the money on actual voting behaviour in the 2011 election was low and not important for the result, and that the 2011 election 'was perhaps the most peaceful and representative of the popular will in several decades'(Conroy-Krutz and Logan, 2012: 627). Conroy-Krutz and Logan remind us that financial resources do not provide the whole story of the 2011 election result. On the other hand, their survey data only look at the effects of goods and money that was distributed directly to the respondents in the survey, focusing on a narrow portion of the financial advantage of the NRM. Arguably, the survey presented by Conroy-Krutz and Logan is not enough to dismiss the importance of money grabbing. This does not mean that the absence of a resource gap would have completely altered the electoral outcome. The NRM and President Museveni have a significant historic legacy in Ugandan politics, related to the bush-war. In addition, the opposition is weak and fragmented. However, this weakness is in part linked to NRM's control of electoral finances. Opposition parties in Uganda are caught in a vicious financial cycle that contributes to the political status quo (Helle, 2011).

13.4 POST-ELECTION INFLATION AND SUBSEQUENT PROTESTS

In the immediate aftermath of the elections Uganda was relatively quiet, although four of the defeated opposition presidential candidates released a joint statement condemning the election (Gibb, 2012). The protests they called for did not materialize in the immediate post-election period. However, after relatively stable macroeconomic growth and controlled rates of inflation in the years leading up to the election, Uganda started to see rising rates of inflation in the months during the election campaign. This trend increased in the following months. Prices on essential goods such as food and fuel as well as essential health and education services grew significantly. The Consumer Price Index (CPI) in Figure 13.1 below highlights that the CPI remained unusually high in the few months preceding and the 6 months after the February election. Members of civil society, local experts and opposition politicians blamed government spending before and during the election campaigns as one of the factors driving this inflation.[11]

   The government and central bank refuted the claims, blaming the rising inflation on a regional food crisis and the global economic outlook. Both of these explanations carry some merit. Globally, 2011 was a year of high inflation, and there was large regional food demand that drove prices of Ugandan agricultural products up. However, Uganda experienced considerably higher inflation than many countries that were more directly affected by this than Uganda: Uganda had the seventh highest inflation rate in 2011 globally. Regionally, the only country with a higher inflation rate was Ethiopia – all other neighbouring countries had lower inflation rates than the 18.7 per cent annual increase in CPI that Uganda experienced. There is thus reason to believe that international conditions

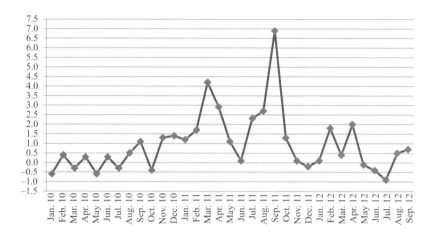

Source: Uganda Bureau of Statistics, September 2012. Available at: http://www.ubos.org/
?st=pagerelations&id=138&p=related%20pages:%20CPI%20%20May%202009 (accessed
10 May 2013).

*Figure 13.1   Monthly percentage change in Consumer Price Index in
             Uganda, January 2010 – September 2012*

were not solely responsible for the inflation experienced after the 2011
election (Kabundi, 2012). Combined with the timing of the increase in
inflation and the fact that the government overspent significantly during
the campaign, the picture of a budget cycle motivated by the election,
which in turn affected the post-election economic stability in Uganda,
emerges.

In the aftermath of the rising food and fuel prices, the Ugandan
opposition drew inspiration from the events unfolding in the Arab
Uprisings and started organizing protest marches against the NRM
government. The protests focused on economic issues, but carried a
strong political component in that they were organized by members of
the opposition parties and mostly split across government/opposition
lines. The army and police forces cracked down hard on the protests,
which the government perceived to be political: several people were
killed and several opposition leaders arrested (Gibb, 2012). After a few
weeks of confrontation the protests died out and President Museveni
maintained control. The protests, nevertheless, highlighted that there was
resentment within the Ugandan public, and that the opposition had the
potential to mobilize important segments of the Ugandan population.

13.5   INCREASING ELECTORAL QUALITY INSTEAD OF QUANTITY

Partly as a result of these adverse effects of unfair elections, some experts have argued that since competitive elections *can be* detrimental to development, they should not be considered an important part of a developmental process (Kelsall et al., 2010; Therkildsen and Bourgouin, 2012). This trend has been particularly prevalent over the past 10 years because some authoritarian regimes have managed to create significant economic growth, while more competitive regimes have not (Cheru, 2012). We do not support this policy prescription. We argue that instead of eliminating accountability through elections both national and international stakeholders should pay attention to the quality of elections rather than simply counting the number of elections.

The focus should be on securing electoral integrity, whereas addressing the issue of political finance is fundamental in order to achieve this goal. The grabbing of state resources by ruling parties must be addressed in a systematic manner. The advice offered by the Global Commission to remedy the situation highlights the complex interplay between rules and actual practices (Annan et al., 2012: 33–37). This report highlights two challenges. First, creating legislation that makes grabbing illegal in terms of clear and unpartisan regulations that leave little room for interpretation and rule-bending; and increasing transparency with regards to political funding, and what this money is spent on. This is increasingly being done, though there is still some work left both in terms of clarity and transparency. Formally, there is legislation in place in Uganda that should prevent many of the practices described in this chapter if implemented properly. This is the second (much harder) challenge: how do you get politicians to enforce compliance if they benefit from non-compliance? This question must be understood in light of the fundamental challenge associated with political power. It calls for an assessment of constitutional design, the function of checks and balances, but also, debate about the state's position in society.

However, in order to increase compliance we also need to address issues related to the costs of losing an election. If controlling the state is the only path to economic prosperity and power, then the stakes around elections are very high. Consequently the incentive to *grab an election* is also higher. The question of election grabbing can therefore not be analysed without looking at the political economy of society as a whole.

NOTES

1. Interviews with General Secretaries and Party Treasurers of Forum for Democratic Change (FDC), Democratic Party (DP), and Uganda Peoples Congress (UPC). Individual interviews carried out in Kampala, December 2010.
2. *Ibid.* Information on the NRM: Interview with National Spokesperson of NRM Ofwono Opondo, Kampala, 17 December 2010.
3. Interview with National Spokesperson of NRM Ofwono Opondo, Kampala, 17th of December 2010. During the interview Mr Opondo was confronted with the allegation that these contributions could be seen as bribes in an attempt to receive future government tenders and favours. He replied that this could be the case, but that the NRM could not do anything with the motive behind the payments.
4. Interview with National Spokesperson of NRM Ofwono Opondo, Kampala, 17 December 2010.
5. The pledges were well-documented in the Ugandan media (Asiimwe, 2010; Njoroge, 2011).
6. See for example Karuaga and Bekunda (2011).
7. The Political Parties and Organisations Act of 2005 requires all political parties to submit their audited accounts and disclose their sources of income to the Electoral Commission of Uganda each year. Compliance has historically been low across the board, but over the past few years most of the opposition parties have handed in their accounts. The NRM had not done it by the end of 2011, and although party sources claimed they were working on it, sources within the Electoral Commission confirmed that they had only submitted one account for the whole 6-year period from 2005 to 2011, and that this had been rejected by the Auditors and the Electoral Commission. It was thus not available for the public.
8. For quotes see Mayanja and Abdallah (2011).
9. Interview with National Spokesperson of NRM Ofwono Opondo, Kampala, 17 December 2010. Also echoed in interview with Assistant to the General Secretary of the NRM, Hippo Twebaze, Kampala, 16 December 2010.
10. The LC (Local Council) system in Uganda is based on five different levels, ranging from Level 1 (the village) to Level 5 (the district). Each level is supposed to have an elected representative body.
11. See Makuma and Akello (2011) for quotes.

REFERENCES

Acemoglu, D. and J. A. Robinson (2012), *Why Nations Fail: The Origins of Power, Prosperity, and Poverty.* London: Profile Books.

Annan, K., E. Z. Ponce de Leon, M. Ahtisaari, M. K. Albright et al. (2012), Deepening democracy: a strategy for improving the integrity of elections worldwide. Report of the Global Commission on Elections, Democracy and Security, Stockholm.

Asiimwe, D. (2010), Bribery or service? Museveni's cash handouts has sparked controversy. *The Independent*, 29 September. Available at: http://www.independent.co.ug/index.php/cover-story/cover-story/82-cover-story/3483-bribery-or-service-museveni-cash-handouts-have-sparked-controversy/.

Casas-Zamora, K. (2005), *Paying for Democracy: Political Finance and State Funding for Parties.* Colchester: ECPR.

Cheru, F. (2012), Democracy and people power in Africa: still searching for the 'political kingdom'. *Third World Quarterly*, **33**, 265–291.

COG (2011), Uganda Presidential and Parliamentary Elections 18 February 2011. Report of the Commonwealth Observer Group. Commonwealth Secretariat, London.

Conroy-Krutz, J. and C. Logan (2012), Museveni and the 2011 Ugandan election: did the money matter? *The Journal of Modern African Studies*, **50**, 625–655.

DEMGroup (2011), *Report on Money in Politics: Pervasive Vote Buying in Uganda Elections*. Kampala: DEMGroup.

EUEOM (2011), Uganda: Final Report General Elections 18 February 2011. European Union Election Observation Mission.

Gerring, J., S. C. Thacker, and R. Alfaro (2012), Democracy and human development. *The Journal of Politics*, **74**, 1–17.

Gibb, R. (2012), Presidential and parliamentary elections in Uganda, February 18, 2011. *Electoral Studies*, **31**, 458–461.

GoU (2005a), Parliamentary Elections Act. Kampala: Government of Uganda.

GoU (2005b), Presidential Elections Act. Kampala: Government of Uganda.

Helle, S.-E. (2011), Living in a material world: Political funding in electoral authoritarian regimes in sub-Saharan Africa. Master in Comparative Politics, University of Bergen.

Izama, A. and M. Wilkerson (2011), Uganda: Museveni's triumph and weakness. *Journal of Democracy*, **22**, 64–78.

Kabundi, A. (2012), Dynamics of inflation in Uganda. Working Paper Series N° 152, African Development Bank.

Karugaba, M. and C. Bekunda (2011), MPs Pass Sh600 Billion Additional Budget. *The East African*, 4 January. Available at: http://allafrica.com/stories/201101050043.html.

Kelsall, T., D. Booth, D. Cammack and F. Golooba-Mutebi (2010), Development Patrimonialism? Questioning the orthodoxy on political governance and economic progress in Africa. Africa Power and Politics Working Paper 9.

Kiiza, J. (2008), Party financing and its implications for democratic governance in Uganda. In J. Kiiza, S. Makara and L. Rakner (eds), *Electoral Democracy in Uganda: Understanding Institutional Processes and Outcomes of the 2006 Multiparty Elections*. Kampala: Fountain Publ., pp. 231–261.

Makuma, R. and J. Akello (2011), Post-election economic woes. Available at: http://www.independent.co.ug/cover-story/4008-post-election-economic-woes (accessed 19 October 2012).

Mayanja, S. and H. Abdallah (2011), Govt is broke, says Bbumba as tough times loom. *The East African*, 14 February. Available at: http://www.theeastafrican.co.ke/news/-/2558/1106116/-/item/0/-/2fs7il/-/index.html.

Museveni, Y. K. (2010), *State of the Nation Address 2010*. Available at: http://www.mediacentre.go.ug/details.php?catId=6&item=886 (accessed 4 October 2012).

Njoroge, J. (2011), Opposition cries foul as Museveni gives Sh 741 million in cash donations. *The Daily Monitor*, 7 January. Available at: http://allafrica.com/stories/201101070114.html.

Saffu, Y. (2003), The funding of political parties and election campaigns in Africa. In R. Austin and M. Tjernström (eds), *Funding of Political Parties and Election Campaigns.* Stockholm: International Institute for Democracy and Electoral Assitance IDEA, pp. 21–33.

Therkildsen, O. and F. Bourgouin (2012), Continuity and change in Tanzania's ruling colition: legacies, crises and weak productive capacity. DIIS Working Paper 6.

Tripp, A. M. (2004), The changing face of authoritarianism in Africa: the case of Uganda. *Africa Today*, **50**, 3–26.

Tumushabe, G. W. (2009), Trends in public administration expenditure in Uganda. *ACODE Policy Research Series*, Kampala.

William, M. (1997), Money and power in Uganda's 1996 elections. *African Journal of Political Science*, **2**, 168–179.

PART IV

Risk of grabbing due to interaction with
international players

14. Elite capture of Kabul Bank

Arne Strand

Afghanistan is entering the most critical period since the overthrow of Taliban back in 2001. The North Atlantic Treaty Organization (NATO) has announced withdrawal of international forces by 2014, and a sharp reduction is expected in funding for development programmes and support for the Government of Afghanistan (GOA). This has led to increasing fear of renewed internal fighting, and major uncertainty if there will be an orderly shift of presidential power as President Karzai's term should end in April 2014 (International Crisis Group, 2012). There are increasing concerns over the high level of corruption and the large amounts of cash being brought abroad as the Afghan elite prepare to secure their financial future.

The overall objective of combating terror, building peace and winning Afghan 'hearts and minds' has, since 2001, frequently come to over-shadow normal development and governance priorities. Key international actors have based their strategy on the presumed loyalty of a small Afghan military and political elite, seeing that as instrumental in securing Afghan support to the international mission. These Afghans have been able to make use of their position to secure generous benefits from the international assistance, and from the opportunities emerging from an economic liberalisation policy that formed part of the peace-building package. The sale of state property, tendering of large security and engineering contracts and a process to tender out major mineral and energy resources left those with political and military connections ideally placed to maximize personal and family income.

This resonates with the literature on peace building and corruption where it has been observed (Cheng, 2012) that:

> while post-conflict environments appear to be especially prone to corruption, and while corruption can compromise peace-building efforts, fighting corruption is not the only objective of peace-building actors – nor is it necessarily the most important one. Enabling corruption might be a price peace builders

have to pay to ensure the participation of warring factions in a peace agreement and to end large-scale violence.

The author (*ibid.*: 11) concludes that:

> in most peace-building concepts there is an implicit trade-off whereby corruption is tolerated in the short term in order to end violence and aid stability, but the foundation for long-term development of state institutions are undermined as the capacity and legitimacy of the state suffer damage.

To be able to capitalize on such short-term opportunities and maintain their influence over the state apparatus, the Afghan elite was in need of access to stable sources of cash. This coincided with the interest of elements in the Afghan banking sector in political alliances to secure access to a continuous cash flow and political backing for their operations. The case of the Kabul Bank fraud illustrates how this was accomplished in a situation where the importance of building peace through an international military operation took precedence over addressing corruption. And where, consequently, the international community and the Afghan population had to foot the bill for a USD 920 million fraud.

Three decades of conflict and massive funding for military operations, the buying of alliances, and humanitarian assistance for victims of war, has left Afghanistan vulnerable to corruption. Since the overthrow of the Taliban regime in 2001 it has been evident that corruption has emerged as a major obstacle to Afghan state-building and the peace-building process. This has been confirmed over the last years through national corruption surveys undertaken by Integrity Watch Afghanistan (2013). The surveys document that corruption not only reduces the scale and impact of development programmes but also the trust the population hold in the GOA and in those elected to govern. Since I have worked for international non-governmental organizations (NGOs) in Afghanistan during the 1980s and '90s, and as researcher and evaluator during the last decade, I have been able to follow these developments closely. Over the last few years, Kabul has been ripe with stories of how key persons in the government have embezzled large sums, and how they have protected each other. Local businessmen conveyed stories of rigged tender processes, and how they had been warned against submitting bids for larger contracts that would compete with companies linked to powerful individuals. Independent media has exposed different forms of corrupt practices, though largely without any consequences for those involved. It was only when the Washington Post exposed the Kabul Bank case in February 2010 that the extent of the political corruption was exposed and became an issue of more general concern. Although several overview articles have been written, which this chapter draws on,[1] and an independent committee has released its report on the case, there are still signs that those responsible will not be held accountable due to their political affiliations (Independent Joint Anti-corruption Monitoring and Evaluation Committee, 2012).

14.1 CREATIVE BANKING

Kabul Bank had a rather unlikely start when it was established back in 2004. The co-founders ending up as Chairman and CEO of the bank were Sherkhan Farnood, a technical operator trusted with the printing of banknotes for one of the Afghan Islamic resistance parties, and Khalil-ullah Ferozi, an internationally renowned poker player with experience from operating the Shaheen Exchange, a *Hawala* banking system operating out of Moscow and later Dubai. Kabul Bank was formally registered with the Afghan Central Bank (Da Afghanistan Bank, DAB), as is the banking requirement, and expanded its presence rapidly throughout Afghanistan with 68 branches in all of Afghanistan's provinces. A major reason for such an expansion was that Kabul Bank managed to secure a USD 1.8 billion annual contract to pay (with international funding through the Afghan Reconstruction Trust Fund) the salaries for about 80 per cent of the employees of the Afghan government. It is estimated that the bank earned up to USD 10 million a year in interest for holding the salaries (Filkins, 2011). Moreover, it managed through effective advertising to receive about USD 1.3 billion as deposits from the Afghan public, making it the largest Afghan private bank (Huffman, 2011).

However, the owners did not intend to rest on their achievements or comply with international and national banking regulations. They rather opted to secure for themselves political connections in the Afghan government to fully utilize the financial opportunities that the bank provided them. In this endeavour they were rather innovative and approached the brothers of President Karzai and First Vice-President Fahim, both active in the Afghan business sector. According to an explanation provided by Mahmoud Karzai, in 2007 he was provided with about USD 6 million in cash, as a gift, from Kabul Bank's Chairman Farnood to buy 7.5 per cent shares in Kabul Bank. This secured for him, and in the same way the vice-president's brother Abdul Haseen Fahim, seats on the board of Kabul Bank. The result was a political affiliation that shielded the bank from government 'interference', but it came at a high financial cost.

The two board members drew on the bank's financial resources to finance their own investments, including the buying up of privatized state property and for having 'cash at hand' when larger procurement processes required companies to provide financial guarantees. What were termed 'loans' to these board members were in reality interest free 'grants' without a repayment schedule or any collateral. Discussions broadcast on Afghan television following the disclosure of the scam suggest that 'grants' for purchases that turned profitable were repaid by the two board members, though if investments failed it was left to Kabul Bank to shoulder the financial losses.

What finally 'broke the camel's back' in 2010 were a series of property investments made by Kabul Bank in Dubai's elite neighbourhood Palm Jumeirah. Houses and flats were offered for the Afghan political elite on 'grant terms'. Some were registered to the CEO of Kabul Bank and some to his wife, while, in reality, they were used by members of the Afghan elite or those they wanted to befriend. One property was held by the former vice-president, Ahmed Zia Masood. According to the US Embassy in Kabul, he was stopped by officials of the United Arab Emirates in 2009 for entering the country with USD 52 million in cash in his luggage. The same authorities had reported that Kabul Bank Chairman Farnood owned 39 properties in Dubai (Steele and Boone, 2010). When the real estate crash came in 2008, these property investments, estimated at USD 160 million, become a major liability for Kabul Bank.

14.2 THE ELECTION GAME

This setback did not prevent Kabul Bank's leadership from trying to secure further influence in Afghan political circles. The presidential elections in 2009, where President Karzai was re-elected after massive election fraud, was seen as an opportunity for them to secure their political influence (Bijlert, 2009, 2010). President Karzai's election team and campaign was headed by Finance Minister Omar Zakilwal, and included several other ministers. Zakilwal publicly acknowledged that they received a contribution from Kabul Bank, and that he personally forwarded a briefcase with cash to the campaign team. He believed the contribution was about USD 0.2 million. This amount, or any other contribution from Kabul Bank, is not registered as required by the Independent Election Commission. Neither does the amount match information provided by other campaign staff or Kabul Bank CEO. The latter has repeatedly told journalists that Kabul Bank provided President Karzai's campaign with up to USD 14 million. Afghan officials moreover allege that money from Kabul Bank was on a number of occasions used by the Karzai government to bribe parliamentarians to secure their votes in cases of importance to the government.

14.3 REAL MONEY FOR FAKE COMPANIES

How did Kabul Bank come to all this cash, and how could their activities go undetected despite an international audit? Journalists, such as Michael Huffman, who have looked into the case have found an intriguing arrangement. Two hundred fake companies had been established by Farnood and Ferozi, and these were granted loans from Kabul Bank. The loans were transferred to the Shaheen Exchange in Dubai and from this company returned back to individuals in Afghanistan through the use of fake names, possibly addressed to a person employed by the real recipient. There were two sets of books, one fake set in Kabul that was made available for the auditors and one real set held by Shaheen Exchange in Dubai.

Both the Chairman and the CEO were actively using Kabul Bank funds in violation of Afghan banking law. All property purchases in Dubai were illegal as banking investments were not allowed outside of Afghanistan. Equally illegal were the purchase and direct running of Afghan businesses by bank officials and board members. One telling example is that of the airline Pamir Air, of which Farnood was the chairman. Their operating license was only revoked in March 2011 following an air crash killing 44 people. The crash investigation revealed that the plane's registration had been forged to avoid safety inspections (Huffman, 2011).

14.4 THE SCANDAL IS OUT

But underneath the polished surface and marketing campaigns, major disagreements were developing between the Chairman Farnood and CEO Ferozi. The Afghan Parliament, the High Office of Oversight and Anti-Corruption, and gradually too the DAB took an increasing interest in Kabul Bank, especially after a 2009 audit report on 'nonperforming loans and loan losses'. In February 2010, Abdul Qadir Fitrat, Director of DAB (Afghan Central Bank), requested that the US Treasury Department conduct a forensic audit of the two largest private banks: Kabul Bank and Azizi Bank. Further pressure emerged as international newspapers, during the same month, revealed the failed investments in Dubai, and the extent of capital taken out of the country via Kabul airport (including by

Pamir Air). Pressure was building on DAB to take a more active role towards Kabul Bank, but they were reportedly hesitant to fully engage due to the expected protection provided through Kabul Bank's political connections. It was Chairman Farnood that finally informed US authorities in July 2010 about the bank's difficult financial situation and the magnitude of the scam. This was possibly done to protect himself, as it was evident that the bank would no longer be able to maintain their operations in the same manner (Huffman, 2011: 9). This raised major concerns in the US camp, to the extent that US (and NATO) Commander General Patraeus called in July for a meeting with President Karzai and Director Fitrat to discuss the financial state of Kabul Bank. Fitrat went on to the Parliament to ask for a USD 200 million 'safety net trust fund for private banks'. While the news was still not public in Afghanistan, pressure was growing on Kabul Bank management. On 30 August Director Fitrat demanded the resignation of Farnood and Ferozi, and appointed DAB's chief financial advisor to oversee Kabul Bank.

This caused panic among Kabul Bank's customers. They lined up to withdraw their deposits: USD 180 million was withdrawn in just 2 days, despite denials from bank staff and even the Finance Minister that there was no reason for concern. Mehmod Karzai denied that losses were as high as the alleged USD 300 million, while President Karzai blamed the media for its negative coverage of the financial situation of Kabul Bank.

The reality could not be hidden and the Afghan government ended up providing a USD 820 million bailout grant for Kabul Bank. This amount confirmed that the extent of the fraud was far beyond what was expected, and later estimates ended up at USD 930 million.

14.5 IMF PRESSURE

Uncertainty over the Afghan government's will to address corruption led, in turn, the International Monetary Fund (IMF) to refuse renewal of the Extended Credit Facility Programme in September 2010, the function of which is to ensure that Afghanistan's financial sector is sound. Their terms were clear. The Afghan government was required to conduct a forensic audit of Kabul Bank and Azizi Bank, to reform their banking and lending laws, to prosecute the officials responsible for Kabul Bank fraud, place the bank under receivership and devise an acceptable plan to recapitalize the government's reserves for the USD 820 million bailout. International development partners added pressure by halting their scheduled transfers to Afghanistan. Despite such pressure, responses were slow on the Afghan side. Karzai tried to avoid having USAID fund the forensic audit as that would provide them the right to insights into the findings. Kabul Bank was only dissolved as a legal entity in April 2011, but with parts of it immediately re-established as 'New Kabul Bank'. Farnood and Fitrat were finally arrested in June 2011, a year after the scandal broke, but released in September the same year without having to stand trial. In October 2011, the Afghan Parliament passed a bill to recapitalize the government's reserves over a period of 8 years, effectively passing on the cost to Afghan taxpayers (and international donors).

14.6 PROTECTIVE POLITICS

When names of those involved emerged and the extent of the fraud became publicly known in April 2011, efforts to protect the president, his family and associates began. For the Afghan government the problem was no longer those who had committed the fraud, it was rather, as they narrated: those who had not detected it early enough or acted upon the information they possessed.

President Karzai announced in April 2011 that the bank would be placed under receivership and that its management could be prosecuted. But, he further informed that the remaining shareholders were offered an amnesty and would be excused if they repaid their loans within 1 month (this was later extended to 3 years). In effect, he was letting his and his vice-president's brother off the hook. Karzai's argument was that the blame had to be placed on the foreign advisors that had provided DAB with inaccurate information, and the auditors (a Pakistani auditing company) that had failed to detect the fraud. He was at this stage expressing his opinion that the fault was not with DAB: they had only been inexperienced.

This statement from the president and the continued pressure from the IMF and other development partners emboldened DAB Governor Fitrat. In late April, he exposed to the Afghan Parliament the names of the top eight shareholders in Kabul Bank and that of two businessmen involved in the fraud. He also informed the parliament that as many as 103 ministers and members of parliament had received money from Kabul Bank. He, however, did not oppose the amnesty President Karzai had announced, but urged the collaboration of the 'grantees' in reclaiming the funds. He noted that Mahmoud Karzai and Abdul Haseen Fahim had a partial repayment agreement with the government, and informed the parliament that he had requested that the government confiscate shareholders' property and set up a special court to try them for the fraud.

The public announcement of the names of the two brothers and the extent of their involvement made Governor Fitrat a threat to President Karzai and his circle. They appointed a commission to review the Kabul Bank case, headed by Azizullah Lodin, the Chairman of the Afghan High Office of Oversight and Anti-Corruption. Their report, released on 29 May 2011, placed the blame for the fraud on DAB due to 'their weak monitoring'. The same report acquitted the shareholders of any wrong-doing, though excluding Chairman Farnood and CEO Ferozi. Chairman Lodin referred in his presentation of the report to the fraud as a 'minor incident' that the donors should not use as a pretext for withholding financial support to Afghanistan.

The IMF maintained the pressure, however, much to the dismay of Finance Minister Zakilwal – who argued that the international community 'were playing politics'. The mounting pressure on Governor Fitrat forced him to flee to the United States. He claimed to know of an assassination plot arranged by the Afghan government and announced his resignation from the governor position. He categorically rejected his own part in the Kabul Bank fraud, but provided further details of the involvement of and benefits taken by the Karzai family.

From this point, it was up to Karzai. He became increasingly negative towards the international community and played up pro-Afghan and anti-Western rhetoric. He ordered, or accepted, that Farnood and Ferozi should be released from custody in September 2011, and did not give in to all demands from the IMF and the other donors. They finally approved a new agreement by November 2011 involving a watered-down list of demands. Almost a year later, on 30 October 2012, President Karzai chaired a government meeting that made the following decision: 'The Ministry of Foreign Affairs and Attorney General Office were tasked to effectively follow up with the United States the issue of the extradition of Abdul Qadir Fitrat, the former DAB governor, who is also accused in the Kabul Bank issue' (Government of Afghanistan, 2012).

This decision fits into a narrative of national pride and independence and the opposition of international pressure. Though, at the same time, Karzai demonstrates to his fellow Afghans his influence over the state. It is not the judicial system but the president who decides who should be taken to court or not, or extradited to stand trial – seemingly with limited evidence. He signalled to his fellow Afghans: do not dare to challenge us; we will use the state against you. This is not least important at a time when Karzai and his vice-presidents are working hard to secure their influence after the 2014 presidential elections, possibly with another Karzai brother or close ally as the new president.

The verdict of the Special Tribunal on the Kabul Bank case announced in early March 2013 does little to increase trust in the willingness of the Afghan government to take corruption seriously. According to Smith (2013), charges against Farnood and Ferozi for money laundering and embezzlement were dropped. They were therefore only sentenced to 5 years in prison, or potentially in 'house detention'. Farnood was ordered to repay USD 279 million and Ferozi USD 531 million, but few believe this money will be paid. Equally disturbing to Smith is the fact that no shareholders but several employees of DAB were sentenced, leading to a comment that 'the similarity of the sentences meted out to the architects and beneficiaries of the fraud with the penalties against officials in the central bank makes a mockery of the judicial process as well' (Smith, 2013).

14.7   POLICY IMPLICATIONS

The policy implications of the Kabul Bank case might be grave in this vulnerable transition period, and beyond. One of the key points in the declaration from the Tokyo conference, signed between donors and the GOA in June 2012, is a requirement that the Afghan government must do its utmost to reduce corruption. This is regarded as the foundation for further international development funding. Donors can demand a strict adherence of the Tokyo Declaration if they observe that the present and future Afghan government is not paying serious attention to corruption issues. This is an opportunity key development partners, such as the United States and UK, might make use of when they no longer have to consider whether such actions could pose increased security risks to their soldiers.

It is not only the Karzai family that received generous support from Kabul Bank: so did other candidates for the presidency and members of the parliament. Thus, the large majority of the present Afghan elite will try to avoid any further attention on the Kabul Bank case. It is impossible for Afghan elite politicians to promote a serious anti-corruption campaign; none of their citizens will believe them. Ironically, this might strengthen support for the Taliban, who curbed both corruption and drug production when in power and chased most of those now holding office out of Afghanistan in the mid-1990s.

When the United States and NATO made themselves dependent on the same elite to overthrow the Taliban in 2001 and to 'build the new Afghan state', in effect they entered a partnership that laid the foundation for malpractices. The elite felt that NATO and the United States depended on them to 'fight terror', a position that emboldened them to make use of all the possibilities to enrich themselves. One obvious lesson is that when military strategies overrule principles of state-building and good governance, this opens up endless opportunities for elite capture and corruption.

Another lesson for peace-building theory is that the Kabul Bank case confirms that efforts to 'buy' short-term peace with political and military elites will not benefit longer-term peace building. On the contrary, the Afghan case demonstrates that it will ruin the foundation for a functional and broadly accepted state. A state and governance structure is needed that can gain and maintain the trust of the population as Afghans are left to cope with their future – and pay the bill for fraud – as the international military withdraws.

NOTES

1. See, for example, Huffman (2011).

REFERENCES

Bijlert, M. v. (2009), Polling day fraud in the Afghan elections. AAN Election Blog. Kabul, Afghanistan Analyst Network.

Bijlert, M. v. (2010), Who controls the vote? Afghanistan's evolving election.Afghanistan Analyst Network Thematic Report 05/2010. Available at: http://www.afghanistan-analysts.net/uploads/AAN-2010-Controlling_the_vote-final.pdf.

Cheng, C. S. and D. Zaum (eds) (2012), *Corruption and Post-Conflict Peacebuilding: Selling the peace? Cass Series on Peacekeeping.* London: Routledge.

Filkins, D. (2011), Letter from Kabul: The Great Afghan Bank Heist. *The New Yorker*, 14 February 2011.

Government of Afghanistan (2012), President Karzai chairs meeting to assess Kabul Bank loan recovery progress. Available at: http://president.gov.af/en/news/14226 (accessed 3 November 2012).

Higgins, A. (2010), In Afghanistan: signs of crony capitalism. *Washington Post*, 22 February.

Huffman, M. (2011), The Kabul Bank scandal and the crisis that followed. USPolicyinabigworld. Available at: http://www.uspolicyinabigworld.com/2011/12/03/the-kabul-bank-scandal-and-the-crisis-that-followed-2/.

Independent Joint Anti-corruption Monitoring and Evaluation Committee (2012), Report of the public inquiry into the Kabul Bank Crisis. Kabul, 15 November 2012.

Integrity Watch Afghanistan (2013), *National Corruption Survey 2012.* Kabul: Integrity Watch Afghanistan.

International Crisis Group (2012), *Afghanistan: The Long, Hard Road to the 2014 Transition.* Kabul/Brussels: International Crisis Group.

Smith, S. (2013), Kabul bankrupt? Verdict portends broad consequences for Afghanistan. Available at: http://www.usip.org/publications/kabul-bankrupt-verdict-portends-broad-consequences-afghanistan (accessed 15 March 2013).

Steele, J. and J. Boone (2010), WikiLeaks: Afghan vice-president landed in Dubai with $52m in cash. *The Guardian*, Thursday 2 December 2010.

15. Don't rock the boat: Norway's difficulties in dealing with corruption in development aid

Eirik G. Jansen

This chapter addresses some of the constraints Norway faces when dealing with corruption in development aid programmes. The issue will be described and analysed in relation to one particular programme, the Management of Natural Resources Programme (MNRP) in Tanzania that Norway supported from 1994 to 2006 with NOK 300 million. An evaluation of MNRP (Cooksey et al., 2006), followed by a detailed forensic audit (Andresen and Bhattbhatt, 2007, 2008), revealed comprehensive and systemic corruption in the programme. The Norwegian government's response was directed primarily at the role of the government of Tanzania in the programme. How Norway as a donor dealt with the corruption in the MNRP and the framework within which this happened has been left largely unaddressed.

The chapter focuses particularly on the role of the Norwegian Embassy in Dar es Salaam in the management of MNRP and how the management and corruption in the programme was handled. I have first-hand knowledge about the way this was done as I was the programme officer at the Embassy for MNRP from 2003–07. After 2007, I closely followed how the Norwegian Embassy in Dar es Salaam and the Ministry of Foreign Affairs (MFA) in Oslo have handled MNRP after the corruption was documented. Some of the questions that will be addressed in the chapter are the following: Why did Norway not discover and react upon the extensive misuse of money and corruption in MNRP earlier? Why was only a small amount of the embezzled money in MNRP repaid by the government of Tanzania to Norway? What are the characteristics associated with the Norwegian aid system and its environment that make it likely that misuse of money and corruption may continue to occur in aid programmes? The last question aims to discuss the more general lessons that can be learnt from MNRP which are relevant for Norwegian development cooperation.

15.1 CORRUPTION, FRAUD AND THEFT IN A DONOR-FUNDED NATURAL RESOURCE MANAGEMENT PROGRAMME

Much of the support under the MNRP was spent on the development of national institutions in the forestry, fisheries and wildlife sectors. Some of the support was spent on infrastructure, but most of the money was allocated for capacity building (seminars and workshops) for the MNRP's own staff, government employees in the districts and the local population, in order for them to learn more about how the various natural resources should be better managed.

For many years MNRP was considered a successful programme for the management of natural resources. During 2006 the picture of MNRP changed as a result of an evaluation that the Norwegian Embassy and the Ministry of Natural Resources and Tourism in Dar es Salaam carried out covering the whole period of MNRP from 1994 to 2006. The evaluation findings were not compatible with the results reported in the previous annual reports and mid-term reviews. The most important finding in the evaluation concerned the financial management of the MNRP. It was decided to conduct an audit of the programme.

The main questions addressed in the two audit reports of 2007 and 2008, carried out by an independent Danish auditor were: How has the allocated money been spent and what kind of documentation exists for the money spent? The Danish auditor and his Tanzanian colleague visited the project offices for 6 of the 11 projects in MNRP in various parts of Tanzania. They spent many days at each project site and went through the accounts and financial management system for each project. There are few Norwegian development programmes where *the flow of financial resources* has been documented in as much detail and where the financial management system has been assessed so closely.

It was found that seminars and workshops were regularly reported to last longer than they actually did, in other words, for seminars lasting only 2 days, costs could be charged for 6 days. In some cases employees of the MNRP had been given double per diems and overtime pay while on holiday. Employees of MNRP had been paid large sums for travel expenses that could not be documented. For one selected project, it was found that 30 per cent of the expenses could not be documented with receipts. MNRP covered the expenses for reports from consultants where there were no agreements with the consultants and no reports. Various types of infrastructure were overpriced and procurement rules were not adhered to when goods and services were purchased. There was no control over the stock of goods in the stores of the various MNRP projects. There was a lack of inventories and lists of equipment. Large sums of money had been transferred from MNRP to the Ministry of Natural Resources and Tourism without explanation, and there were no documents that justified these transfers. The financial accounts for the projects were not set up according to the standard format for accounts. The *internal* and *external* mechanisms for controlling the financial management system did not function well. The internal control mechanism, the audit unit of the Ministry, did not identify the poor financial management system of MNRP. Neither did the *external* mechanisms, the Controller and Auditor General (CAG) and the Norwegian Embassy. The most serious problem was that the CAG received all the reports and accounts from the Ministry and accepted them with only minor changes.

There were also other areas in which the auditors had critical comments (Jansen, 2009). Bearing in mind the large amount of money which may have been mismanaged, the Danish auditor was asked whether half of the total allocated funds (USD 30 million from a total USD 60 million), might have been mismanaged and used for corrupt purposes. The Danish auditor replied that this sum might not be far from the truth.[1]

15.2 HOW DID THE EMBASSY DEAL WITH THE CORRUPTION IN MNRP?

The issue of corruption in MNRP became particularly apparent in the latter part of 2006 and in 2007. At that time various versions of the evaluation report of MNRP were submitted to the Norwegian Embassy. The reactions to the report and subsequent internal memos and discussions were mixed. Some gave strong support and said that it is important to follow up, while others were more evasive; 'don't rock the boat' was one comment that summarized several similar comments about not pursuing the matter in detail.

In 2008, information about the extensive corruption in MNRP came into the public domain both in Tanzania and in Norway. The major Tanzanian and Norwegian newspapers wrote about MNRP and the corruption in the programme was referred to in the Tanzanian and

Norwegian parliaments. The Norwegian Minister of International Development declared, 'We must get to the bottom of this case' (Bistandsaktuelt, no 3, 2008). For those of us who had been concerned about the extensive corruption in MNRP for years, the minister's statement was encouraging. It became a test case for taking the principle of *zero-tolerance for corruption* seriously. The two audit reports by the Danish auditor contained leads to many specific issues and areas where corruption could be found and documented. The two reports formed an excellent point of departure for further investigations.

Over 2 years the Norwegian Embassy had meetings with the Ministry of Natural Resources and Tourism about the mismanagement of funds in MNRP. During this period a separate investigation was carried out about the financial management of MNRP. Since there was so much public awareness about the case, many were interested in the progress of the investigations into MNRP. How much of the NOK 300 million would be considered to have been used for corrupt purposes? In June 2010, it became clear that Norway would be refunded about NOK 10.9 million by the government of Tanzania. Of this amount about NOK 10.2 million consisted of value added tax that Norway had paid by an administrative mistake and that the government of Tanzania by omission had not discovered. This amount was not labelled as corrupt use of aid money. The investigation found that there was only sufficient documentation to claim that NOK 750 000 could be labelled as the corrupt use of funds.[2] When the NOK 10.9 million was repaid from the government of Tanzania to the government of Norway towards the end of 2010, the Ministry of Foreign Affairs in Oslo hailed this as a victory and as clear evidence that the anti-corruption approach in the embassy and the MFA was working.[3] For those of us who knew the MNRP and had followed the case closely, the final result of the investigation was a disappointment. The zero-tolerance for corruption that all persons in the MFA, Norad and the embassies were told to adhere to, appeared to be a joke.

The investigation report had not got to the bottom of the corruption, according to a Norwegian auditor who read the investigation report about MNRP submitted to the embassy in 2009.[4] It is clear that the terms of reference for the investigation were narrow, the time allocated for the study was short, and many of the contentious issues in MNRP identified by the two audit reports were not followed up.

It is still necessary to consider, however, why Norway acted as if it did not want to get to the bottom of this case. One potential explanation was the importance of continuing to have good diplomatic relations with Tanzania. Another reason may have been that Norway planned to launch a forest and climate programme (REDD+) in which Tanzania would be a major partner. NOK 500 million were in the planned pipeline for the REDD+ programme in Tanzania and it would be difficult to implement this without a good relationship with the government of Tanzania. The comment 'don't rock the boat' should been seen in this light.

15.3 ANALYSIS: SEVEN GENERAL LESSONS

There are also other reasons why one did not get to the bottom of the corruption in MNRP and why the corruption was discovered at such a late stage in the programme. Below, I outline seven explanatory factors that, in different ways, made it difficult to combat corruption in MNRP and in other on-going aid projects. All factors are highly relevant for understanding the constraints Norway faces when fighting corruption in development aid more broadly.

15.3.1 Recipient Responsibility

The end of the 1980s and the 1990s saw a new aid ideology where *recipient responsibility* was a key concept. Norway advocated strongly for the implementation of this concept. In the case of MNRP, the Norwegian Embassy in Dar es Salaam gradually handed over responsibility for planning and implementation to the Ministry of Natural Resources and Tourism. As for the MNRP's accounts and financial management, Norway adhered to the concept of recipient responsibility and used the Tanzanian authorities' own systems. The Ministry's own auditing system was used, and the CAG gave final approval to the programme accounts. Yet it was still Norway's role to approve MNRP's annual reports, plans and accounts.

One reason why Norway did not discover the amount of money that had been mismanaged in the programme was the trust placed in the ministry and CAG auditing system, and the comments the Norwegian Embassy received from PriceWaterhouseCoopers on the CAG's audit report. The Danish audit report shows clearly that the internal and external control mechanisms, including those of the Ministry and the CAG, did not work.

15.3.2 Focus on Plans for the Future and Not on Implementation

A consequence of applying the principle of recipient responsibility was that Norway took several steps back from actual implementation of the project and assumed the role of a dialogue partner with the Tanzanian authorities. A focus was placed on future policy and overall planning. As programme officer for the MNRP, almost all my work time was spent in Dar es Salaam, and much of it was used for planning, coordinating and harmonizing with other development partners on how to support Tanzania in managing its natural resources. Colleagues both within the Norwegian Embassy and in other countries' embassies were little exposed to the field where their projects were implemented. Only a few days per year were spent learning about project implementation in the field. The *distance* to actual programmes seemed long. There was thus a limited ability to learn and receive feedback from the reality in which programmes were implemented and where the final objectives of the programme were to be achieved. In line with the concept of recipient responsibility there was no 'hands-on' oversight concerning programme implementation.

15.3.3 Pipeline Problems and Heavy Workload

'The pipeline problem' is well known in development aid work. It means that allocated funds must be paid out within set timeframes and by the end of the financial year. Towards the end of the year the pipeline problem is among the largest challenges at embassies dealing with development aid. Staff work hard to obtain new agreements and disbursements by the end of the year. If one knows little about the risks a programme might be exposed to, it is easier to approve a planning document, work out an agreement and make disbursements. In such pressurized situations it can be easier to trivialize and explain away what may be seen as isolated irregularities in a programme.

15.3.4 A Strong Culture Concerning Internal Administration and Reporting Back to MFA

The Norwegian Embassy in Dar es Salaam had acquired a high level of competence in planning and coordination at national level. The embassy had also developed competence in their own internal administrative routines. This was supported by visits of teams from Norad conducting administrative management reviews[5] in all embassies dealing with development cooperation. In addition, various courses in archive systems and administration were mandatory for all employees. These efforts in promoting improved administration were important and necessary for improving the efficiency of development cooperation. It appears, however, that too much attention and time was spent on the performance of administration at the expense of substantive and technical work, and of obtaining a broader understanding of development processes. The 'successful' programme officer would be a person who managed the programmes well in an administrative technical sense, signed agreements and made disbursement on time, reporting back to Norway on progress. There was a strong *administrative culture* emphasizing the need to 'do things right'. The main incentives in the system leading to a successful career seemed to be to master and follow the administrative rules laid down.

In his book *The White Man's Burden*, William Easterly distinguishes between *planners* and *searchers* (Easterly, 2006). *Planners* have much of the aid partners' future-oriented attitude that is described above. *Searchers* are more retrospective. They try to understand what has taken place and receive feedback from the reality in which the programmes have been implemented. From an internal perspective, working inside various parts of the Norwegian development aid system, it appears that knowledge of internal administrative routines is highly valued, but there is little stimulus and recognition for critical reflection on the work done.

The attitude about how to deal with potentially difficult aspects of development programmes must also be considered in relation to the administrative and technical resources at the embassy. The workload was heavy for all staff at the embassy in Dar es Salaam. Most programme officers would be responsible for several different programmes, each involving meetings with government, coordination with other development partners, meetings with consultants and reporting back to the embassy and MFA. Spending too much time dealing with one programme would have implications for how much time could be allocated to other programmes. There were, in essence, too few people at the embassy to secure responsible follow up of the NOK 750 million annual budget, dispersed through a large number of projects and activities.

15.3.5 Lack of Contextual Understanding

One of the main reasons why corruption in MNRP was so extensive is that there was a poor understanding of the context in which the programme was taking place. Programme staff were not sufficiently informed about the corruption in Tanzania's bureaucracy and how it works. We also knew too little about the power structures at various levels of the state administration and in the villages where the projects were implemented. There was not enough analysis of actors and networks that could explain what took place in MNRP. Too little was known about what Goran Hyden refers to as *the power aspect of politics* in Tanzania (Hyden, 2006).

The annual reports from MNRP gave little impression of the many conflicts among different actors when managing natural resources. In the eyes of MNRP, win–win situations were everywhere and society was understood in terms of simple harmony models. This was despite the documentation presented in the media and research literature of strong competition between different actors concerning property rights and rights to different natural resources. The possibility that public servants might engage in corruption in their management of natural resources was not presented in the reports from MNRP.

Development partners' attitudes were also characterized by over-simplistic understanding of how to solve the problems of managing natural resources. Capacity building seemed to make up much of the answer. If only everyone was given proper training on the significance of sustainable management, the problems would be nearly solved. The power aspect and conflicting interests between the various players were not a part of the model and vocabulary used in planning environmental and natural resource programmes (Brockington, 2008).

Many consider it to be the recipient authorities' task to communicate feedback to development partners, while development partners are removed from implementation, concentrating on future plans and coordination. Development partners could justify this if they received thorough and analytical reports from the authorities on the implementation of programmes. Yet the reports the embassy received from MNRP were mechanical, simplistic and maintained the same format year after year. They were output oriented and reported on the number of seminars held, the number of patrol trips conducted, the number of trees planted, and so on. They contained little discussion and analysis of the complex world where projects were taking place. Corruption and mismanagement of natural resources were not discussed.

15.3.6 Fighting Corruption in a Future-oriented Perspective

During the last 10 to 15 years corruption has, however, been very much on the policy agenda in Tanzania. The media has exposed a number of grand corruption cases. Development partners have supported the establishment of the Prevention and Combating of Corruption Bureau (PCCB), the development of anti-corruption strategies, and capacity building work for anti-corruption measures. Many donors refer to the support of these activities as evidence of how seriously they take the fight against corruption. But development partners appear more comfortable in supporting institutions and activities that prevent corruption from taking place in the future. It is more uncomfortable both for the government of

Tanzania and for the development partners to critically assess corruption that has already occurred or is taking place in ongoing projects.

15.3.7 The Lack of Independent Reviews

Another factor that has weakened a critical perspective is that people have worn many different hats in the MNRP. Many of those who have taken part in reviews and planning have sat at all sides of the table within MNRP and the Ministry. The Ministry often nominated former and retired directors in the Ministry to participate in mid-term reviews. In light of the Danish audit reports there is little doubt that it would have been useful to include people who were more independent and critical, without a background and interests in MNRP.

15.4 CONCLUSION AND GENERAL LESSONS TO BE LEARNED FROM MNRP

How representative is the story of MNRP for other development aid programmes? MNRP was unusual in the sense that it was subject to a forensic audit that revealed large-scale corruption and systemic weaknesses in its financial management and audit system. If similar audits were carried out in other aid programmes it is not unlikely that the findings in many cases would be the same. However, the issues discussed above are important factors in explaining why there could be mismanagement and corruption in other development aid programmes.

From the above analysis, there are some clear lessons. The Norwegian aid system should be much more knowledgeable about the often corrupt contexts within which it operates. Given the context in which many programmes are executed, independent audits should be carried out more frequently.

A greater focus should be placed on the implementation side of programmes, and embassy staff should develop an understanding of what happens in the field where programmes operate. Field visits, including by embassy staff, should be compulsory both in programmes funded through general budget support and through programme support. In other words, more time should be spent in obtaining feedback from the field at the expense of internal administration and reporting back to Norway. More time should also be spent on learning from the past than on focusing on planning for the future. Finally, monitoring, reviews and evaluations should, to a larger extent, be conducted by independent persons who have no stake in the programmes they assess.

NOTES

1. Information obtained in a conversation with the Danish auditor, Arthur F. Andreasen, on 6 November 2007 in Dar es Salaam. Later in the Norwegian press, Mr Andreasen reiterated that he estimates that 50 per cent of the money allocated for MNRP was mismanaged and used for corrupt purposes, see inter alia, www. Bistandsaktuelt. no. 3, 2008.
2. See Nettavisen Dagbladet, 29 June 2010.
3. See Nettavisen, op. cit.
4. See interview with Einar Døssland in Aftenposten, 30 October 2011.
5. Norwegian: forvaltningsgjennomganger.

REFERENCES

Andresen, A. F. and K. K. Bhattbhatt (2007), Re-evaluation of Mafia Island Marine Park. Report prepared for the Ministry of Natural Resources and Tourism and the Royal Norwegian Embassy, Dar es Salaam.

Andresen, A. F. and K. K. Bhattbhatt (2008), Management of Natural Resources Programme, Tanzania – Financial review of five Projects under MNRP. Report prepared for the Ministry of Natural Resources and Tourism and the Royal Norwegian Embassy.

Bistandsaktuelt (2008), Interview with the Minister for International Development Cooperation. *Bistandsaktuelt*, no. 3.

Brockington, D (2008), Corruption, Taxation and Natural Resources Management in Tanzania. *Journal of Development Studies*, **44** (1), 103–126.

Cooksey, B., L. Anthony, J. Egoe, K. Forrester, G. Kajembe, B. Mbano, I. von Oertzen and S. Riedmiller (2006), Management of the Natural Resources Programme, Tanzania, TAN-0092. Final Revised report, Oslo: Norwegian Agency for International Development Cooperation.

Easterly, W (2006), *The White Man's Burden: Why the West's Efforts to Aid the Rest Have Done So Much Ill and So Little Good*. New York: The Penguin Press.

Hyden, G (2006), Beyond governance: bringing power into policy analysis. *Forum for Development Studies*, **33** (2), 215–236.

Jansen, E. G. (2009), Does Aid Work? Reflections on a natural resources programme in Tanzania. U4 Issue 2009, 2, Chr. Michelsen Institute, Bergen.

16. When per diems take over: training and travel as extra pay

Ingvild Aagedal Skage, Tina Søreide and Arne Tostensen

Weak access to basic services and poor framework conditions for the private sector impede development. Low-quality service provision for example in health, education, utility supply, industry regulation or law enforcement can often be explained by inefficiencies in state administration. This is why many governments offer extensive training to build capacity or to introduce new approaches and strategies. Training programmes are often organized in collaboration with development partners and as complements to development interventions. As a result, a significant share of budgets is allocated to seminars and workshops. Higher competence among civil servants at all ranks is expected to strengthen bureaucratic efficiency and thus improve sector performance for better development. In the same vein, heightened awareness with regard to salient issues such as gender, transparency, HIV and AIDS, microfinance, and so on, is also expected to improve performance.

Whether the many training programmes, workshops and seminars actually enhance efficiency and performance depends on the manner in which they are organized and how receptive the participants are to learning. While it is often assumed that training programmes lead to better performance, research suggests that training programmes are often organized and attended for the mere purpose of obtaining extra pay rather than for their substance (see Cooksey, 2007, 2010; Jansen 2009a, b; Vian, 2009). Civil servants who attend seminars and workshops are offered per diem payment in line with existing travel compensation systems, which means that they are offered non-salary daily subsistence allowances intended to cover extra expenses when on duty travel away from office. The compensation is normally set at standardized rates, payable according to stipulated rules and regulations. While per diem payments were initially meant to be compensatory only, they tend to assume the character of additional salary payments in countries where salary levels are generally low (Policy Forum, 2009). In a developing country, where civil servants draw low wages – even in the upper echelons – these extra emoluments may contribute significantly to total income. Indeed, the incentives embodied in these non-salary allowances may bear decisively on decisions about whether or not to travel and participate in seminars, workshops and conferences.

When such emoluments significantly increase their monthly pay, civil servants may become unduly preoccupied with pursuing such allowances, and pay less attention to the contents of the events.[1] Some may even prefer attending seminars and obtain extra payment instead of discharging their regular work. If this is so, the incentives inherent in travel compensation systems can prevent governments from reaching the full potential of their training programmes, and worse, the training programmes themselves may indeed become a source of inefficiency. For this reason we need better knowledge about the problem of *per diem grabbing* and how to improve the efficiency of travel compensation systems. This chapter presents some of the results of a qualitative study on per diem manipulation and fraud in three developing countries.

16.1 PER DIEM GRABBING IN THREE COUNTRIES

At the request of Norad, the Norwegian Agency for Development Cooperation, the authors conducted a study of the phenomenon of per diem irregularities and fraud in Tanzania, Ethiopia and Malawi, a project carried out during 2011–12.[2] The study specifically addressed the misuse of the systems as it plays out in practice.[3] Apart from publicly available secondary material and data provided by the institutions visited – including national statistics and national budgets/expenditures; circulars and staff manuals; audit information from the offices of auditors-general; and surveys by line ministries and donor agencies – we relied primarily on semi-structured, qualitative in-depth interviews with key informants representing a wide range of institutions and stakeholders, including academia, civil society organizations (CSOs) and the media (120 respondents in total). Corroboration of information was sought to establish relatively firm inferences, notwithstanding the sensitive nature of the topic. The public sector in the three countries has adopted standardized travel reimbursement systems, with rates and rules on how compensation should vary with rank and city or area, standardized forms for the request of reimbursement and rules regarding supporting documentation such as original receipts. Management approval is needed prior to travel in all of the countries, and all have a system of internal and external audit.

Formally, the travel compensation systems in the three countries are similar and resemble international best practice when it comes to these kinds of systems. It was remarkable, therefore, to see how differently they work in practice, which suggests that contextual factors are important, such as low salary levels.

16.1.1 Ethiopia

A main reason why it is difficult to ensure that the Ethiopian travel compensation system works efficiently is the meagre per diem rates. The official rates (Council of Ministers, 1993, 2001, 2008) are far below the real costs of meals and accommodation which are estimated to be three to four times higher than the maximum per diem rate.[4] For this reason, a civil servant is hesitant to travel, unless he or she has been reassured that the number of reported days on travel may be inflated to match the actual expenses. The civil servant is thus paid for more days on travel than has actually taken place. This practice is condoned and defended by government officials as a way of maintaining flexibility with regard to expenses in a situation with uncertain budgets and high inflation. However, it also provides significant room for managerial discretion, which may be misused by leaders who want to favour certain employees or promote party loyalty in a polity perceived by Human Rights Watch (2010) and Freedom House (2011) as a repressive one-party state. The practice seems to have created a culture of increasing tolerance of irregularities and malpractices. Civil servants who are loyal and efficient expect their managers to use the opportunities offered by the system to secure them something extra.

Different development partners negotiate per diem rates on the programmes they finance on a case-by-case basis (Ministry of Finance and Economic Development, 2008). These negotiated higher rates make sure that externally funded programmes are carried out as intended. For this reason, it has become more popular for civil servants to work on programmes financed by development partners, leaving a bias against ordinary government-financed programmes. In effect, the differences in the per diem rates seem to influence how government institutions allocate their staff resources.

16.1.2 Tanzania

Although Tanzania has been commended for its macroeconomic development, political stability and a growing private sector, the country has a long way to go to ensure that its travel compensation system works efficiently. The reason is not only the functioning of the travel compensation system itself. Just as important is a range of discretionary allowances offered to motivate staff or incentivize extra performance, including special duty allowance, honoraria for outstanding performance and sitting allowances for attending certain meetings. Many civil servants seem to consider the travel reimbursements as just another source of extra pay. During our study we were given examples of civil servants who could obtain per diem payments for more days than they had actually travelled, reimbursements for more expenses than what they had incurred, or for meetings not attended.[5] However, the rates are significantly higher in Tanzania than for example in Ethiopia, and the civil servants do not have to inflate the number of days to gain something extra from travelling. We cannot report the magnitude of fraud and mismanagement in the system. However, the total government wage bill accounted for 32 per cent of the 2010/11 budget. Allowances accounted for 16.2 per cent of the total wage bill, of which duty-facilitating allowances made up 10.2 per cent, remunerative allowances 6 per cent and domestic per diems 4 per cent. The total absolute allocation for allowances amounted to TZS 269 billion (USD 165 million).

16.1.3 Malawi

When reforming their staff compensation system in 2004, Malawi incorporated into a 'clean salary' many extra allowances previously payable to civil servants. Travel-related per diem is currently the only allowance remaining at a manager's discretion. Although this was a wise reform, it may have led some managers who want to offer their employees something extra to 'stretch' the travel compensation system a bit too far. For example, a manager satisfied with a department's performance may offer the whole department 2 days of travel compensation – as a bonus – even if no trips or training courses have taken place.[6] A 2010 review of travel-related expenditure showed that excessive amounts were being spent on travel-related allowances, accounting for 21.9 per cent of salaries. Over the period 2006/07–2010/11, the total travel budget (the sum of domestic and foreign travel) was on average 9.2 per cent of the total national budget (Peprah and Mangani, 2010). Malawi's high travel expenditures aggravate the country's budget deficit, which has been hovering around 5 per cent of GDP in recent years. The travel-related allowances constitute a large proportion of the total emoluments of civil servants and quite certainly take on the character of salary supplement rather than reimbursement of expenses.

16.1.4 General Findings

In all three countries we got the impression that per diem grabbing is a phenomenon of significant magnitude. The different practices and consequences can be placed in three categories of mechanisms that could lead to managers' 'per diem misuse' as opposed to the intended, efficient travel compensation in a strict sense: (1) indirect, *informal performance reward*: per diem payments are used as a bonus; (2) unintended *distortion of incentives* for those involved (less time in office, too much time spent on seminars); and (3) *outright fraud* and corruption. These categories will obviously have different impacts on development. The many training initiatives financed by development partners or the governments expand opportunities for extra payments through the travel compensation system, although the risk of fraud is present also on duty travel which is not part of a competence-raising programme. We could not obtain data indicating the volume of fraud or the impact on training outcomes. However, interviews with more than 120 respondents in key positions provided numerous examples of how grabbing is carried out in practice by organizers of training events as well as by the civil servants attending them.

The travel compensation systems and how they are applied in practice are not trivial issues. They impact significantly on the work environment, staff motivation and work priorities, and hence on the quality of public service delivery. The degree to which a travel compensation system can be a source of extra emoluments differs across countries, institutions and rank. The fact that government rates in Tanzania (and Malawi) are sufficiently high to provide an economic reward from participating in training activities create different distortionary incentives than in Ethiopia where the low government rates lead to consistent manipulation of budgets on a discretionary basis. In all three countries, however, there is a de facto opportunity to benefit more in donor-financed programmes, partly because the rates are higher and partly because the allowances are sometimes seen as a means to attract participants to the seminars. One consequence is that when similar training is replicated by different agencies there is still an economic incentive to participate in all of them to obtain more payment, instead of prioritizing other work tasks.

16.2 EXPLANATORY FACTORS

Civil servant salaries are very low in all three case countries. At lower levels, poverty must be understood as a driving force underlying individuals' per diem grabbing, but there are no indications that malpractice decreases at higher echelons of government (Fjeldstad, 2005). From a government perspective, it is clearly a problem of organization as well. This implies that a large proportion of staff emoluments is allocated informally, which is typically less controlled and fair than what formal payment would be. Why does per diem grabbing persist in a state administration, even if the problem is well known to the government?

16.2.1 Lack of Control

Manipulation of travel expenses is irregular and a form of fraud and thus, intuitively, a problem of weak control. Such a view assumes principal-agent characteristics of the problem, where the main reason why the problem continues is lack of information by the principal (Rose-Ackerman, 1975; Mookherjee and Png, 1992). Whether the principal is a manager within a given institution or a separate controlling institution, such as a ministry, a principal-agent problem can be solved with better monitoring efforts and/or incentive schemes connected to staff perform-ance. There are strong reasons to consider lack of control an important part of the problem. In all three case countries, staff as well as managers could forge receipts and produce fake seminar attendance sheets. In addition, in many training events it was possible for civil servants to attend just long enough to obtain the offered allowance, and then leave. Besides, some managers told us they would show up unexpectedly at seminars, simply to check how many staff were actually present. In all three countries, the National Audit Office was well aware of the challenges, and apparently, did what could be done to report attempted fraud. However, there are many means of per diem grabbing from funding intended for capacity-raising programmes. They include faking non-existent training events, when in reality the money has been pocketed by the organizers of the events. Careful auditing of capacity-raising programmes will often require some form of performance evaluation in order to check whether the training has had the intended impact on institutional efficiency, a form of control which requires broad competence and resources on the part of the auditors. Concerns about the need for such monitoring challenges uttered in interviews indicated clearly that the problem of per diem grabbing has principal-agent characteristics.

16.2.2 A Management Problem

We found, however, that weak control is not the whole explanation. There were too many cases where managers had allowed per diem

irregularities to happen or continue, or accepted the obviously opportunistic organization of seminars (in other words, primarily to maximize per
diem payments). They misused the system to offer extra payments to
staff, and inflated their unit's budget to create financial space for
manipulation of the travel compensation system. There were even cases
of managers reimbursing staff for more days than staff members had
requested. These findings were surprising given the assumption that most
managers are rewarded in some way if their unit performs well.

It appeared, however, that many managers had a strong interest in
keeping the extra discretionary authority given to them by the travel
compensation system. Correspondingly, for many staff members it would
be important to be included among those allowed to attend seminars or to
travel, simply because of the extra emoluments. The manager's authority
to make such decisions would afford him or her with an opportunity not
only to demand added commitment by subordinates, but also to demand
loyalty. Such expectations on the part of managers apply regardless of
how he or she performed or what form of irregularity was involved. As
mentioned above, this authority could also be used to reward loyalty to
the incumbent political party. This fact, combined with a general tolerance of such forms of misuse across government institutions, suggests
that the problem should also be seen as a collective action issue.[7]

General resistance to reform of the travel compensation system – from
too much discretionary authority and lax controls to less discretion and
more stringent controls – was rather unconvincingly justified by the need
for financial flexibility. There seems to be little understanding of how
discretion itself could be a significant cost, particularly in terms of
influencing staff incentives (Olson, 1996). However, by keeping the
system 'flexible' financially, the managers were not only given added
authority; but also the opportunity for increased personal income. In all
three countries, the per diem rate varies by rank or seniority. Managers in
government institutions benefitted most from generous per diem payment. They had incentives to keep the status quo, particularly since these
emoluments were tax exempt.

16.2.3 Donor Interests

International donor agencies play an important role in financing and
designing development programmes and training events. Several development partners have tried to harmonize their rates and systems with those
of recipient countries, but in practice, these attempts are undermined if
the donors effectively compete for participants. The offered allowance is
a means of attracting the most relevant or senior staff from government

institutions. One international organization told us that they would not reach their internal targets for training programmes – which might also, in turn, jeopardize future funding – unless potential participants were offered generous allowances for attending. Apparently, their targets were set as the sheer number of participants attending training events or the number of activities, rather than the demonstrated learning and service delivery outcomes expected to ensue. Surprisingly, another international organization would not divulge the rates they offered workshop partici-pants since this was considered confidential information.[8] Several man-agers of government institutions were annoyed that development partners would not inform them or were negligent about informing them about what staff would be offered when attending training events. Such lack of information could easily lead to a situation in which staff would be compensated twice (from their government institution *and* the develop-ment partner). With respect to control of expenses for training events, there was significant variation across development partners and embas-sies. Some would insist on using government systems, which means, in effect, that hardly any independent control was conducted on behalf of the development partner. Others, however, would demand detailed infor-mation and control by independent auditors.[9]

In general, however, we found representatives of development partners who considered the problem of per diem grabbing an insignificant problem. The way these emoluments could distort development pro-grammes, the impact of training events, and the function of government institutions seemed not to be fully comprehended among development partners. Nor did they seem to appreciate the role of development aid in compounding and aggravating the problem. This neglect on the part of development partners is surprising in view of the large amounts of money that are allocated to activities susceptible to per diem irregularities, and might be explained by the donors' own incentive problems as described above.

16.3 POLICY DISCUSSION

Following from the principal-agent perspective on the problem of per diem grabbing, improved monitoring of how seminars and workshops are organized and financed will be an important part of a solution. Control can be facilitated by standardizing and harmonizing per diem systems. Information about rates, rules and the amounts spent on travel expenses should be transparent and made publicly available to establish rates that are compensatory only, as distortionary incentives are created by rates at all levels. Lessons may be learned from results-based domestic CSOs that cannot afford to waste scarce resources.[10] In addition to internal control routines, training programmes and travel expenses should be subject to external auditing as well. The National Audit Offices in all three case countries told us that they would be interested in closer collaboration with development partners to control public institutions' expenditures and the funding of training programmes.

However, bureaucratic efficiency hinges on a balance between trust and control. Discretion is a prerequisite for flexibility, and 100 per cent control will never be cost-efficient. For this reason, there will always be a modicum of risk of mismanagement and fraud in travel compensation systems, and control initiatives have to take place within framework conditions that keep civil servants motivated. Better control systems should therefore be combined with some form of recognition of performance. Unless the intrinsic motivation of civil servants is in line with the goal of better service provision, there will always be inefficiencies of some sort. In Tanzania, the state administration is about to introduce performance-based pay. This may be a step in the right direction, but it is difficult to predict how it will play out in practice if existing allowance systems remain the same. One important vehicle of directing focus at performance, however, would be to evaluate the impact of training programmes on improved service delivery, not merely by counting how many participants have received per diem allowances.

In addition, it will be important to change the widespread acceptance of per diem allowances as a source of extra pay – in other words, a move away from the current per diem culture that seems entrenched in many countries. Civil servants at all levels need to understand that travel compensation systems are meant for reimbursement of *travel expenses only*. Furthermore, they need to act on that understanding. The monetary per diem benefits accruing to staff should be channelled into a formal wage. Managers should be instructed never to use per diem allowances as a device for incentivizing performance in office or for buying loyalty from their subordinates. Likewise, the development partners should not condone such irregularities. They should not allow the inflation of the daily allowances offered for the purpose of attracting participants to training activities, as this leads to replication and waste. Moreover, they should ensure that training programmes are subjected to independent auditing, at least until perceptions of these kinds of payments have changed and the system is cleaned up.

NOTES

1. For a discussion of how payments may distort intrinsic motivation, see Frey (1997).
2. This chapter presents a snapshot of results with particular focus on *grabbing*. The comprehensive results of literature reviews, data collection and interviews are available in a separate report: Søreide, Tostensen and Skage (2012), downloadable at http://www.norad.no. We wish to thank Norad for the opportunity to conduct the study and our local consultants, Mekonnen Gebeyehu in Ethiopia, Tom Kavinya in Malawi and Samuel Wangwe in Tanzania. We are also grateful to Michael Davies and Odd-Helge Fjeldstad for useful advice and comments on the main report.
3. The magnitude of the problem could not be ascertained precisely with hard data. The focus on mismanagement and misuse of the system should not be construed to mean that misuse happens consistently across and within all public institutions in the countries concerned. The extent of abuse varies, which suggests that management is important at the institutional level.
4. At the time of fieldwork in Ethiopia the maximum rate was ETB 70, equivalent to about USD 4.1 at the exchange rate at that time. In general, the availability of and access to budget information and national statistics in Ethiopia was very limited.
5. See Vian et al. (2011) for similar findings.
6. In one extreme case investigated for fraud, one and the same person had claimed per diem allowances for 1057 days in one calendar year. The case was part of a larger scam in the Ministry of Agriculture and Food Security, involving 20 civil servants (*Daily Times* (Blantyre), 10 November 2008).
7. A study of corruption in an aid-financed family planning programme in Nigeria (Smith, 2003) associates per diem fraud with patronage systems and a lax attitude to spending and control in aid-financed projects.
8. Details are available in Søreide et al. (2012).
9. If stricter controls were instituted, the reputation would spread that it was harder to misuse the travel compensation system for training events financed by the (strict) development partner in question.
10. Although this chapter focuses on government institutions, CSOs were also covered by the study upon which this chapter is based.

REFERENCES

Cooksey, B. (2010), Allowances in Tanzania. Mimeo, a study conducted for Norad.

Cooksey, B., L. Anthony, J. Egoe, K. Forrester, Kajembe, B. Mbano, I. von Oertzen, S. Riedmiller (2007), Management of Natural Resources Programme, Tanzania TAN-0092, Final Evaluation, Oslo, Norwegian Agency for Development Cooperation, (Norad Collected Reviews 1/2007).

Council of Ministers (1993), Council of Ministers' Directive on the Daily Allowance of Government Employees, Addis Ababa.

Council of Ministers (2001), Revised Council of Ministers' Directive on the Daily Allowance of Government employees, Addis Ababa.

Council of Ministers (2008), Council of Ministers' Directive on the Determination of the Daily Allowances for Foreign Business Trips, Addis Ababa.

Daily Times Reporter (2008), ACB arrest three more in K40 million scam. *Daily Times*, 10 November, Blantyre, Blantyre Newspapers Limited.

Fjeldstad, O.-H. (2003), Fighting fiscal corruption, lessons from the Tanzania Revenue Authority. *Public Administration and Development*, **23** (2), 165–175.

Freedom House (2011), Country Report, Ethiopia. Available at: http://freedom house.org/template.cfm?page=22&year=2011&country=8036 (accessed 2 October 2011).

Frey, B. S. (1997), *Not Just For the Money, An Economic Theory of Motivation.* Cheltenham, UK and Northampton, MA: Edward Elgar.

Human Rights Watch (2010), Development without freedom, how aid underwrites repression in Ethiopia. Human Rights Watch, New York.

Jansen, E. (2009a), Monitoring Aid, Lessons from a Natural Resources Programme in Tanzania. U4 Practice Insight 2009, 1, U4 Anti-Corruption Resource Centre, Bergen.

Jansen, E. (2009b), Does aid work? Reflections on a natural resources programme in Tanzania. U4 Issue Paper 2009, 2, U4 Anti-Corruption Resource Centre, Bergen.

Ministry of Finance and Economic Development (2008), Ministry of Finance and Economic Development Directive on the Channel and Budgetary Projects Expenditure Payment System, Addis Ababa.

Mookherjee, D. and I. P. L Png (1992), Monitoring vis-a-vis investigation in enforcement of law. *American Economic Review*, **82** (3), 556–565.

Olson, M. (1996), Big bills left on the sidewalk: why some nations are rich, and others poor. *Journal of Economic Perspectives*, **10**, 3–24.

Peprah, I. and R. Mangani (2010), *Government of Malawi, Public Expenditure Review of Travel* (Study Funded by DFID Malawi), Lilongwe, Malawi: Government of Malawi.

Policy Forum (in collaboration with Twaweza) (2009), Reforming allowances: a win–win approach to improved service delivery, higher salaries for civil servants and saving money. Policy Brief No. 9, Dar es Salaam, Policy Forum.

Rose-Ackerman, S. (1975), The economics of corruption. *Journal of Public Economics*, **4**, 187–203.

Smith, D. J. (2003), Patronage, per diems and the 'workshop mentality', the practice of family planning programs in Southeastern Nigeria', *World Development*, **31** (4), 703–715.

Søreide, T., A. Tostensen and I. A. Skage. (2011), *Hunting for per diem, The uses and abuses of travel compensation in three developing countries,* Norad Evaluation Department, Report 2/2012 Study. Norwegian Agency for Development Cooperation, Oslo.

Vian, T. (2009), Benefits and drawbacks of per diems, do allowances distort good governance in the health sector? U4 Brief No. 29. U4 Anti-Corruption Resource Centre. Bergen, Chr. Michelsen Institute.

Vian, T., C. Miller, Z. Themba and P. Bukuluki (2011), Perceptions of per diems in the health sector, Evidence and implications. U4 Issue 2011, 6. U4 Anti-Corruption Resource Centre. Chr. Michelsen Institute, Bergen.

Index